Child Psychiatric Units

At the Crossroads

of related interest

Group Work with Children and Adolescents
A Handbook
Edited by Kedar Nath Dwivedi
Foreword by Robin Skynner
ISBN 1 85302 157 1

Play Therapy
Where the Sky Meets the Underworld
Ann Cattanach
ISBN 1 85302 211 X

Play Therapy with Abused Children
Ann Cattanach
ISBN 1 85302 193 8 pb
ISBN 1 85302 120 2 hb

Interventions with Bereaved Children
Susan C. Smith and Sister Margaret Pennells
ISBN 1 85302 285 3

Child Welfare Services
Developments in Law, Policy, Practice and Research
Edited by Malcolm HIll and Jane Aldgate
ISBN 1 85302 316 7

Legislating for Harmony
Partnership under the Children Act 1989
Edited by Felicity Kaganas, Michael King and Christine Piper
ISBN 1 85302 328 0

Chain Reaction
Children and Divorce
Ofra Ayalon and Adina Flasher
ISBN 1 85302 136 9

Meeting the Needs of the Ethnic Minority Children
Edited by Kedar N Dwivedi and Ved Varma
ISBN 1 85302 294 2

Child Psychiatric Units

At the Crossroads

Edited by Rosemary Chesson and Douglas Chisholm

Jessica Kingsley Publishers
London and Bristol, Pennsylvania

First published in the United Kingdom in 1996 by
Jessica Kingsley Publishers Ltd
116 Pentonville Road
London N1 9JB, England
and
1900 Frost Road, Suite 101
Bristol, PA 19007, U S A

Copyright © 1996 The publishers and the contributors

Library of Congress Cataloguing in Publication Data
Child psychiatric units: at the crossroads/edited by
Rosemary Chesson and Douglas Chisolm
p.cm
Includes bibliographical references and index
ISBN 1 85302 329 9 (alk. paper)
1. Child psychotherapy – residential treatment – Great Britain
2. Psychiatric hospital care – Great Britain. I. Chesson. Rosemary.
1945- II. Chisholm, Douglas 1941
(DNLM: 1. Psychiatric Department, Hospital – Great Britain)
2. Child Health Services – Great Britain. 3. Mental Disorders – in
infancy & childhood – Great Britain. WS 27 FA1 C5 1995]
RJ504.5 CA7 1995
362.2 1 083--dc30
DNLM/DLC
for Library of Congress

British Library Cataloguing in Publication Data
A CIP catalogue record for this book is available from the British Library

ISBN 1 85302 329 9

Printed and Bound in Great Britain by
Cromwell Press, Melksham, Wiltshire

Contents

Acknowledgements

We would like to thank all those who have contributed to the production of this volume, including all our colleagues in the Lowit Unit and the Department of Child and Family Psychiatry, The Royal Aberdeen Children's Hospital. In particular our thanks are due to Mrs Marjorie Reid and Miss Aileen Campbell who typed early drafts of chapters and to Mrs Julia Riddoch who was responsible for bringing together the whole book in the final stages of the operation and who met our often unreasonable deadlines. The help of Ms Susan Ramsay was invaluable also in checking data and rogue references! We owe a debt of gratitude, too, to Dr Andrew Leahy for his helpful comments on Chapter 8. Finally we should like to express our thanks to our partners, Andrew and Rosemary, for their forbearance over the past months and years.

Acknowledgement is made to Grampian Health Board Endowments, who funded the research project, which led to this volume.

Rosemary Chesson
Douglas Chisholm

Preface

It is widely acknowledged that a need exists in the 1990s for a comprehensive review of British child in-patient psychiatric units. This volume seeks to address that need. Although a number of transatlantic publications appeared in the 1980s, this has not been the case in the UK, where heavy reliance continues to be placed on Barker's *The Residential Psychiatric Treatment of Children*, some twenty years after its first publication date. Yet, today child psychiatric in-patient treatment is subject to scrutiny to a greater extent than ever before. Reflecting this, in-patient units currently exist in a very different social, political and healthcare milieu to that of previous decades. The recent NHS reforms and emphasis on care in the community, together with the Children Act, 1989, have major implications for units and staff working within them.

If in-patient units are to survive, it is necessary to be clear regarding that which they can offer, and as to why they are an essential part of child mental health service provision. Unless arguments for units' survival are supported by detailed, up-to-date information on their functions, treatment processes and outcomes, then purchasers may not be prepared to support these seemingly costly facilities. This volume sets out to examine the nature and extent of in-patient child psychiatric provision, both nationally and locally, and to describe practice within units, in particular by considering in depth the work of one – the Lowit Unit, part of the Royal Aberdeen Children's Hospital. The detailed case studies provided in many of the chapters demonstrate the complexity and multifaceted nature of the work, which is carried out by members of the multi-disciplinary network.

The fact that this volume has been produced by members across a wide range of professions well reflects the nature of in-patient care. It is important to note, furthermore, that this book developed from a research project – critical dimensions of therapeutic input – a joint initiative of the two editors, a child psychiatrist (DC) and a sociologist (RC). This therefore has had a major influence on the content and direction of this volume, with its focus on treatment within a social and organisational context, rather than for example on psychopharmacological therapy.

In addition it was our intention that this contribution should reflect both continuity and change. Those chapters tracing the development of units serve also to remind us a need for in-patient treatment exists. It is evident, as well, from the historical review that units, particularly in Britain, have always had strong links with their communities, and that boundaries between hospital and community have been blurred, unlike perhaps some specialist wards for treating physical illness. Units since their inception have been a locus where health and social workers, together with their educational colleagues meet to help the child overcome his or her difficulties – seamless care has for long been an objective. Moreover, from the earliest days in-patient treatment has been no more than a part of a total treatment package.

Finally it is to be hoped that the specialist reviews included in this volume may assist a wide range of professionals in the production of practice guidelines for child psychiatric residential treatment.

Rosemary Chesson
Douglas Chisholm

CHAPTER 1

Child Psychiatric Residential Units
Setting the Scene

Victor O'Loughlin

Introduction

Psychiatric in-patient units for children were first developed in the United States in the years after the World War I, in the wake of the horrendous panencephalitis epidemic (American Psychiatric Association 1957). The first child psychiatric in-patient unit in the United States was created, in fact, in 1923 at the Bellevue Hospital in New York. Shortly thereafter, similar units were opened at the King's Park State Hospital in New York and the Franklin School of Philadelphia (American Psychiatric Association 1957). With the decline in the incidence of behavioural disorders consequent on the encephalitis epidemic, units increasingly came to be seen as the setting of choice for the management of children with a variety of emotional problems who could not be effectively treated on an out-patient basis (Hersov and Bentovim 1985).

Prior to the opening of the child psychiatric in-patient units, there had been residential provision for children in the form of orphanage-type institutions providing principally custodial-type care, the aim of which was to provide a physical and a moral upbringing. Childcare was handled largely by women, who were selected for their domestic abilities, rather than interest in childcare. By the mid-eighteenth century, schools to improve the social and emotional well-being of delinquent and destitute children were beginning to be established and in the second half of the nineteenth century, residential schools for mental defectives were developed (Howlin 1985).

Training schools for the rehabilitation of delinquent youngsters had been set up, however, prior to the late nineteenth century and early twentieth century. These schools tended to have an authoritarian and punitive regime and meet with varying success (Harper and Geraty 1987; Jemerin and Phillips 1988).

Treatment Approaches

It was not until the 1930s that residential units with a therapeutic orientation but without a medical base were in operation. In general, these were inspired initially by the work of Aichorn (1935) who, in the 1920s in Vienna, applied psychoanalytic principles to the management of delinquent boys. This work was continued later by Bettleheim (1950) and Redl and Wineman (1957) in the USA. Bettleheim described how all aspects of the child's living experience had to be considered in therapy (Bettleheim and Sylvester 1948; Bettleheim 1950) and how the milieu should afford the child unconditional gratification to enable personality growth to occur.

Redl (1966) emphasised the primary treatment of children by child care workers in the residential environment through the 'life space interview', a set of verbal interventions initiated in response to events in the child's daily life. While techniques were analytically based, they were expressed in practical terms and intended for use by para-professionals.

The child guidance model, emphasising the therapeutic importance of the treatment team, generally comprising psychiatrist, psychologist and social worker, was seen by Whittaker by the late 1970s as having become the mainstream of analytically-based residential treatment (Whittaker 1979). Both individual and group psychotherapy were perceived to be the primary focus of treatment. While the psychoanalytical model had been dominant throughout the first half of the twentieth century, its limited applicability to some client populations and the general lack of empirical evidence for its effectiveness encouraged a search for alternative approaches. Despite the high regard in which Bettleheim's work and writings have been held, Irwin (1982) believed that, at this time, very few establishments were employing this approach. While in part this is because a longer stay was required than had become the norm, more fundamentally it was because such treatment was considered unnecessary to promote personality growth. In addition, it was acknowledged that such techniques might prove harmful since some children may not be able to relinquish their need for unconditional gratification.

Residential treatment programmes based on the principles of learning theory became more popular as psychoanalytic concepts became more generally challenged within mental health. Behaviourally-oriented programmes shared a focus on the child's overt behaviour, rather than on such elements as inner personality states or intra-psychic conflicts. In contrast to the child guidance model which emphasised the prime role of the 'core' psychiatric team in treatment, the behavioural model stressed the role of the residential staff as the primary treatment agents.

Writers such as Johnson (1982) have noted, however, that behavioural approaches now share with psychodynamic approaches an emphasis on the importance of the relationships that develop between child and family members and that different models are commonly reconciled in practice. Reflecting this, the psychoeducational model was another influential model (Hobbs 1966). This, like the behavioural model, stressed the teaching of more appropriate behaviours and coping skills to children and adolescents. Community involvement was emphasised as was continued contact between the child and family, aiming to promote the generalisation of treatment effects to the home environment.

Polsky (1962) has stressed the importance of peer influences in residential treatment which could often operate to the detriment of treatment efforts by staff. Based on this recognition Vorrath and Brendtro (1974) and others developed approaches using formal or informal peer group discussion as a way of reinforcing positive behaviour. The peer group model has been particularly taken up by in-patient programmes dealing primarily with adolescent substance abusers.

Use of Residential Treatment

Starting in the 1970s there was a burgeoning in the number of residential treatment centres in the United States. Between 1969 and 1981 there was a doubling in the numbers of children in residential treatment settings (Taube and Barrett 1985). By 1986 a further increase of up to 32 per cent was anticipated, and it was estimated that by 1995 there would be over 30,000 children in such units (Wells 1991).

Hospital Psychiatric Units

During a similar period, that is during the last 20 years, there has been a rapid increase in the number of hospital psychiatric units for children. Jemerin and Philips (1988) noted that, with regard to the USA, this was in part due to changes in funding with an increased reluctance on the part of health care insurers to fund treatment in non-medical settings, but also to an increasing disillusionment with the results of long term residential treatment. Similarly, there had been an increasing awareness of the differences emerging between in-patient child psychiatric units and non-hospital-based residential treatment centres.

Robinson (1957) has defined an in-patient psychiatric unit in broad terms as: (1) being primarily focused on diagnosis, and treatment, and, (2) located in a medical facility.

Irwin (1982) in reviewing the literature concludes that, in effect, in former years there has been little differentiation between in-patient psychiatric and residential treatment. As with Marsden, McDermott and Miner (1970) he notes that in-patient psychiatric units could be differentiated, in a number of aspects, from other residential units by

(1) having fewer children

(2) being less likely to exclude psychotic, suicidal and more complex cases

(3) tending to be more restrictive and located in closed settings

(4) length of stay tending to be shorter in that in-patient care is seen as just one aspect of overall treatment and care

(5) more individualised treatment being provided because a wider range of therapies is available

(6) being located in medical settings (and being in close proximity to out-patient departments, which allow for the continuation of treatment following discharge from the unit).

With the growing awareness of the differences between child psychiatric in-patient units and residential treatment centres, together with the financial pressures towards shorter stays, child psychiatric in-patient units in the 1980s became primarily diagnostic treatment centres with a reduced emphasis on aftercare and limited work with families. The change in practice resulted, however, in the number of readmissions to hospital increasing and concerns being raised lest the 'revolving door' syndrome was to creep into child psychiatric practice (Jemerin and Phillips 1986).

Research and Evaluation

Research regarding both the outcome of residential treatment in child psychiatry and into therapeutic influences on residential treatment in child psychiatry has been dogged by methodological pitfalls and lack of funding (Quay 1986). Maluccio and Marlow (1972) in their review of the literature state that research in this area has been characterised by 'insufficient conceptual clarity, fragmentation of practice, theory and limited substantive research'. For decades, Maluccio and Marlow (1972) argue, questions related to selection criteria and the relative effectiveness of different treatment programmes have remained unanswered.

Research, moreover, has also been severely limited by the paucity of controlled studies (Curry 1991). The majority of investigations to date have been descriptive, concern small numbers of children and are short term. Furthermore, there has been a lack of clarity regarding definition of residential care and delineation of in-patient psychiatric treatment (Irwin 1982). Hersov and Bentovim (1985) highlight the not inconsiderable problems in attempting to compare different treatment packages, different settings and different groups.

Curry (1991) recommends that research should rely on more powerful designs, employ more sophisticated measures of children's problems and competencies and focus on specific treatment components and outcome over time. Curry (1991) has also drawn attention to the fact that although the majority of former patients appear to be functioning adequately at follow-up, residential treatment is clearly only one of several treatment experiences that will affect their development. Indeed Maluccio and Marlow (1972) as long ago as 1972, pointed out that there is evidence to suggest that the support and availability of services post discharge is more significantly related to eventual outcome, than the degree of disturbance at the point of admission or discharge.

Wells (1991) has called for 'research to inform the placement process' and drawn attention to the need for empirical investigations that test the relationships between child characteristics, treatment experiences and outcomes. Particular emphasis, it is agreed, needs to be placed on how children are functioning after discharge, and what experiences, once hospitalisation is complete, promote and maintain adaptation.

Current Role of In-patient Units

It is accepted today that with increased emphasis on shorter periods of hospitalisation and no definitive evidence suggesting that there are clear advantages accruing to intensive out-patient treatment (Blotcky, Dimperio and Gosset 1984; Braun et al. 1981; Hoult et al. 1983), in-patient treatment must be seen as just one of the many services that a child might need or receive throughout childhood and adolescence. As has been long recognised 'despite there being many advocates for in-patient and residential treatment the efficacy of the treatment is in doubt' (Maluccio and Marlow 1972). Furthermore, while the literature suggests that a significant proportion of children do improve, the proportion of children with similar psychiatric diagnoses who do not receive the same intensive treatment but who go on to become well-adjusted, functioning adults remains unknown. Thus, longitudinal investigations of children are needed as well as more in depth research relating to residential treatment itself to produce more accurate assessments of their treatment needs and of treatment effectiveness (Wells 1991).

References

Aichorn, A. (1935) *Wayward Youth.* New York: Viking.

American Psychiatric Association (1957) *Psychiatric In-patient Treatment of Children.* Baltimore: Lord Baltimore Press.

Bettelheim B. and Sylvester E. (1948) 'A therapeutic milieu.' *American Journal of Orthopsychiatry 18,* 191–206.

Bettelheim, B. (1950) *Love is not Enough.* New York: Free Press.

Blotcky, M.J., Dimperio, T.L. and Gosset, J.I. (1984) 'Follow-up of children treated in psychiatric hospitals. A review of studies.' *American Journal of Psychiatry 141,* 1499–1507.

Braun, P., Kochansky, G., Shapiro, R., Greenburg, S., Gudeman, J.E., Johnson, S. and Shore, M.F. (1981) 'Overview: deinstitutionalisation of psychiatric patients, a critical review of outcome studies.' *American Journal of Psychiatry 138*, 6, 736–749.

Curry, J.F. (1991) 'Outcome research on residential treatment: implications and suggested directions.' *American Journal of Orthopsychiatry 61*, 3, 348–357.

Harper, G. and Geraty, R. (1987) 'Hospital and residential treatment.' In R. Michels and J.O. Cavenar (eds) *Psychiatry 2*. New York: Basic Books.

Hersov, L. and Bentovim, A. (1985) 'In-patient and day hospital units.' In M. Rutter and L. Hersov *Child and Adolescent Psychiatry, Modern Approaches*. Second edition. Oxford: Blackwell Scientific Publications.

Hobbs, N. (1966) 'Helping disturbed children; psychological and ecological strategies.' *American Psychologist 21*, 1105–1151.

Hoult, J., Reynolds, I., Charbonneau-Powis, M., Weekes, P. and Briggs, J. (1983) 'Psychiatric hospital versus community treatment: the results of a randomised trial.' *Australian New Zealand Journal of Psychiatry 17*, 2, 160–167.

Howlin, P. (1985) 'Special educational treatment.' In M. Rutter and L. Hersov (eds) *Child and Adolescent Psychiatry – Modern Approaches*. Second edition. Oxford: Blackwell.

Irwin, M. (1982) 'Literature review.' In J.L. Schulman and M. Irwin (eds) *Psychiatric Hospitalisation of Children*. Springfield, III: Charles C. Thomas.

Jemerin, J. and Philips, I. (1988) 'Changes in in-patient child psychiatry. Consequences and recommendations.' *Journal of American Academy of Child and Adolescent Psychiatry 27*, 397–403.

Johnson, S. (1982) 'Residential treatment for emotionally disturbed children and adolescents: a review of the literature.' *Canada's Mental Health*, March, 5–8.

Maluccio, A. and Marlow, W. (1972) 'Residential treatment of emotionally disturbed children. A review of the literature.' *Social Service Review 46*, 230–250.

Marsden, G., McDermott, J.F. and Miner, D. (1970) 'Residential treatment of children: A survey of institutional characteristics.' *Journal of the American Academy of Child and Adolescent Psychiatry 9*, 332–356.

Noshpitz, J.D. (1975) 'Residential treatment of emotionally disturbed children'. In S. Arieti. *American Handbook of Psychiatry*, Revised edition, Vol V: Treatment, D.X. Freedman and J.E. Dyrud (eds) New York: Basic Books.

Polsky, H.W. (1962) *Cottage Six: The Social System of Delinquent Boys in Residential Treatment*. New York: Russel Sage Foundation.

Quay, H. (1986) 'Residential treatment.' In H. Quay and J.S. Werry (eds) *Psychopathological Disorders of Childhood*. Third edition. New York. John Wiley.

Redl, F. (1966) *When We Deal With Children*. New York: Free Press.

Redl, F. and Wineman, D. (1957) *The Aggressive Child*. New York: Free Press.

Robinson, J.F. (Ed) (1957) *Psychiatric In-Patient Treatment of Children.* Washington DC: American Psychiatric Association.

Taube, C.A. and Barret, S.A. (1985) *Mental Health, United States, 1985.* Rockville, M.D.: National Institute of Mental Health.

Vorrath, H.H. and Brendtro, L.K. (1974) *Positive Peer Culture.* Chicago: Aldine.

Wells, K. (1991) 'Placement of emotionally disturbed children in residential treatment; A review of placement criteria.' *American Journal of Orthopsychiatry 61,* 3, 339–347.

Whittaker, J.K. (1979) *Caring for Troubled Children.* San Francisco: Jossey-Bass.

CHAPTER 2

Historical Precursors

Douglas Chisholm

Introduction

By the time the first child psychiatric in-patient unit opened in Britain, non-hospital residential treatment of disturbed children had already been taking place for some time. In addition, many child psychiatric in-patient units were already in operation in the USA. In these ways, a considerable body of knowledge had been accumulated prior to the British units operating (Barker 1974) and it is clear that the development of child psychiatric in-patient practice in Britain can only be understood against a background of:

(1) the history of non-hospital residential provision in North America, as is discussed briefly by O'Loughlin in Chapter 1.

(2) the history of non-hospital residential provision in Britain which is considered in the present chapter, including:

   (a) schools for children with emotional and behavioural difficulties, previously known as schools for maladjusted children; and

   (b) Children's Homes and other provision for children who require care away from their homes.

(3) the development of hospital child psychiatric in-patient treatment in North America. The salient points of this are outlined in Chapter 3, prior to a relatively fuller account of the development of British child psychiatric in-patient practice.

In these accounts the published literature is not covered comprehensively, a task Barker (1974) had viewed as scarcely practicable twenty years ago. Thus, areas considered to have been influential are concentrated on, although as Wardle (1991) points out with regard to admission procedures and management, it is not possible for all to be identified. Some of the influences on the development of child psychiatric residential units will have been mediated through the literature, but others have been through discussion at conferences, visits such as that made by Dr. Mildred Creak to the USA in 1932/3 (Wardle 1991) and

8

some through working at other centres. That British child psychiatrists have normally trained first in adult psychiatry including taking the Membership of the Royal College of Psychiatrists (or a diploma prior to the founding of the College) has also been a channel of influence.

With regard, too, to British non-hospital residential treatment, developments are described when there are reasonably close parallels to in-patient treatment even when the links may have been quite indirect, for example through the awareness of members of the multi-disciplinary team other than doctors and nurses, of developments in their own professions, or even through changes in the expectations of parents. Recent developments that may still have an impact are also described. As the Lowit Unit lies in North East Scotland it has also been seen as appropriate to identify some of the differences between Scotland and England and to comment briefly on some local relevant developments.

History of Residential Provision in Britain

(1) Residential Schools for Children with Emotional and Behavioural Difficulties
THE BLEAK EARLY PICTURE

In Britain, as in the USA, non-hospital residential units preceded the opening of in-patient psychiatric units. Barker (1974) points out that both before and since the establishment of child psychiatric units disturbed children have been catered for in a variety of types of schools and children's homes, in mental subnormality hospitals and in foster homes. Parry-Jones (1989) observes that surprisingly little is known about what happened to disturbed children in the nineteenth century but that their admission to workhouses and asylums was widespread. There was little differentiation between the effects of deprivation, mental illness and mental handicap and West (1967) comments on the lack of distinction between young paupers and criminals and makes it clear that they would receive, by modern day standards, very harsh treatment. Indeed, prior to the middle of the nineteenth century the law did not distinguish between child and adult offenders and children could be executed for such offences as stealing (Sheldrick 1985; West 1967).

SOME EARLY SCOTTISH INITIATIVES

In contrast to this harsh environment, however, a Report by a Working Party of the North East of Scotland Joint Consultative Committee (NESJCC) on Residential Child Care Services (1973) describes in the North East of Scotland an enlightened pioneering tradition dating at least from the 1840s and gives a number of examples. One of these was the introduction of a Child's Asylum Committee which sought 'to avoid stamping the child for life with the character of a convicted felon' as stated in an early annual report. The committee tried also to make decisions in 'the best interests of the child'. This, while ante-dating it by some 120 years, was similar in some respects to the Children's Hearing system introduced in Scotland following the Kilbrandon Report (1966). This system dealing with offenders without involving the courts or punitive measures, and attending to social factors and their impact on the family (Webb and Wistow 1987) has itself been a highly regarded form of provision for child and adolescent offenders (Miller 1993). In 1854, too, The Old Mill Reformatory, near Aberdeen, was unique in the liberality of its regime, including an experiment in self-government among the boys. It took day-boys as well as boarders and it was indeed in the 1840s and 1850s that the first experiments in comprehensive day-care took place in North East Scotland in what were called industrial feeding schools. These day schools recognised the importance of avoiding unnecessary separation of a child from his home.

Sheriff Watson in Aberdeen introduced compulsory attendance for child vagrants and beggars, and the schools in Aberdeen were said to have almost cleared the streets of juvenile delinquents. These initiatives were influential in developments elsewhere and Mary Carpenter (see below) was aware of them and referred most favourably to their value (Bridgeland 1971; Carpenter 1879; NESJCC 1973).

KEY INITIATIVES IN ENGLAND

Bridgeland (1971) in his comprehensive and thoughtful text *Pioneer Work with Maladjusted Children*, which is frequent drawn upon here, also describes other early enlightened initiatives. These included the opening of ragged day schools which catered for deprived and delinquent children, so that by 1851 when the Ragged Schools Union was formed there were over 60 such schools in existence. These schools differed from the industrial feeding schools described above in that they did not regularly distribute food, and attendance was voluntary. The earliest provision for delinquent youth had occurred when the Marine Society (1756) established a school for convicts' children (Parry-Jones 1994).

The first ragged school in Bristol (Balbernie 1966) was opened in 1846 by Mary Carpenter whom Bridgeland (1971) credits with a major influence on the government. He considers that it was largely through her writing and propagandising that not only were school boards empowered to establish day feeding schools but also to give private reform schools legal recognition so that they could receive grants and become subject to inspection. By the time of her death she had established the structure of child care for deprived and delinquent children for the next century. Her views and understanding were ahead of her time. She emphasised the child's need for affection and firm non-punitive discipline and had a clear concept of the difficulty of some emotionally deprived youngsters in forming affectionate bonds and of the primary importance of facilitating them doing so. She stressed the key importance of quality of staff, was concerned that the physical health of the children was attended to, and recognised the need for good after-care (Carpenter 1879; Saywell 1964).

The residential reform schools, which included the first reformatory for girls, where she put her views into practice can reasonably be viewed as early precursors of schools for maladjusted children, although there were a considerable number of intervening developments and it was over forty years after her death before the first of these was opened. It was, in fact, in the late 1920s that a number of independent boarding schools began to be set up to cater for nervous and difficult children (Underwood 1955). The industrial training schools and reformatories made provision in the intervening years for juveniles that kept them from being incarcerated in prison but as Wills (1971) describes they often saw a harshly disciplinarian training environment as what was required rather than a more therapeutic one as might have fitted with Mary Carpenter's enlightened viewpoint. Ultimately, they gave rise to approved schools.

Bridgeland (1971) notes that theorists in the late nineteenth century stressed respect for the whole child and established a basis for the treatment of the deviant child with special educational problems but that, although public schools were liberalised to some extent in the nineteenth century, there was little movement towards the development of special educational provision for the maladjusted. Nonetheless he does mention the schools Mr. E. Sargent and Alexander Devine opened in 1888 and 1894 as examples of sympathetic and imaginative individual ventures.

EARLY THERAPEUTIC COMMUNITIES

The work of men and women of vision was carried forward into the twentieth century by Leila Rendel who played the central role in the development of the Caldicott community, which can be seen as an early version of a therapeutic community. According to Fees (1990), however, it was at the Little Commonwealth in Dorset set up by Homer Lane in 1913 that work with disturbed, deprived and delinquent children as fellow members of a community was first tried in England. Lane imported some of his ideas about self-government from the USA, where he had experience of working in that way himself. He saw himself as a Freudian, a noteworthy aspect of his thinking in view of the subsequent influence of psychoanalytic ideas on provisions for disturbed children. The Little Commonwealth was an inspiration and, in many respects, a model for a great deal in the way of group work in residential and day provisions for children and adolescents with difficulties but it failed to have much impact on social service and Home Office provision (Bridgeland 1971; Fees 1990; Wardle 1991).

'PROGRESSIVE' SCHOOLS

A major part of Lane's contribution to the development of progressive education was through his impact on other pioneers in the field. Among these was A.S. Neill who, already disillusioned with education along formal and traditional lines by the time he met him (Neill 1915), was strengthened and advanced in his thinking about the needs of children by the contact. Neill went on to establish in 1921 his famous but controversial Summerhill School with its radical and uncompromising rejection of the imposition of education and its emphasis on freedom, permissiveness and self-government (Neill 1961). Neill, in his turn, influenced in major ways other pioneers in progressive education such as Otto Shaw, at Redhill School, Lucy Francis at Kingsmuir School, John Aitkenhead at Kilquhanity School and the attempt in more recent years in Aberdeen by R.F. Mackenzie, to run a local authority mainstream comprehensive school on somewhat similar principles. The failure of this venture despite being much valued by some of its pupils and staff stemmed in part at least from a relative lack of acceptance of its approach and values by the wider community, including parents of children there and some staff members.

SCHOOL PRINCIPAL AS THERAPIST

A.S. Neill was much influenced by psychoanalytic ideas, first those of Freud and later those of Reich, and initially tried to act both as therapist and school principal. The attempt to do so had played a part in the downfall of Lane and Neill's experience led to the view that the child's therapist should be based outside the school (Neill 1961). Combining the roles has not been much practised since, but that it can be done successfully was shown by Otto Shaw at Redhill School and by workers in the USA, Barbara Docker-Drysdale, as well, acted as co-principal and as therapist to the children (and consultant to the staff) at Mulberry Bush School but she makes it clear that she felt this was only possible for her because her husband and co-principal established and supported the therapeutic environment and administration of the school (Docker-Drysdale 1968). It is clear that combining the roles raises complex issues for the children who may have to relate to the therapist-principal in two very different ways. It has pitfalls for the therapist-principal who will certainly need to have well-developed skills in both roles and probably appropriate support available. This is an issue discussed further below with reference to psychiatrists.

PLANNED ENVIRONMENT THERAPY AND RELATED CONCEPTS

Another influential figure in the development of maladjusted education was David Wills who, although he was like Neill much influenced by Homer Lane and psychoanalytic ideas, took up the clear position that it was inappropriate for the roles of principal and therapist to be combined. Wills' own approach, including his belief in the healing power of love and his opposition to punishment, was largely attributed by him to his Quakerism. More than these concepts, however, it has been those he developed with his co-worker, Dr. Marjorie Franklin, of shared responsibility and planned environment therapy that have attracted most interest and discussion. Shared responsibility, although involving a considerable measure of self-government, differed from some forms of it in that it was acknowledged that decision-making was shared between staff and children. The aim was considered to be both therapeutic and educational and suitable only for children over 10 years old (Franklin 1962, 1980).

Righton (1975), defining the concept widely, distinguishes the following three types of planned environment therapy:

(1) Planned environment therapy as developed by Wills and Franklin. This stemmed from the work of Sigmund Freud, Aichorn, Homer Lane and A.S. Neill.

(2) Milieu therapy. This also stemmed from the work of Sigmund Freud and Aichorn, but then in America drew from the ego psychology of Anna Freud, Lewin's group dynamics, and work on the sociology of social organisations. Practitioners in North America working along these lines include Bettelheim, Redl and Vineman and Brown. In Britain, Bion's work on social group theory (Bion 1961) and the work from the Tavistock on organisation and management have provided a theoretical under-pinning for similar developments. The prominent practitioners in Britain of this approach include the Docker-Drysdales at Mulberry Bush School, Richard Balbernie at the Cotswold Community and Melvyn Rose at Peper-Harrow.

(3) Social or community psychiatry. This was developed by Maxwell Jones, who set up therapeutic communities at Henderson Hospital and Dingleton and has been described by Robert Rapaport (1960). In Aberdeen, J.K.V. Morrice, who had worked with Maxwell Jones, utilised these ideas both to change the lot of patients in long-stay psychiatric wards and in a Day Hospital where it was combined with an emphasis on group psychotherapy.

Righton considered that the milieu therapy approach differs from the planned environment therapy as developed by Wills and Franklin by placing more of an emphasis on the small group and less on individual therapy; more of a focus on planning the environment to serve the therapeutic process and by making more of an effort to make it testable and, if possible, modifiable. He also saw in this a move towards working with the current interactions of the child and away from working with the child's unconscious and past experience. The therapeutic community model was largely developed with adults and differs in that more of an emphasis is placed on the healing powers of the community as a whole. Kennard (1983) considers that in a therapeutic community for adults a lesser need for substitute parenting reduces the need for specific therapeutic relationships to be distinguished from other relationships in the community.

Kennard (1983) includes in a sub-group of therapeutic communities those inspired by Rudolf Steiner. His anthroposophy led Dr. Karl Konig, an Austrian physician, to provide the impetus in 1939 in Aberdeenshire for the establishment of the first Camphill Community. This gave rise to the Camphill Movement and the Camphill Rudolf-Steiner and related schools which have catered for mentally handicapped, delinquent, maladjusted, autistic and normal children for many years. The anthroposophical approach to education and development was part of a comprehensive philosophy of life and included curative eurhythmy which emphasised the links between speech and movement and a belief in the therapeutic value of creative work, of the arts, including music, and of religion. It was also considered important to attend to diet, clothes and the physical surroundings. Despite large elements that many would find unacceptably mystical, Camphill schools share in practice and philosophy a great deal with other communities. These include an emphasis on both staff and children being members of the community and sharing tasks, a belief that all of them have a helpful contribution to make (and this would include quite severely handicapped children helping maladjusted children with their relationship difficulties) and a view of the community as central to the therapeutic process. A particular strength has been that these schools have had their own training course in curative education for workers with handicapped and maladjusted children in Camphill, Aberdeen, since 1949.

SCHOOLS FOR MALADJUSTED CHILDREN AND PSYCHIATRY

There have been important links between schools for maladjusted children and psychiatry from their earliest days but these have taken a number of different forms and have changed over the years. Bridgeland (1971) points out that some of the earliest schools for disturbed children sprung from early workers in child psychiatry seeing a need to prevent gains from treatment being lost through parents' difficulties. Dr. F.H. Dodd, who had been physician in charge of the Psychological Department of the Eastern Dispensary in London before moving to the Tavistock Clinic, was interested in the relationship between physical ill-health and psychological difficulties and set up and ran, from 1920 to 1940, what can be viewed as the first school for maladjusted children (Barker 1974; Bridgeland 1971). Another psychiatrist to adopt Dodd's response to the problem of children losing the gains they had made from treatment through exposure to parents' problems was Dr. Albert Fitch who, from 1935 to 1952, opened and ran a school for maladjusted children first at Dunnow Hall on the Yorkshire-Lancashire border and then at Ledston Hall near Castleford. It is of interest that neither of these psychiatrists undertook much in the way of formal individual psychotherapy with their pupils but concentrated on providing an environment which would meet the parenting and educational needs of the children.

In contrast, Dr. Ida Saxby, who was qualified in mathematics, philosophy and psychoanalysis, as well as medicine, tried unsuccessfully at Rest Harrow Abbey School near Haslemere to combine being therapist and school principal.

Dr Marjorie Franklin, a psychiatrist and psychoanalyst, who was founder, secretary of the management committee and consultant of Hawkspur Camp where planned environment therapy was developed, also established an experimental school for maladjusted children at Arlesford Place, where planned environment therapy would be given expression and the results systematically assessed. This was an unsuccessful venture, partly at least because the warden of the school was not fully in sympathy with Dr Franklin's approach. It is to be noted that a somewhat similar factor also contributed to the problems at Rest Harrow Abbey School.

Dr Franklin, however, went on to found the Planned Environment Therapy Trust. She also described a role for visiting psychiatrists to schools for maladjusted children, seeing it as including consultation to the staff and individual therapy for the children but also requiring the psychiatrists to be familiar with the school environment and in sympathy with the approach used. Barbara Docker-Drysdale, too, whose conceptualisations owed much to the work of Winnicott, indicates that she used him for support and consultation (Docker-Drysdale 1968). Acting as consultant to the staff either on an individual or on a group basis and contributing to the assessment and treatment of the children have become the roles fulfilled by psychiatrists in relation to schools for maladjusted children.

Barker (1974) expressed the view that the polarisation between schools for the maladjusted, and child psychiatric in-patient units, was such as to make it unlikely that a child psychiatrist would become principal of a school for maladjusted children again. It is clearly the case that the training of the child psychiatrist is geared to his or her becoming a therapist or consultant and not a school principal. In addition, keeping to the therapist-consultant role avoids what has previously been mentioned as the particularly difficult combination of being both principal and therapist. The parallel problem for psychiatrists (or other therapists) in in-patient units or providing both therapy and leadership or direction to the unit has been much discussed (for example Irwin 1982). Barker (1974) states the view that undoubtedly schools and child psychiatric units can each learn much from the other, and experience as regards the above issue would be one such area.

CHANGING PERSPECTIVES AND FINANCIAL PRESSURES

Schools such as those described by Docker-Drysdale (1968), Wills (1971) and Balbernie (1966) were therapeutic establishments influenced by psychoanalytic ideas utilising planned environment therapy and aimed at a fundamental personality regrowth for often seriously disturbed children. Commenting on centres such as these Barker (1982) says it is uncertain whether what they provide is better than other forms of treatment but that they are impressive and seem to obtain good results. Writing about one of them, the Cotswold Community, Wills (1971) contrasts it with most approved schools, but also warns that it does not follow that its model is appropriate for all such establishments. In view of the lack of research evidence that schools run on psychotherapeutic lines (including therapeutic communities) have a great deal of success in treating delinquents, and some indication that a firm but not harsh regime may be best, but that no residential treatment for delinquents is very successful (Rutter and Giller 1983; Clarke and Cornish 1978) this is clearly a wise caveat. Wills also makes the important point that there is a shortage of suitably trained staff to meet the needs of the children, and expresses the view that the best that would be likely for many would be a holding operation.

Wrate *et al.* (1985) comment on the relative lack of success that the schools for maladjusted children in their study seemed to have, but relate this to the entrenched nature of the difficulties of many of the children and conclude that they are an essential part of the range of provision. Howlin (1994) refers to the difficulties in interpreting follow-up studies of children attending these schools and suggests that residential schools for maladjusted children sometimes have a role, when family problems or inadequacies are largely contributing to their difficulties.

Certainly, what happened throughout the 1980s is that there was a rise in the number of children in schools for children with emotional and behavioural difficulties (EBD) – as maladjusted children were called after the 1981 Education Act, which was designed to give expression to some of the recommendations of the Warnock Report (1978). The number of children in EBD day schools accounted for much of the increase but residential EBD schools were also used to an greater extent (Cliffe with Berridge 1991; Howlin 1994). This increase occurred despite the influence of the Warnock Report (1978) which envisaged children with special educational needs having these met in mainstream schools on the basis of comprehensive individual assessments. An attempt has been made to analyse the reasons for the sustained growth in the number of children in EBD schools. Suggested reasons include: attempts to protect the smooth-running of mainstream schools from disruption of disturbed children; limited resources to support children in mainstream schools; and, arguably, the closing of Children's Homes (see below). While it is unclear whether or not these changes are a positive development, it has been pointed out that the very wide variations among local authorities in the use of day and residential EBD schools, which cannot be explained on the basis of regional differences in numbers of disturbed children, are a cause for concern.

The Education Act 1981 and the Education (Scotland) Act 1981 have been seen as beneficial through empowering parents and making professionals more accountable, but have been criticised as bureaucratic and time consuming. Much of this debate centres around the procedures known as 'statementing' in England and Wales and 'recording' in Scotland which includes documentation of the pupil's needs as identified by multi-disciplinary assessment and of the measures being taken to meet these needs. A study of the reactions of parents and professionals to the recording procedures of the Education (Scotland) Act 1981 as regards visually impaired children identified a strong feeling that the procedures could be streamlined while a similar quality of parental involvement was preserved. The Act was seen as having sharpened up the accountability of special educational provision (Thomson, Budge, Buultgens and Lee 1986). It is likely that a similar study as regards EBD children would arrive at similar conclusions.

Rimmer (1992) writing at the time of closure of Red Hill School of which he was Principal, notes that other independent schools were closing or under threat of closure, and suggests some of the reasons lie not just in expense, but in advantages being perceived in EBD schools being local provisions provided by Local Education Authorities. He queries whether such provisions as will emerge will meet the needs of all children but considers that it will not lead to much reduction in places. He notes that placement in an independent school outwith an area cannot easily be reconciled with a model of a 'cluster' of schools with a range of provision, and a consistent team overviewing assessment, review and discharge.

THE SCOTTISH SCENE

In Scotland, development of schools for maladjusted children took place much more slowly and to a more limited extent than in England. Despite the enlightened initiatives of the nineteenth century and the work of those influenced by A.S. Neill, himself a Scot, described previously, the Scottish tradition of an emphasis on strict discipline and high academic standards was reflected in children with behavioural difficulties being seen as requiring correction and training rather than treatment or therapeutic education (Bridgeland 1971). Such provision as there has been has tended to be run by voluntary bodies such as Barnardo's and Save the Children Fund, although they did receive grants from the Scottish Education Department (McNair 1968). Provision for secondary school pupils was even more limited with Lendrick Muir School when it was opened in 1961 being the only grant aided secondary school for maladjusted children (and then only for those of above average ability) (Bridgeland 1971). One response to the lack of provision for maladjusted children in a few cases was to accommodate them at residential schools that were not primarily for the maladjusted, for example Kilquhanity School and Camphill Rudolf Steiner Schools or to send them to schools for maladjusted children in England. There were, of course, many maladjusted children in approved schools often without this being explicitly acknowledged. This was, in essence, the case in England as well, as there is overlap and lack of differentiation between the two groups but it was necessarily more so in Scotland in view of the lack of alternatives.

In 1944, the Report of the Working Party on the Ascertainment of Maladjusted Children called for a marked improvement in the provision of day and residential schools, particularly for adolescents. The need was accepted by the Scottish Education Department who also pointed out that these schools could be planned on a regional basis with educational authorities taking into account the needs of neighbouring authorities. Improvements in provisions took some years to be accomplished. For example, when Cordyce School, a regional residential school for maladjusted children which set out to be part of a fully integrated comprehensive service to troubled youngsters (Michie 1971) was opened in 1973 outside Aberdeen, there was no strictly comparable establishment in Scotland.

As was indicated in the 1991 Save The Children Fund document *Harmeny School —The Future* more recently the policy of educational authorities in Scotland has changed towards keeping EBD children of primary school age at home if at all possible, even in the face of a considerable level of disturbance. If their families were unable to provide adequate care, substitute care was to be provided through the social work department. This led to the closure of some residential EBD schools and for a tendency for children to go to residential EBD schools only as a last resort, often with problems deeply entrenched. Closer involvement between EBD schools and the community was, as in England, seen as desirable. Developments have occurred as regards this, both through greater involvement of families in schools and through staff from the schools undertaking outreach work in the community.

(2) Children's Homes and Other Forms of Residential Care
ANOTHER BLEAK EARLY PICTURE

Berridge (1985) considers the historical antecedents of Children's Homes and differentiates between England and Scotland. He points out that in the sixteenth and seventeenth century in England there was an increase in destitution and vagrancy and parishes had to take on an increasing responsibility for the poor. One response was the creation of workhouses where children and parents could reside. In the eighteenth and nineteenth centuries it was realised that many of the children grew up to become beggars and vagrants themselves, and an attempt to prevent this entailed providing education and training. However, it was also part of the philosophy to discourage entry to the workhouses and dependency on them. It was considered desirable, therefore, that these institutions have bleak harsh environments with the children often separated from their parents. Despite this there tended to be insufficient places, and the same residential establishments had to cater for disturbed, handicapped and deprived children and adolescents, irrespective of whether they were long-stay or short-stay admissions, so that the task of those in charge was daunting. The almost unavoidable consequence was that throughout the nineteenth century control of children and adolescents in care was emphasised. Unfortunately, the education and training that was provided was not appropriate for survival outside the institutions, and most attempts to settle boys and girls in apprenticeship or service were unsuccessful.

CHILDREN'S HOMES, FOSTER CARE AND CHILDREN'S OWN FAMILIES:
CHANGES IN POLICY AND IDEOLOGY

It was only in the twentieth century that the needs and rights of children were taken into account. Changes acknowledging these took place only slowly, and in 1946 the Curtis Committee criticised Children's Homes as showing a lack of personal interest and affection for the children and advocated more use of foster care. There is now a general acceptance that children should not normally remain for long periods in Children's Homes and that placement with a foster family is a more effective way of meeting their needs. In addition to the Report of the Curtis Committee other influences supporting this change were feelings about Children's Homes stemming from their harsh Poor Law origins, the writings of R.D. Laing (1960) and Szasz (1961), the perceived lesser expense of foster care (although the difference is less if all related expenses are considered) and Bowlby's ideas about the harmful effects of extended mother–child separation (Cliffe with Berridge 1991).

As was to be expected, between the 1950s and the 1990s numbers of children in residential care, that is those in Children's Homes, residential schools, NHS establishments and secure institutions, have fallen and numbers in foster care have risen. The numbers in care overall have also fallen and the drop in the proportion of children in residential care relative to the proportion in foster care is marked. However, this overall pattern hides important fluctuations over the years. These include such factors as:

- a drop in the number of children in the community

- legal changes so that 'in care' orders were not used for criminal cases

- the creation of unified social services departments which took on long term responsibility even if that entailed the use of compulsory measures

- research showing that children in care longer than six weeks tended to stay long term

- greater efforts to keep children in their own homes and to return them to them

- permanency planning (aimed at settling all children in care with a permanent family).

It has been pointed out that occupancy of residential care gives an inaccurate picture of the extent to which residential care is still used. There is substantial movement in and out of residential care and Utting (1991) comments that many, perhaps most, children in care have been in residential care at some point.

THE CHILDREN IN RESIDENTIAL CARE

The characteristics of children admitted to Children's Homes have changed over the years. For most of this century delinquent children have been managed separately (in approved schools) from those admitted to Children's Homes because their parents could not provide adequate physical and psychological care. However, following the Children and Young Person Act 1969, the view was taken that the needs of both were similar and both types of provision became 'community homes' (Wolkind and Rushton 1994). Subsequently, many of the 'community homes with education' that replaced approved schools have closed (Parker 1988). With wider use, too, of foster care and adoption including of older children, and treating children in their own homes when possible being accepted, children's homes have received concentrations of adolescents who frequently come from dysfunctional families including abusive and seriously neglectful ones. It is known that children in care are a group with an increased incidence of educational, developmental, physical and mental health problems and of social deviance, and that in the past admission to care has sometimes increased these problems rather than remedied them. Since the youngsters in residential establishments are frequently those who have been hard to place elsewhere or for whom placements have broken down they are a group with even more difficulties than the rest (Utting 1991). Often with these youngsters the aim may still be, despite all their problems and those of their families, to return them home after no longer a stay than is unavoidable.

STAFFING ISSUES

For stays in the Homes to be constructive experiences staff have therefore had to become skilful in managing groups of often seriously disturbed young people. They also had to develop skills in working actively with them, and with their families to enable them to make the changes necessary for reintegration home to have a chance to succeed. Alternatively, they have had to work towards preparing the child for a foster or adoptive placement. Unfortunately, much of this work has had to be undertaken by unqualified staff. This has quite often applied even to officers-in-charge and to most or all other staff members in many establishments. This is recognised as a deplorable state of affairs and a target of having all officers-in-charge qualified within three years has been set (Utting 1991).

Consideration is also given to the requirements of other staff and the same report suggests that some of the training requires to broaden its scope and identifies training for residential staff as a priority. It is also acknowledged that measures are required to improve the morale and standing of residential care staff. Staffing levels have improved but still seem inadequate to meet the needs of some of the difficult youngsters.

THE CHILDREN ACT AND CURRENT POLICY

The Children Act (1989) has been described as 'the most important piece of legislation affecting children this century' (Utting 1991) (see also Chapter 11). Wolkind (1991) points out that no group of children will be more affected by the Act than those 'being looked after by the local authority' as they are to be called in attempt to reduce the stigma of being 'in care'. It has considerable implications for the residential care of children. It is clear from publications commissioned from the Department of Health that residential care is seen as 'a positive and desirable way of providing stability and care for some children which they themselves often prefer to other kinds of placement' (Department of Health 1990). Moreover, this continues to be the case, despite the widespread concerns about residential care following reports on the Pindown Experience (Levy and Kahan 1991) and about the vulnerability to abuse of children in residential care (Department of Health 1991; Utting 1991). Barker (1988) makes a distinction between residential care and treatment, but Skinner (1992) states that residential child care can be seen as including both care and treatment, and Utting (1991) sees a need for sophisticated and expert treatment in a residential setting as one of the factors making residential care the preferred, best or only option for certain children.

PARTNERSHIP WITH PARENTS AND FAMILIES

The Children Act 1989 and the related publications (particularly Department of Health 1991; Utting 1991) draw on research into residential child care and make recommendations as to how the child's welfare can be promoted, in partnership with parents and carers and on policies, planning and decision making. It is made clear that the voluntary route into care is to be chosen unless it would be damaging to the child. Voluntary care (now to be called accommodation) is seen as a way of sustaining families, not as substituting for them, and it is proposed that it should operate rather like respite care does for children with disabilities. It is pointed out that compulsory measures have not in the past meant better planning and security, but have been associated with difficulties in the relationship between parents and social workers with feelings of upset, anger and helplessness on the part of parents and increased difficulties in sustaining family ties. While the links need not be causal ones, forming a partnership with parents and carers is seen as the way forward. It is underlined that such a partnership will only be achieved through being worked for and not just through avoiding the use of compulsion. Written contracts with parents, involvement of parents in reviews, case conferences and planning meetings, and efforts to establish shared perceptions of problems and the responses to them are seen as contributing to successful partnerships. The need to consider siblings and the extended family more fully than has been often done in the past is highlighted.

AVOIDING CHILD ABUSE

The impact of other children in residential care has been studied and found to be more often a source of stress or aggression than a helpful influence (Colton 1988). The right of children for protection from other residents and not to be left to fight their own battles is advocated, and it is recommended that victims of abuse and abusers should not be accommodated together (Utting 1991), Skinner (1992), however, considers that this will not always be realistic in view of the numbers involved and points out the difficulties in identifying abusers and the risk that victims may become abusers themselves. The need for management to be alert to the risk of abuse by staff while supporting them having appropriate physical contact with children has also been recognised (Utting 1991).

GOOD PLANNING AND LISTENING TO CHILDREN

As regards planning and decision-making for individual children Utting (1991) referred to evidence that the following are required:

(1) improved planning, including specifying in writing what is needed, who should carry it out and by when;

(2) ascertainment of the child's views and perceptions with due weight being given to them;

(3) attention to relevant research;

(4) careful collection of reliable data including observations; and

(5) consideration of the history of the child and the family. Worrying evidence is quoted of the gap between children's concerns and workers' perceptions, including lack of awareness of children's concern about their angry and aggressive behaviour.

RESIDENTIAL CARE AS PART OF OVERALL CHILD CARE STRATEGY

The Wagner Report (1988) emphasised residential child care being considered in the context of a national and local child care strategy and as part of community-based provision. Residential care should be a positive choice. Kendrick and Fraser (1992) while endorsing this last point suggest that residential care establishments can be viewed in two clusters – one locally-based community provision including small Children's Homes and respite facilities, and the other enclosed residential communities such as secure units and therapeutic communities. This division does not imply that in the latter cluster work with the family or with the child at home should not be undertaken but that the former group are much more permeable to the wider community. This permeability to the community fits well with the picture Utting (1991) paints of some homes vigorously developing outreach work or acting as a base for activities such as after care, day care, intermediate treatment.

THE SCOTTISH SCENE

The historical background to current provision for children in the care of the local authority is significantly different in Scotland from in England. Berridge (1985) suggests that residential care developed more slowly in Scotland than in England because the smaller number of large towns or cities made raising the money required more difficult. The Calvinistic religious attitudes stressed the importance of the family and the lack of a tradition of sending boys to boarding school meant the idea of residential care did not occur so readily. The Poor Law provision was even less generous than in England and boarding out or fostering was favoured on the basis that it was less expensive and that the children could do useful work on the land. Good local schools meant that there was less need to have education provided in institutions.

Despite the long tradition of foster care in Scotland residential establishments did over time come to care for substantial numbers of children. More recently, there has been, as in England, a move towards a reduction in the numbers of children in residential care and an increased emphasis on supporting children in their own homes or in foster care, or placing them for adoption. This was shown by a reduction from 36 per cent of children in care being in residential care in 1976 to only 18 per cent in 1990 (Skinner 1992). As in England, residential care became a provision predominantly for adolescents and, indeed, in Scotland, the same document talks of children under 12 being placed in residential care only in exceptional circumstances.

The legislation covering being in care in Scotland differs from in England. Generally, in Scotland, children are in residential care either subject to a statutory residential supervision requirement from a Children's Hearing or they are there on a voluntary basis. In fact, the proportion of children in care on a voluntary basis has fallen from 45 per cent in 1977 to 13 per cent in 1990. This latter figure contrasts with 37 per cent of children in care in England being there on a voluntary basis. The adverse effects of compulsion on partnership with parents has already been discussed and avoiding its use when possible is advocated for Scotland as for England (Skinner 1992).

Conclusion

Complex relationships exist between EBD schools, Children's Homes and child psychiatric in-patient units. Not only are children with similar difficulties found in all three, but the same children may move from one to the other, sometimes, indeed, with one child making several such moves. Aspects of the Children Act 1989, moreover, apply to all three types of establishments and are likely to increase the extent to which there are similar issues to be dealt with in all of them. Some of these are considered with reference to child psychiatric in-patient units in Chapter 14. It was to be anticipated, therefore, that lessons could be drawn from experiences in one type of establishment which could be applied in another. Some of these are referred to in this chapter and in a number of other chapters. With reference to the Lowit Unit in particular, the contribution of social work to the changes that have occurred is referred to in Chapter 11.

Changes occurring as regards the extent or the nature of provision in EBD schools, or in Children's Homes, or in child psychiatric in-patient units can have an impact on all three. For example, delaying discharging children from in-patient units because of lack of provision in schools for maladjusted children was referred to by Barker (1974) and is still an issue at times today. On the other hand, purchasers refusing to accept children remaining longer in in-patient units than would otherwise be the case because of shortage of educational provision can increase the demands for EBD school places.

A recommendation (Skinner 1992) that children under 12 years of age should only exceptionally be placed in residential care can have an impact on demands for places and length of stay in both EBD schools and child psychiatric units. This effect can be mitigated by the development of specialised foster placements in sufficient numbers. However, as Wolkind and Rushton (1994) point out, there are likely to be limits to the number of foster parents who can be recruited in any community. Moreover, the concept of residential care as a positive choice (Wagner 1988) has already been mentioned and it is arguable that this should continue to be a possibility for certain children under 12 years of age. As regards child psychiatric in-patient units, too, as children who would previously have been managed in Children's Homes are now being managed in foster care, more of the co-operative work has to be with foster parents rather than with residential social workers.

Hersov (1994) points out that over the last decade there has been a trend in the USA to admit to hospital, on occasion, without first considering the appropriateness of less restrictive treatment resources. This has been rightly condemned by professional organisations there. The importance of avoiding misuse of in-patient units has long been recognised (Hersov and Bentovim 1976) but pressures to make inappropriate admissions can sometimes occur. It remains to be seen how, if joint purchasing between the NHS purchasers and local authorities is introduced, it will affect the pressures.

References

Aichorn, A. (1935) *Wayward Youth*. New York: Viking Press.

Balbernie, R. (1966) *Residential work with Children* (rev. ed.) London: Chaucer Publishing Company Ltd.

Barker, P. (1974) *The Residential Psychiatric Treatment of Children*. London: Crosby, Lockwood and Staples.

Barker, P. (1982) 'Residential treatment for disturbed children: its place in the '80s.' *Canadian Journal of Psychiatry 27*, 8, 634–638.

Barker, P. (1988) 'The future of residential treatment for children.' In C. Schaefer and A. Swanson (eds) *Children in Residential Care: Critical Issues for Treatment.* New York: Von Nostrand Reinhold.

Berridge, D. (1985) *Children's Homes.* Oxford: Basil Blackwell.

Bion, W.R. (1961) *Experience in Groups.* London: Tavistock.

Bridgeland, M. (1971) *Pioneer Work with Maladjusted Children.* London: Staples Press.

Carpenter, J.E. (1879) *The Life and Work of Mary Carpenter.* London: Macmillan and Co.

Clarke, R.V.G. and Cornish, D.B. (1978) 'The effectiveness of residential treatment for delinquents.' In L.A. Hersov, M. Berger and D. Shaffer (eds) *Aggression and Anti-social Behaviour in Childhood and Adolescence 1,* 143–159. Oxford: Pergaman Press.

Cliffe, D. with Berridge, D. (1991) *Closing Children's Homes. An End to Residential Child Care?* London: National Children's Bureau.

Colton, M. (1988) 'Dimensions of foster and residential care practice.' *Journal of Child Psychology and Psychiatry 29,* 5, 589–600.

Department of Health (1990) *The Care of Children: Principles and Practice in Regulations and Guidance.* London: HMSO.

Department of Health (1991) *Patterns and Outcomes in Child Placement. Messages from Current Research and their Implications.* London: HMSO.

Docker-Drysdale, B. (1968) *Therapy in Child Care.* London: Longman Green.

Fees, C. (1990) 'Reflections of a folklorist in a residential therapeutic community for emotionally deprived and disturbed children.' *Maladjustment and Therapeutic Education 8,* 2, 68–73.

Franklin, M. (1980) 'Clinical aspects of his work with David Wills'. *Journal of the Association of Workers for Maladjusted Children 8,* 2, 73–80.

Franklin, M. (1968) 'The work of W. David Wills – An appreciation.' *Newsletter of Association of Workers for Maladjusted Children 10,* 2, 17–37.

Hersov, L. and Bentovim, A. (1976) 'Inpatient units and day-hospitals.' In *Child Psychiatry, Modern Approaches.* London: Blackwell.

Hersov, L. (1994) 'Inpatient and day hospital units.' In M. Rutter, E. Taylor and L. Hersov. *Child and Adolescent Psychiatry, Modern Approaches.* 3rd edition. London: Blackwell.

Howlin, P. (1994) 'Special educational treatment.' In M. Rutter, E. Taylor and L. Hersov (eds) *Child and adolescent Psychiatry – Modern Approaches.* Third edition. Oxford: Blackwell.

Irwin, M. (1982) 'Literature review.' In J.L Schulman and M. Irwin (ed) *Psychiatric Hospitalisation of Children.* Springfield: Charles C. Thomas.

Jones, M. (1952) *Social Psychiatry.* London: Tavistock.

Jones, M. (1968) *Social Psychiatry in Practice.* Hammondsworth: Penguin.

Kendrick, A. and Fraser, S. (1992) 'Summary of the literature review.' Appendix B to Skinner, A. A Review of Residential Child Care. Edinburgh: HMSO.

Kennard, D. (1983) An Introduction to Therapeutic Communities. London: Routledge and Kegan Paul.

Kilbrandon Report (1966) Children and Young Persons. Scotland, Edinburgh: HMSO.

Laing, R.D. (1960) The Divided Self. London: Penguin.

Levy, A. and Kahan, B.A. (1991) The Pindown Experience and the Protection of Children. Staffordshire: Staffordshire County Council.

McNair, H. (1968) A Survey of Children in Residential Schools for the Maladjusted in Scotland. Edinburgh: Oliver and Boyd.

Michie, J. (1971) 'The proposed regional school for the maladjusted.' Education in the North 8, 87–90.

Miller, A. (1993) 'Children's hearing – emergency measures.' Scottish Child. April/May, 7.

Neill, A.S. (1915) A Dominies' Log. London: Herbert Jenkins.

Neill, A.S. (1961) Summerhill. Harmondsworth: Pelican.

North East of Scotland Joint Consultative Committee on Residential Child Care Services (1973) The Distribution and Use of Residential Child Care Services in North East Scotland. Aberdeen: Aberdeen Peoples Press.

Parker, R. (1988) 'A historical background.' In I. Sinclair (ed) Residential Care. The Research Reviewed. London: HMSO.

Parry-Jones, W.L.I. (1989) 'The history of child and adolescent psychiatry: its present day relevance.' Journal of Child Psychology and Psychiatry 30, 1, 3–11.

Parry-Jones, W.L.I. (1994) 'History of child and adolescent psychiatry.' In M. Rutter, E. Taylor and L. Hersov (eds) Child and Adolescent Psychiatry: Modern Approaches. Third edition. Oxford: Blackwell.

Rapoport, R. (1960) Community as Doctor: New Perspectives on a Therapeutic Community. London: Tavistock.

Righton, P. (1975) 'Planned environment therapy: a reappraisal.' The Journal of the Association of Workers for Maladjusted Children 3, 1, 3–12.

Rimmer, A. (1992) 'Death of a school.' Therapeutic Care and Education 10, 1, 55–59.

Rutter, M. and Giller, H. (1983) Juvenile Delinquency: Trends and Perspectives. Harmondsworth, Middlesex: Penguin.

Save The Children Fund (1991) Harmeny School: The Future. Unpublished report.

Saywell, R.J. (1964) 'Mary Carpenter of Bristol.' Historical Association Bristol Branch Local History. Pamphlets No. 9. Bristol: Bristol University.

Sheldrick, C. (1985) 'Treatment of delinquents.' In M. Rutter and L. Hersov (eds) Child and Adolescent Psychiatry: Modern Approaches. Second edition. Oxford: Blackwell.

Skinner, A. (1992) *The Social Work Services Inspectorate for Scotland A Review of Residential Child Care.* Edinburgh: HMSO.

Szasz, T. (1961) *The Myth of Mental Illness.* New York: Hoeber-Harper.

Thomson, G., Budge, A., Buultjens, M. and Lee, M. (1986) 'Scotland and the 1981 Education Act.' *British Journal of Special Education 13*, 3, 115–118.

The Faculty of Curative Education (1981) Curative Education. *Report of Working Party on Camphill Course for Curative Education.* Aberdeen: Aberdeen University Press.

Underwood, J.E.A. (1955) *Report of the Committee on Maladjusted Children.* London: HMSO.

Utting, W. (1991) Social Work Services Inspectorate Children in the Public Care. *A Review of Residential Child Care.* London: HMSO.

Wagner, G. (1988) *Residential care: A positive choice.* London: HMSO.

Wardle, C.J. (1991) 'Twentieth century influences on the development in Britain of services for child and adolescent psychiatry.' *British Journal of Psychiatry 159*, 53–68.

Warnock, L.M. (1978) *Special education needs.* Report of the Committee of Enquiry into the Education of Handicapped Children and Young People. London: HMSO.

Webb, A. and Wistow, G. (1987) *Social Work, Social Care and Social Planning: The personal social services since Seebohm.* London: Longman.

Weihs, T.J. (1971) *Children in Need of Special Care.* London: Souvenir.

West, D.J. (1967) *The Young Offender.* Harmondsworth: Penguin.

Wills, W.D. (1971) *Spare the Child. The story of an experimental approved school.* Harmondsworth: Penguin.

Wolkind, S. (1991) 'Child placement.' *British Medical Journal 303*, 48.

Wolkind, S. and Rushton, A. (1994) 'Residential and foster family care.' In M. Rutter, E. Taylor and L. Harsov (eds) *Child and Adolescent Psychiatry: Modern Approaches.* Oxford: Blackwell.

Wrate, R.M., Kolvin, I., Garside, R.F., Wolstenholme, F., Hulbert, C.M. and Leitch, I.M. (1985) 'Helping seriously disturbed children.' In A.R. Nicol (ed) *Longitudinal Studies on Child Psychology and Psychiatry: Practical Lessons from Research Experience.* Chichester: John Wiley and Sons.

CHAPTER 3

The Development of Child Psychiatric In-Patient Practice
Past, Present and Future

Douglas Chisholm

The North American Picture

From Containment, Through Psychoanalytically Orientated Treatment, to Eclecticism and Early Discharge

Child psychiatric in-patient units have existed in the USA since the early 1920s catering initially primarily for children with post-encephalitic behaviour disorders (Barker 1974; Harper and Geraty 1987) and children suffering from autism and schizophrenia (Hendren and Berlin 1991). These units were initially seen as providing containment (Jemerin and Philips 1988) but as they extended their role to cater for a wider range of child psychiatric disorders they took on a more therapeutic role. Certainly by the 1930s a great deal of expertise had been built up and a substantial body of knowledge accumulated. One early view of them was as providers of a benign, neutral setting to offset the adverse influence that got in the way of psychotherapy (Hersov and Bentovim 1985). Bender (1937) describes how group therapy including use of the living experience in such units can be a main plank of treatment and, as has been described with reference to non-hospital residential units, greater appreciation of the therapeutic potential of the living experience followed. The models of therapeutic milieu mentioned in Chapters 1 and 2 could also be applied to in-patient units with many of the units being centred round individual psychotherapy as the key treatment for the child (Robinson, Maxwell and Dominguez 1947). However, for many, individual psychotherapy was just one treatment modality, albeit often one that was seen as of particular importance and Jemerin and Philips (1988) talk of child psychiatric in-patient units eventually centring round 'the ideal of a developmentally oriented milieu program with individualised goals for each child, embodying individual dynamic and group psychotherapy, occupational and sensimotor therapy, special education and collaborative work with parents' (p.397).

Expansion of In-patient Child Psychiatric Provision and Associated Changes

By the 1970s there was some disillusionment with the results of long-term residential treatment as evidence accumulated that gains made during admissions were often not maintained after discharge (Lewis *et al.* 1980). Because of this, for financial reasons, and because of greater attention to biological approaches to explaining and treating child psychiatric disorders, there was a rapid increase in the numbers of child psychiatric in-patient units. These have developed over recent years into specialised units for comprehensive diagnostic evaluation and brief treatment very different from the residential treatment centres many had come to resemble previously (Jemerin and Philips 1988). Indeed, this resemblance between in-patient units and residential treatment centres was so marked that much of the literature did not distinguish between the two (Irwin 1982). Although Perry (1989) suggests that child psychiatric units treat much the same children as they always did Jemerin and Philips (1988) and Hendren and Berlin (1991) describe how, in response to changes in families and in society, and to the shortage of other provisions, units have had to assess and treat many more aggressive children with severe conduct disorders including many who had suffered physical or sexual abuse. It seems likely that, although the problems that individual children present are not dissimilar from those that had to be coped with in the past, the frequency with which children with particularly difficult management problems are admitted has increased. This change together with the move to shorter admissions has led to changes in practice including earlier use of physical restraint, 'time-out', and seclusion, more work with families to facilitate earlier return home of the child and more frequent re-admissions to hospital. Lack of appropriate residential facilities in the community has also increased the tendency to re-admit to psychiatric units. These pressures together with growth in knowledge in paediatric psychopharmacology have led to increased use of medication.

Length of Stay and Outcome

The issue of length of stay has evoked a great deal of discussion. This has been partly because of the lack of evidence as to what length of stay constitutes the best treatment but has also been fuelled by pressure from payers for shorter treatment time (Barber and Allen 1992). In addition, there is the imbalance between the number of places available and the number of children who it is thought would benefit from in-patient admission. Whereas Moultrie and Carek (1982) cautiously welcome brief treatment, seeing children and families as previously at risk of over-diagnosis and over-treatment, when Jemerin and Philips (1988) describe these changes they include some of the adverse consequences, such as fragmentation of care. They also make recommendations for action including the development of a full spectrum of rehabilitative services co-ordinated by a central agency.

Blotcky, Dimperio and Gosset (1984) from a review of hospital and non-hospital studies conclude that length of stay sufficient to meet treatment goals is correlated with a better outcome. Pfeiffer and Strzlecki (1990) by a statistical analysis of a number of outcome studies show a modest correlation between length of stay and a favourable outcome but note that a specialist treatment programme for the child while in the unit plus good aftercare were stronger positive influences. Inadequacies of the follow-up studies so far carried out are however acknowledged by Pfeiffer and Strzlecki. In a recent study, Kolko (1992), for example found no relationship between length of stay and a positive outcome.

Some units have taken the concept of brief treatment further and admit on a time-limited basis with arrangements for discharge a condition of admission (Ney, Adam, Hanton and Brindad 1988). Taking the full range of child psychiatric disorders including the most severe, and with a length of stay of only 29 days, they found that in contrast to the increase in re-admissions noted elsewhere they had a reduced re-admission rate. They considered that their results provided evidence that the short pre-determined admission period was an effective form of treatment but acknowledged that the improvements shown might be due to other factors. They argue, however, that knowing the date of discharge increased the motivation of families to co-operate in treatment. Gray et al. (1992), however, have found the use of a fixed discharge date for this purpose only occasionally necessary and see little justification for routine use of the same fixed length of stay for all patients. They consider, however, that knowledge of the likely time scale for treatment of children with specific categories of disorder is very useful.

Further Developments and the Future

Other developments in treatment are the emphasis on: the need to attend to multi-cultural issues (Hendren and Berlin 1991); goal directed treatment by Nurcombe (1989); and on a single focal problem by Harper (1989) while Woolston (1989) suggests that short and intermediate treatment should be conceptualised as catalysing improvement in the fit between the child and his or her family (and other key individuals). Perry (1989) views the future of child psychiatric in-patient units as lying in their capacity both to provide for acutely disturbed children and to carry out on an elective basis comprehensive assessments utilising advances in biochemistry and imaging as appropriate to elucidate the physical contribution to children's difficulties.

The British Picture

Developments Before the First British In-patient Unit

To understand the development of British child psychiatric in-patient units it is necessary to consider how disturbed children were catered for before such units were in existence. As has already been described, and as is already still the case, most provision for disturbed children was, in fact, non-medical. Nonetheless, a small but increasing number of youngsters were admitted to adult lunatic asylums from the early nineteenth century onwards (von Gontard 1988). For example, it is known that from 1815 to 1899, excluding the years 1825 to 1829 for which information is lacking, 235 children aged between six and 16 were admitted to Bethlem Royal Hospital (Wilkins 1987). While much of the treatment at that time of those considered insane, including children, was harsh and inhumane (von Gontard 1988), a study of juveniles up to 19 years in Oxfordshire asylums showed this was not necessarily the case (Parry-Jones 1989).

Although there was not a smooth forward progression, and child psychiatric opinion later reacted against the asylums with their associated organic perspective, the experiences of adult psychiatrists in looking after children and young people gave child psychiatry a medical foundation. Child psychiatry was also influenced by the development of paediatrics as a medical speciality, while experience in organising the mentally handicapped in wards, and assessing and classifying them was also found helpful (von Gontard 1988; Parry-Jones 1989). Von Gontard (1988) also refers to the contributions of other medical specialties such as neurology, genetics and sexology. Other important early influences came from psychoanalysis, psychology, social work, education including remedial teaching, criminology, the mental hygiene movement and the child guidance movement with its emphasis on the multi-disciplinary team (von Gontard 1988; Parry-Jones 1989; Wardle 1991). From these roots child psychiatry in England developed along two different paths, in child guidance clinics of the local education authorities and in hospital-based child psychiatry departments. Although practice in both was along multi-disciplinary lines it was in the latter that the child psychiatrist's leadership role was most clearly established, and it was in association with hospital-based out-patient services that in-patient units developed. They reflected, too, both child psychiatry's medical roots and its broadly based multi-disciplinary ethos.

The First British Hospital Child Psychiatric In-patient Unit

The first hospital child psychiatric in-patient unit in Britain was the Children's In-patient Department of the Maudsley Hospital which opened in 1947, although Creak had by that time already started an in-patient unit in the evacuated Mount Girls' School in Mill Hill. In his description of the unit at the Maudsley Hospital after it had been running for two years, it is striking that much of what Kenneth Cameron says is as applicable today as it was then, and that some of the points made are seen as requiring emphasis by other psychiatrists at much later dates. Cameron stresses the importance in treatment of appreciation of the biopsychosocial unity of the child. Assessment should cover all of these dimensions, and, while he makes the very practical point that treatment has to focus on the aspects that can be changed, whether or not they brought about the condition in the first place, he argues that 'total treatment' is always required. It is clear that he considers that the latter includes the child's home and family. Cameron also emphasises that hospitalisation is *only a phase of treatment* and that work with discharged cases is required if the benefits of in-patient treatment are not to be lost.

Cameron states that they quickly found that adults could not 'supervise' children but must 'work with' them. He explains this difference with an electrical analogy of tension in the supervised group of interacting children rising as if the connections were of cells in series while with adults intermixed and working with the children the tension was at a lower level as if the cells were in parallel. This phenomenon is well understood by those with practical experience of working with disturbed children but poorly described in the literature.

To guide them in their work with children, nurses at the unit at the Maudsley Hospital were given a typescript with four basic principles:

(1) that children have a biological need for affection

(2) that the infant abandons demands for immediate gratification to retain the approval of the mother who gives it affection and it was on a similar basis that nurses should look for conformity from the children to reasonable demands

(3) that each child requires emotional, imaginative and physical outlets

(4) that nurses were also encouraged to use their authority when appropriate, although the first three principles provided the basis.

A stable routine was also seen as helpful and he underlines the need for nurses to feel secure.

The First Child Psychiatric Unit in Scotland

Other early in-patient units were at St. James' (Portsmouth), Mapperley and Hill End but the first child psychiatric unit in Scotland was Ladyfield at Crichton Royal Hospital, Dumfries. It opened in 1951 in a moderate sized country house standing in its own grounds outside the hospital, and catered for twelve boys and eight girls from five to fourteen years.

In 1954 Rogers stated that life there resembled as much as possible an ordinary residential school with, in addition to school, occupational therapy such as woodwork and sewing, and a special event such as an outing each day.

The routine was seen as important in the children's management. The unit was seen as practising 'role' therapy with the assistant matron as a mother figure, the male charge nurse a father figure and the cadet nurses elder sisters. Rogers (1954) expressed the view that psychotherapy with children needed real people to act as, for instance, parents, sisters, while in working with adults the psychiatrist could assume all these roles and help the patient to understand them.

By 1965 Rogers gives a much fuller account of the work of Ladyfield based on his experience of over 10 years. By then there were two houses of 17 to 18 children of normal intelligence with all kinds of psychiatric disorder divided flexibly by age with much of overlap; and a third house of 25 disturbed children with mental and in some cases physical handicap. This unit was able to offer less intensive treatment than the other two but was at that time being integrated more closely with them.

Rogers saw comprehensive diagnosis as a major function of the unit and considered that it could take up to three months. It was his view that a statement of the child's assets should form at least half of the diagnostic assessment and formulation. The child's capacity for change was another area that he saw as of particular importance. The second function of the unit he saw as short term treatment in which the child was removed from home to defuse a crisis and to allow treatment to be commenced with a view to it continuing on an out-patient basis. The third function was to provide long-term treatment mainly for children with severe neurotic disorders, severe psychotic disorders or brain damage often with epilepsy.

Rogers was aware of therapy and the ward routine as being closely inter-twined and talks of staff functioning together as a therapeutic community with good communication as essential. His conception of the importance of the personnel in the unit was reflected in his view that ward maids should as far as possible not be employed as they would be outwith the therapeutic team. (Other centres including the Lowit Unit (Lowit 1967), have tried to address this problem by including such staff in community meetings (Maxwell Jones 1952), but success with this has varied).

Rogers saw nursing care as the basis of the whole plan of treatment. He did not see it as appropriate for there to be a set of rules by which nursing staff should handle the children but saw certain principles as important. These included:

(1) confidence, especially when the child first came in, that he or she would improve

(2) a simple basic structure to the child's day

(3) ignoring and tolerating bad language, verbal abuse and cheek to allow free communication and trusting relationships to develop with the expectation that these behaviours would respond later, when the

child felt safe and happy with the staff, to gentle admonitions. This form of management entailed allowing regression to occur to a level at which the child could function happily with gradual retraining of the child occurring thereafter.

(4) individualisation of treatment of the children depending on the needs of each and his or her treatment plan.

Drug treatment was used but mainly to tide children over crises. All children were seen for individual therapy or group therapy was undertaken. School was seen as an important strand in treatment and casework with parents was undertaken by social workers. Behaviour therapy was also being used to some extent and Rogers was optimistic regarding its future use.

Other Descriptions of the Work of Child Psychiatric Units

The first account of the work of a regional unit catering for the needs of a defined population was that of Barker and Jamieson (1967) of the Liff House Children's Unit, Dundee which served the whole area covered by the Eastern Regional Hospital Board. They specifically describe the unit as aiming at providing a therapeutic milieu with a warm, accepting emotional climate, definite though relatively few limits, and treatment geared to the needs of each child. At least once weekly individual therapy was the norm. Drug use was limited to anti-convulsants for epilepsy, night sedation, phenothiazines and anti-depressants, mainly, amitriptyline in a few cases.

In 1983, Mathi and Lewis published a 15 year review of the same unit. The main change they focus on is an increased length of stay, partly reflecting admission of children with more chronic problems, with increased out-patient resources reducing the need for short term assessment and treatment, and partly difficulty in finding long-term placements and the long waiting lists for these. The treatment modalities utilised remained similar. There is, however, specific mention of psychodrama, and they comment that work with parents and families was not a major part of treatment while children were in the unit (though they add that that was changing gradually). That work with parents and families was not a major part of treatment is surprising in the light of the unit having changed to a five day unit in 1967. It may, however, have seemed less necessary, or less likely to be productive for those children for whom return home immediately after leaving the unit was not considered likely or where extensive work with the family had already failed.

Mathi and Lewis (1983) conclude that some other child psychiatric units describe a contrasting pattern of greater turnover of children (Copus and Walker 1972; Fitzpatrick 1981). Copus and Walker (1972) describe a child psychiatric ward in Bristol where children were admitted for either

(1) diagnosis or short-term treatment for up to three months, on a day-patient or in-patient basis

or infrequently

(2) longer term treatment for up to six to nine months, as day-patients only. The treatment modalities were similar to those described in the other units mentioned above but they particularly mention the use of the 'life-space interview' (Redl 1959).

There is further discussion of this in the consideration of milieu therapy below. They discuss, too, the impact on nurses of nurse–patient relationships being frequently formed and broken, an issue also commented on by Jemerin and Philips (1988). They consider intensive case work with the family as essential. They particularly mention the need to ensure that the family environment is not worse than when the child was admitted as a result of the complex feelings the admission arouses in parents, and the changes in the family functioning that may follow. The child is kept at home at least part of the time, a manoeuvre that they see as requiring a great deal of social work input and they query whether insufficient social work staffing may be leading to re-admissions. On the other hand they also view re-admission as sometimes making a positive contribution to maintaining therapy.

Barker's 1974 Review of British Child Psychiatric In-Patient Practice

In 1974, *The Residential Psychiatric Treatment of Children* edited by Barker was published. This book gave a broad picture of British child psychiatric in-patient practice at that time and, as the only at all comprehensive publication on this subject in the UK, has undoubtedly been influential in subsequent practice in the field in this country. It considers the history and future of in-patient child psychiatric treatment; the aims, nature and results of such treatment; the work of a Regional child psychiatric in-patient unit; and in-patient treatment of children with particular syndromes. Barker expresses the view that some agreement about the running of child psychiatric in-patient units had emerged. From the different contributors to the book, from the other work he refers to and indeed from the other work previously referred to, some principles about child psychiatric in-patient treatment emerge. These include at least the following:

(1) The therapeutic milieu is of central importance.

(2) The implications of the temporary separation of the child from his or her parents must be closely attended to.

(3) The nursing staff are key therapeutic agents through the relationships they form with the children.

(4) The management of each child has to be specific to his particular needs (while considering the impact on the others).

(5) Work with the parents is essential.

(6) In-patient treatment (or day-patient treatment) allows the child to experience a variety of other treatments. Each of these could be given on an out-patient basis but, in practice, they can only be delivered in a co-ordinated way in an in-patient (or day-patient setting) and then require a well-functioning multi-disciplinary team with good communication.

(7) The capacity of staff to work effectively with disturbed children can be impeded or facilitated by the feelings (often strong feelings) aroused in them by the children and their behaviour. This can be responded to by providing various forms of support or supervision often in the form of staff groups. As nursing staff have the most extensive involvement with the children such provision is arguably particularly essential for them.

Predictions in 1974 about the Future

Barker also considered what were likely to be future developments of child psychiatric in-patient units. It is of interest to look at these in the light of what has in the event occurred in the years since the book was published. His predictions were as follows:

(1) He saw the usefulness of these units as generally accepted and the need for them as increasing.

(2) He suggested that units were moving in the direction of as free communication as possible with authority being shared as appropriate among all members of the community. As regards this he pointed out that a Maxwell Jones style therapeutic community could not apply with children as they were not able to take full responsibility for themselves. It is to be noted that, as was mentioned in Chapter 2, planned environmental therapy as developed by Wills and Franklin was considered unsuitable for children under ten years of age. (Franklin 1968 and 1980)

(3) There would be further developments in nurse training including some training for non-registered nurses.

(4) Units would become part of a community psychiatric service.

(5) There would be increased availability of day care.

(6) Greater involvement of parents in therapy possibly including in decision-making about their child in the unit would be introduced.

(7) He saw this as possibly leading to a situation whereby in-patient or day-patient provision only took over the care of the child from the parents to the minimum level necessary.

(8) He commented on the need to review and develop treatment methods and viewed behaviour therapy as promising to be of real value.

Have these Predictions been Fulfilled?

(1) In considering developments in child psychiatric in-patient units in Britain since Barker made these comments there is a lack of information available. However, it is clear that the future of the units is less secure than he envisaged and a number have closed and others have fewer patients (Hersov 1986; Wardle 1991; Wolkind and Gent 1987). This has been most worryingly due to financial pressures which continue. However, there has also been a fresh questioning of their value stemming partly from an anti-institutional philosophy, partly from a climate of opinion favouring work in the community by child psychiatrists (Wolkind and Gent 1987) and partly from the lack of research into the functioning and results of in-patient units. The tendency of child psychiatrists to favour work in the community has been increased by the successes achieved by family therapy and behaviour therapy. The result has been a change in the character of admissions so that more severe and intractable problems, which may be seen as less rewarding to work with, constitute a larger proportion of admissions to some units (Mathi and Lewis 1983; Wolkind and Gent 1987).

It has been suggested that it is not now acceptable for the philosophy of each in-patient unit to be determined by the outlook, personalities and beliefs of its senior staff (Wrate and Wolkind 1991). This comment is very different, at least in its tone, from Rogers' (1965) comment that it was impossible to be dogmatic about the structure, composition and organisation of an in-patient child psychiatric unit.

In 1973 a working party of the Scottish Division of the Royal College of Psychiatrists envisaged child psychiatric units as providing short-term, long-term, or parent and child care (Royal College of Psychiatrists 1973) but this has not happened in any planned way. As regards long-term provision, however, the need for provision for new young chronic patients has been raised (Research Committee of Royal College of Psychiatrists 1991).

(2) Barker's prediction that units were moving towards as free communication as possible with authority being shared as appropriate among all members of the community is even more

difficult to comment on as it concerns qualitative aspects of the work of the units that have not been much described in recent years. The limitations on how far this could be achieved with children were referred to by Barker, himself. However, as regards parents and staff, Wilkinson's important book on child and adolescent psychiatric nursing (1983) gives a picture that is consistent with it and Chesson's study reported in this volume tends to support it.

(3) The situation about nurse training is a complicated one with the picture being very mixed with some encouraging developments but many other disappointing aspects. It is discussed further in a subsequent chapter.

(4) As Barker suggested the picture now tends to be one of units having become part of the community's psychiatric service (Hersov and Bentovim 1985). It is less clear whether he also envisaged closer co-ordination of the units and child psychiatric services in general with non-medical services for disturbed children in the spirit of the Mapstone Report *Crossing the Boundaries* (Mapstone 1983). This was of course also recommended in the USA (Harper and Geraty 1987; Jemerin and Philip 1988). To date, (as far as is known), this closer co-ordination has not occurred in Britain to any substantial extent. It is likely that if it did happen it would ease problems such as the difficulty in organising placements for children who are ready to leave the unit but not able to return home or to mainstream schooling. It would also be likely to increase the chances of the children, who would be most appropriately treated in an in-patient child psychiatric unit, being identified at an early stage.

(5) It appears to be the case that there is increased availability of day-patient treatment as Barker suggested would occur, and that the value of a child being able to move flexibly from in-patient to day-patient to out-patient status is recognised (Hersov and Bentovim 1985; Wolkind and Gent 1987).

(6) As regards increased involvement of parents in therapy and decision-making it is clear from Hersov and Bentovim's overview of day-patient units that this occurs in many such units and, indeed, they speak of a risk of the needs of parents with psychiatric disorders themselves getting in the way of meeting the needs of the children. In in-patient work Hildebrand and her colleagues describe the introduction of a full family orientation in a child psychiatric in-patient unit (Hildebrand, Jenkins, Carter and Lask 1981) and Jenkins and Loader (1984) discuss the need to maintain a family perspective as regards locus of the problem when family therapy is utilised in an in-patient child psychiatric unit. Wilkinson (1983), too,

makes it clear that nurses undertake many parent tasks but are not parenting substitutes and emphasises the need for nurses to have good working relationships with parents.

This indeed applies to a varying extent to all staff in child psychiatric in-patient units. All of them have to share in the difficult task of combining on the one hand the creation of a therapeutic milieu for the children in the ward and so outwith the family with, on the other hand, work with the family in preparation for the child's return home. This Janus faced position, as Green (1992) aptly puts it, is facilitated by careful work prior to admission involving parents, child, hospital and outside agencies (Wardle 1991). It is important that this leads to clarity and agreement about what admission can realistically aim to achieve (and what it cannot) and what will be required of workers, child and parents in the child's management. From the outset issues about discharge and alternatives to admission are confronted (Bruggen, Byng-Hall and Pitt-Aitkens 1973; Green 1992; Hersov and Bentovim 1985; Wardle 1991). This is one aspect of establishing a partnership with parents, a central theme implied in the Children Act 1989. Maintaining that partnership throughout the child's treatment involves workers in putting any lingering tendencies towards a paternalistic stance aside, and developing new skills in communicating about the children. It also involves them in finding new ways to discuss the sometimes quite complex strengths and weaknesses of different options in meetings with parents and colleagues together. It is to be recognised that this closer involvement of parents reflects a change that is also occurring in society as regards the relationship of individuals to professionals. This is highlighted in recent community care legislation and national policy (The Scottish Office Social Work Services Group 1991; Skinner 1992).

(7) These developments and the greater availability of day care do indeed give scope for the child to be out of his or her parents' care for the minimum time necessary as Barker predicted would occur. There are insufficient data available, however, to say to what extent this has been translated into shorter stays. One factor militating against shorter lengths of stay has been difficulty in finding long term placements for children when required (Gray *et al.* 1992; Mathi and Lewis 1983).

(8) Barker's comments on the need to review and develop treatment methods are still as true today as when he wrote them. As he predicted behaviour therapy now makes a substantial contribution to the management of the children in most child psychiatric units with

cognitive therapy and social skills training adding to this. There have been other advances in treatment including the greater use of family therapy with in-patients as well as out-patients, the introduction of a systems model in conceptualising aspects of treatment (Blotcky, Dimperio, Blotcky and Looney 1987) and advances in the psychopharmacology of childhood psychiatric disorders.

This last, however, is less emphasised in Britain than in the USA. Wilkinson (1979) in this country, however, describes the use of nursing recordings in a drug trial to assess response to a specific treatment and concludes that nurses can with guidance produce reliable and constant results despite more than one recorder being used.

Current Concerns and Future Challenges

Despite some positive developments since Barker's book was published, the overall impression as regards in-patient child psychiatry is that the major developments took place prior to then and, indeed, that many of the important principles of good practice were recognised when Cameron (1949) described the first two years' experience at the Maudsley Hospital. In some respects a key development has lain in greater recognition of the limitations of what can be achieved outwith the family home (Rutter 1986) since a clearer view of in-patient treatment, as one phase in the management of the child, usually undertaken along with the parents or family, follows from this. There has been little progress in service research in child psychiatry in general (Research Committee of Royal College of Psychiatrists 1991) and child in-patient units are recognised as one area where research is particularly required. It seems likely that in well-functioning units clinicians have concentrated on enhancing the quality of the service given, including attending to the needs of staff for training and support.

In past years, despite financial pressures practice has not generally been dominated in this country by considerations about funding in the way it has in the USA. However, it is clear that this situation has changed to a considerable extent and that these changes are continuing (Hersov 1994; Hoare 1994; Mant and Bucher 1994). Nevertheless, writing of psychiatry in general, Parry-Jones (1989) points out that the increased emphasis on performance measures and cost-benefit analyses can be turned to good effect if there is a forward-looking and constructive response to the challenge. Zeitlen (1995) too, although pointing out that services have become increasingly finance driven, still manages to find room for optimism that the future will bring increased recognition of the need for cooperative and multi-disciplinary working and planning. These issues are also considered in Chapters 14 and 15.

Despite the decline in in-patient child psychiatric provision mentioned previously, there is agreement that there will be a continuing need for some child psychiatric units for the foreseeable future (Rutter 1986; Wolkind and Gent 1989; Green 1992). Rutter (1986) looking 30 years ahead envisages the units being required for some of the most serious disorders, for some of those that complicate physical illness, for certain investigations and for high intensity treatment. He particularly emphasises the part an admission can play in helping parents with their parenting skills. Green (1992) stresses the need to be responsive to the requirements of referrers. It is clear, too, that for child psychiatric in-patient units to develop in ways geared to meeting the needs of the patients, and for them to be given the opportunity to do so requires there to be a positive and sustained response to the recent call for systematic description of the work of the units and for work to demonstrate their effectiveness to be undertaken (Wrate and Wolkind 1991).

References

Barber, C.C. and Allen, J. (1992) 'Optimal length of stay in child and adolescent psychiatric hospitalisation: a study of clinical opinion.' *American Journal of Orthopsychiatry 62*, 3, 458–463.

Barker, P. (1974) *The Residential Psychiatric Treatment of Children.* London: Crosby, Lockwood and Staples.

Barker, P. and Jamieson, R. (1967) 'Two years' admissions to a regional child psychiatry unit.' *British Medical Journal 2*, 103–106.

Bender, L. (1937) 'Group activities on a children's ward as methods of psychotherapy.' *American Journal of Orthopsychiatry 7*, 1151–1173.

Blotcky, M.J., Dimperio, T.L., and Gosset, J.I. (1984) 'Follow-up of children treated in psychiatric hospitals: a review of studies.' *American Journal of Psychiatry 141*, 1499–1507.

Blotcky, M.J., Dimperio, T.L., Blotcky, A.D. and Looney, J.G. (1987) 'A systems model for residential treatment of children.' *Residential Treatment for Children and Youth 5*, 1, 55–66.

Bruggen, P., Byng-Hall, J. and Pitt-Aitkens, T. (1973) 'The reason for admission as a focus of work for an adolescent unit.' *British Journal of Psychiatry 122*, 319–329.

Cameron, K.A. (1949) 'A psychiatric in-patient department for children.' *Journal of Mental Science 95*, 560–566.

Copus, P.E. and Walker, L.W. (1972) 'The psychiatric ward in a children's hospital. A review of the first 2 years.' *British Journal of Psychiatry 121*, 323–326.

Fitzpatrick, C. (1981) '3 year review of admissions to a child psychiatry unit.' *Irish Medical Journal 74*, 169–170.

Franklin, M. (1980) 'Clincical aspects of the work of David Wills.' *The Journal of the Association of Workers for Maladjusted Children 8*, 2, 73–80.

Franklin, M. (1968) 'The work of W. David Wills – An appreciation.' *Newsletter of Association of Workers for Maladjusted Children 10*, 2, 17–37.

Gray, C., Chisholm, D., Smith, P., Brown, M., McKay, C. (1992) 'The role of the child psychiatric ward in health care: experiences with different types of admission over a period of 21 years.' *Irish Journal of Psychological Medicine 9*, 17–23.

Green, J. (1992) 'In-patient psychiatry units.' *Archives of Disease in Childhood 67*, 1120–1123.

Harper, G. and Geraty, R. (1987) 'Hospital and residential treatment.' In R. Michels and J.O. Cavenar Jr. *Psychiatry*. Vol 2. New York: Basic Books.

Harper, G. (1989) 'Focal in-patient treatment planning.' *Journal of the American Academy of Child and Adolescent Psychiatry 28*, 30–37.

Hendren, R.L. and Berlin, I.W. (1991) (eds) *Psychiatric In-patient Care of Children and Adolescents. A Multi-cultural Approach*. New York: Wiley.

Hersov, L. (1986) 'Child Psychiatry in Britain – the last 30 years.' *Journal of Child Psychology and Psychiatry 27*, 6, 781–801.

Hersov, L. (1994) 'In-patient and day patient units.' In M. Rutter, E. Taylor and L. Hersov. *Child and Adolescent Psychiatry: Modern Approached* (3rd Ed) Oxford: Blackwell.

Hersov, L. and Bentovim, A. (1985) 'In-patient and day-patient units.' In M. Rutter and L. Hersov (eds) *Child and Adolescent Psychiatry: Modern Approaches* (2nd Ed.) Oxford: Blackwell.

Hildebrand, J., Jenkins, J., Carter, D. and Lask, B. (1981) 'The introduction of a full family orientation in a child psychiatric in-patient unit.' *Journal of Family Therapy 3*, 2, 139–152.

Hoare, P. (1994) 'Child and adolescent services in Scotland.' In C. Dean (ed) *A Slow Train Coming: Bringing the Mental Revolution to Scotland*. Glasgow: The Greater Glasgow Community and Mental Health Services NHS Trust.

Irwin, M. (1982) 'Literature review.' In J.L. Schulman and M. Irwin (ed) *Psychiatric Hospitalisation of Children*. Springfield: Charles C. Thomas.

Jemerin, J.M. and Philips, I. (1988) 'Changes in in-patient child psychiatry: consequences and recommendations.' *Journal of the American Academy of Child and Adolescent Psychiatry 27*, 397– 403.

Jenkins, J. and Loader, P. (1984) 'Family therapy in an in-patient unit – whose problem is it anyway?' In E.J. Anthony (ed) *Yearbook of Child Psychiatry*. Chichester: Wiley.

Jones, M. (1952) *Social Psychiatry*. London: Tavistock.

Kolko, D.J. (1992) 'Short-term follow-up of child psychiatric hospitalisation: clinical description, predictors, and correlates.' *Journal of the American Academy of Child and Adolescent Psychiatry 31*, 4, 719–727.

Lewis, M., Lewis, D.O., Shanok, S.S., Klatskin, E. and Osborne, J.R. (1980) 'The undoing of residential treatment. A follow study of 51 adolescents.' *Journal of the American Academy of Child Psychiatry 19*, 160–171.

Lowit, I.M. (1967) Report on First Eighteen Months of Work of Aberdeen In-Patient Unit of Child Psychiatry (Unpublished).

Mant, J. and Bucher, J. (1994) 'Is there a market for regional units in child and adolescent psychiatry?' *Journal of Public Health 16*, 3, 305–309.

Mapstone, E. (1983) 'Crossing the Boundaries: New Directions in Mental Health Services for Children and Young People in Scotland.' *Report of a Working Group of the Advisory Council on Social Work and the Scottish Health Services Planning Council.* Edinburgh: H.M.S.O.

Mathai, J. and Lewis, C. (1983) 'Review of 15 years admissions to a regional child psychiatric unit.' *Newsletter of The Association for Child Psychology and Psychiatry 16*, Autumn, 2–6.

Moultrie, M.B. and Carek, D.J. (1983) 'Short term in-patient treatment of children and adolescents.' *Journal of the South Carolina Medical Association.* January, 30–32

Ney, P.G., Adam, R.R., Hanton, B.R. and Brindad, E.S. (1988) 'The effectiveness of a child psychiatric unit: a follow-up study.' *Canadian Journal of Psychiatry 33*, 793–799.

Nurcombe, B. (1989) 'Goal directed treatment planning and the principles of brief hospitalisation.' *Journal of the American Academy of Child and Adolescent Psychiatry 28*, 26–30.

Parry-Jones, W.L. (1989) 'The history of child and adolescent psychiatry:its present day relevance.' *Journal of Child Psychology and Psychiatry 30*, 1, 3–11.

Perry, R. (1989) 'The medical in-patient model.' In R.D. Lyman, S. Prentice-Dunn and S. Gabel (eds) *Residential and In-Patient Treatment of Children and Adolescents.* New York: Plenum Press.

Pfeiffer, S.I. and Strzelecki, S.C. (1990) 'In-patient psychiatric treatment of children and adolescents: a review of outcome studies.' *Journal of the American Academy of Child and Adolescent Psychiatry 29*, 847–853.

Redl, F. (1959) 'Strategy and techniques of the life space interview.' *American Journal of Orthopsychiatry 29*, 1–18.

Research Committee of Royal College of Psychiatrists (1991) 'Future directions for research in child and adolescent psychiatry.' *Psychiatric Bulletin of Royal College of Psychiatrists 15*, 5, 308–310.

Robinson, J.F., Maxwell, A. and Dominguez, K.E. (1947) 'Resident psychiatric treatment with children.' *American Journal of Orthopsychiatry 17*, 458–467.

Rogers, W.J.B. (1954) 'A children's psychiatric unit in a mental hospital.' Paper read to Psychiatric Section of the Royal Society of Medicine with the Society's president, Dr. W.M. Mayer Gross in the chair. Reported in *British Medical Journal.* December 25, 1544–1545.

Rogers, W.J.B. (1965) 'Childrens' in-patient psychiatric units.' In J.G. Howell (ed) *Modern Perspectives in Child Psychiatry*. Edinburgh: Oliver and Boyd.

Royal College of Psychiatrists (Scottish Division) (1973) *The Future of the Psychiatric services in Scotland*. Report of Working Party. A.C. Tait (Chairman). Royal College of Psychiatrists. Edinburgh.

Rutter, M. (1986) 'Child psychiatry: looking 30 years ahead.' *Journal of Child Psychology and Psychiatry 27*, 6, 803–840.

Scottish Office Social Work Services Group (1991) *Getting to Know You. The Involvement of Users and Carers in Social Care Assessment*. Edinburgh: HMSO.

Skinner, A. (1992) *Another kind of home: The Social Work Services Inspectorate for Scotland. A Review of Residential Child Care*. Edinburgh: HMSO.

Von Gontard, A. (1988) 'The development of child psychiatry in 19th century Britain.' *Journal of Child Psychology and Psychiatry 29*, 5, 569–588.

Wardle, C.J. (1991) 'Twentieth century influences on the development in Britain of services for child and adolescent psychiatry.' *British Journal of Psychiatry 159*, 53–68.

Wilkins, R. (1987) 'Hallucinations in children and teenagers admitted to Bethlem Royal Hospital in the nineteenth century and their possible relevance to the incidence of schizophrenia.' *Journal of Child Psychology and Psychiatry 28*, 4, 569–580.

Wilkinson, T. (1979) 'The problems and the values of objective nursing observations in psychiatric nursing care.' *Journal of Advanced Nursing 4*, 151–159.

Wilkinson, T. (1983) *Child and Adolescent Psychiatric Nursing*. Oxford: Blackhill Scientific Publications.

Wills, W.D. (1971) *Spare the Child. The Story of an Experimental Approved School*. Harmondsworth: Penguin.

Wolkind, S. and Gent, M. (1987) 'Children's psychiatric in-patient units: present functions and future directions.' *Maladjustment and Therapeutic Education 5*, 2, 54–64.

Woolston, J.C. (1989) 'Transitional risk model for short and intermediate term psychiatric in-patient treatment of children.' *Journal of the American Academy of Child and Adolescent Psychiatry 28*, 38–41.

Woolston, J.L. (1989) 'Issues in child and adolescent psychiatric hospitalisation.' *Journal of the American Academy of Child and Adolescent Psychiatry 28*, 20.

Wrate, R.M. and Wolkind, S. (1991) 'Child and adolescent psychiatry in-patient units.' *Psychiatric Bulletin 15*, 1, 37–38.

Zeitlen, H. (1995) 'The health service review: can we tell the future from the past and present? Four years on.' *Association of Child Psychology and Psychiatry Review and Newsletter 17*, 1, 24–28.

CHAPTER 4

Day Patient Treatment

Madeline Brown

Development of British Day Patient Treatment

The first psychiatric day hospital in the UK was set up for adults in 1951 (Bierer 1951), and was rapidly followed by others throughout the country, in that decade. The first child psychiatric day unit at 'Tiverlands', (near Newcastle) was established in 1957 by Connell in line with similar developments in France and Denmark in the 1950s (Connell 1961). At that time, there were no residential facilities for disturbed children in the North East of England, either psychiatric or educational. Thus the regional hospital board, in conjunction with the University of Durham, created an out-patient unit for disturbed children in a converted private house near Newcastle, as part of the department of psychological medicine, which also provided services to adults. The first in-patient units had already opened in London and Dumfries by that time, so there was clearly an impetus to provide child psychiatric services. Whether the Newcastle day unit was seen largely as a less costly venture, or a deliberate choice as relating to the suitability of treatment is unclear.

The staff of Tiverlands, which at first comprised a medical director, a senior psychologist, a nurse, a secretary and a cleaner, also served the adult services. There were places for 16 children, and the unit offered observation and assessment of behavioural difficulties, and treatment by structured play and medication. Schooling was an integral part of the treatment. There is no recorded information, however, regarding length of stay.

Connell considered that the advantages of day treatment were:

(1) its flexibility in terms of the number of days attendance per week

(2) the avoidance of the trauma of separation from home

(3) the continuity with community services already involved

(4) the possibility of manipulating the child's environment (Connell 1961).

Accounts indicate that at first the patients had little input from the medical profession, and there was very little time available for their consultation with nursing staff. The need for greater input was recognised, however, and with time delivered, subsequent to an increase in medical staffing.

The provision of a warm accepting climate within the unit was considered important, as was some internal structure. Connell (1961) advocated that a day unit should be part of a service, which included an in-patient unit for children. Those who failed to respond to the day patient approach might then be hospitalised, but Connell does not indicate which cases might not respond to day patient treatment.

There are few further reports on day patient units in the UK until the 1970s. Barker, in *Residential Psychiatric Treatment of Children*, also mentions day patients, but more in the context of day patients attending an in-patient unit, whose admission might be as planned day patients only, or as day patients before or after in-patient treatment. Interestingly, he states that those patients whose problems were mainly language based were more likely to remain day patients throughout their stay in his unit (Barker 1974).

By 1972 in the UK there was a total of 60 in-patient units, two day patient only units, and 17 units with both day and in-patients (Copus and Walker 1972). In Copus and Walker's unit, day patients, who formed 50 per cent of admissions, had an average length of stay of three months; movement from in-patient to day patient was also possible. Copus and Walker (1972) also identified the factors determining day patient or in-patient status, such as

(1) the degree of stress in the home, and the possibility of change there

(2) the danger of total rejection of the child if she or he became an in-patient

(3) the amount of assessment needed,

(4) practical considerations, such as the distance of the home from the unit.

By 1973, Bentovim and Lansdown (1973) were reporting on seven day patient units for pre school children in London, and by 1977 were commenting on the wide variation in day patient services available, depending on unit policy. Day units could serve a large catchment area, or a small one; be free standing, or part of an in-patient or out-patient unit; be purpose built or be in converted premises; cater for four to forty children, with or without their parents and siblings; provide for specific diagnostic groups, or all groups; cater for specific age ranges or all ranges; and offer one day per week attendance up to seven days per week, for a length of stay of a few weeks up to several years. The two common factors identified were the provision of a therapeutic community, and attendance for several hours per day. Hersov and Bentovim (1985) described the functions of a day patient unit as follows:

(1) observation

(2) assessment (including family relationships)

(3) determination of developmental level

(4) the provision of a therapeutic milieu in order to reduce behavioural disturbances in the unit by containing them.

Day patient services were viewed as especially useful for specific categories of patients and their parents namely:

(1) children with pre-school problems

(2) parenting breakdown and child abuse

(3) psychoses of childhood

(4) autistic children.

The North American Experience

In North America, the history of day patient units was in many ways similar to that of the UK (Grizenko and Sayegh 1990). From 1961 to 1981 there was a rapid rise in day patient units from 10 to 353 in the USA, due to an enthusiasm for community mental health services rather than in-patient services. In the 1980s there was a decrease in numbers and a decline in their use, due mainly to a change in funding which made day patient treatment less well paid for the psychiatrists involved, compared with in-patient treatment. Escalating costs of running in-patient units in the 1990s forced a re-evaluation of the situation, and so day patient units are again gaining in popularity due to their lower cost. Even for severe behavioural problems, Grizenko and Papineau's (1992) study showed that there were similar outcomes for in-patients and day patients using a wide range of standardised measurements, with the added advantage of lower cost and a shorter stay in the day patient unit. They commented that often referrers had a mistaken belief that in-patient treatment would be more intensive.

Westman (1979) believe successful day patient units are those with a coherent treatment philosophy, led by a broadly trained experienced director with ultimate responsibility for the budget and personnel. In a five year follow up study of in-patients and day patients at the Ittleson centre at Riverside, New York, it was revealed that children without organic pathology did best as in-patients because of their family psychopathology, while the reverse was true of patients with organic pathology.

Westman (1979) emphasised that a day unit needs a wide range of therapeutic inputs under one roof such as is only likely to be available in a hospital. He also suggested that such varied inputs need co-ordination such as a psychiatrist could provide, as well as a role for the psychiatrist in providing staff support, since disturbed children 'drain' staff members emotionally.

The child psychiatric day care centre in Colorado described by Zimet and Farley (1991) used psychodynamic, learning theory, sociocultural, and other theoretical models on an *ad hoc* basis, in terms of their perceived usefulness in an 'ongoing scientific evaluation'. They reviewed the development of their unit over the decades as follows. In the 1960s the emphasis was on community involvement and group approaches; in the 1970s on more individual approaches and on educational difficulties; in the 1980s on biological and psychopharmacological approaches with 50 per cent of their patients on medication. In the 1990s they feel that the cold winds of restricted finances may impose a need for greater consideration of cost effectiveness to influence practice.

Evaluating British Day Patient Treatment

One of the first controlled evaluations of the therapeutic effectiveness of a psychiatric day centre for pre-school children appeared in 1978 (Woolacott, Graham and Stevenson 1978). Woolacott and colleagues compared a group comprising 10–14 pre-school children with developmental delays and behavioural disturbances who attended one or two days per week, along with their mothers or fathers or both parents, plus their siblings for an average of 26 weeks, with a similar control group, not treated. No difference in outcome between the treated and untreated groups at one year follow up was found. However, the groups were not strictly comparable, due to an excess of more disturbed and physically ill children in the study group. Indeed, Hersov and Bentovim (1985) have acknowledged the difficulty of outcome studies in terms of finding suitable control groups, determining which outcome measures to use, and trying to decide which of the many inputs were effective.

Richman, Graham and Stevenson (1983) in the second phase extension of the above study, which included a second control group with language difficulties, found at five year follow up there was still no difference in outcome between the groups, but they too commented on the difficulties in evaluation of the effectiveness of treatments which included many different elements, and of the difficulty in obtaining matched control groups. Short term effectiveness of focused treatments for specific target behaviours were seen as important to examine, as significant 'within group' responses might be lost in broad outcome measures. They also commented on the likelihood of day patients continuing to require specialised help after discharge, despite two thirds of the patients showing some improvement.

Bentovim and Boston (1973) describing the same pre-school day patient unit at Great Ormond Street hospital, emphasised group as well as individual psychiatric help for the mothers of the day patients. The precise nature of that psychiatric help is nevertheless not specified.

A more recent study (Place, Rajah and Crake 1990), also highlighted the value of day patient treatment. A one day/week day patient placement combined with family therapy was evaluated and it was found that the day patient component of the treatment made a considerable impact on clinical outcome.

It is evident from this review that work to date has concentrated mainly on day patient only units, and there is a dearth of studies of day patients in mixed day patient/in-patient units. This is surprising as most day patients were in mixed units, the proportions being 1:2:2 for day patient only units: in-patient only units: mixed units (Association of Child Psychology and Psychiatry (ACPP) Directory 1990). Nevertheless, since the numbers of patients in most units, whether mixed or not, are small, suitable numbers of day patients to study, and be statistically significant, from a single unit are unlikely to be found. The Scottish National Child Psychiatry Audit Project, which is aggregating data from several units, should be helpful in this respect.

As regards admission criteria for day patients, age, diagnosis, precariousness of place in the family, parental wishes and distance of home from the unit, are all important, but confounding, variables.

The Need for In-patient Treatment

In the Lowit Unit at Aberdeen, day patients can be admitted from age four onwards, whereas in-patients are usually admitted from age six, on the grounds that, developmentally, it is inappropriate to expect the child under six to settle at night without family members present. The child's diagnosis also influences the decision of patient status: usually the more severe conditions such as anorexia nervosa, psychosis, suicidal intent and intractable school phobia necessitate in-patient admission only, at the start of treatment. Where there are complex conditions in younger children such as hyperkinetic syndrome, motor learning difficulties, developmental delays and specific learning difficulties, as well as considerable family reaction to the difficulties, day patient treatment would be recommended, but in-patient treatment could also be appropriate, especially in children living 20–30 miles or more away. Intractable elimination problems, often accompanied by other difficulties which have not responded to out-patient treatment, usually require in-patient treatment in order to facilitate the promotion of patient–staff relationships, essential to the child's co-operation to achieve continence, but pre-school soilers may sometimes manage to achieve bowel control through day treatment only.

Where the child's place in the family is somewhat precarious and considerable scapegoating has occurred, day patient treatment is indicated, in order that the child keeps his or her place in the family. Parental wishes also need to be considered. Some find it intolerable for their child to be an in-patient. In these circumstances, rather than have the child miss out on treatment, a day patient place may be offered, whilst making it clear to the family that progress may be slower. In Grampian region, since some patients live 50 miles or more from the Unit, day treatment may be impractical.

As regards day patient treatment, the therapeutic milieu is more difficult to implement, because of the shorter time spent in the Unit and also because school takes up a considerable portion of the day. Relationships with nursing staff, therefore, take longer to build. In-patient treatment is therefore not necessarily more intense than day patient treatment – it is just that there is more of it throughout the 24 hours, and the same applies to milieu therapy. The other components of treatment, for example psychiatric, individual, group or family treatment, psychological treatment including behaviour therapy, speech and language treatment, occupational therapy and remedial education are all available during the working day and, therefore, available to day patients also. Daily contact with severe family psychopathology, however, may work against treatment of day patients and therefore render it less effective. For example, the child's self-esteem may be carefully built up in the unit by day, only to be demolished by rejecting or scapegoating parents every evening.

In the Lowit Unit, there have always been day patients (Gray et al. 1992). A third of patients are usually day patients, but in 1991 a natural experiment occurred since the unit could admit only day patients for nine months of the year due to staffing difficulties. This illustrated some of the advantages of day patient treatment but also reinforced the necessity for in-patient treatment. For instance a six-year-old who could not be expected to travel 50 miles twice a day had to await in-patient status. Some patients never came for treatment since other measures had to be taken in the interim and the impetus for treatment was lost; one went into care instead, one went to a general adult psychiatric ward, very inappropriately, and an anorexic's treatment was much longer (and less satisfactory) than usual and had to be shared with a paediatric ward. Worthy of note is that parents of our patients were under considerable stress when in-patient treatment could not be offered. There were also, however, one or two patients (younger children who had behavioural difficulties at home and at school) who managed well as day patients even though it was thought they would need in-patient treatment.

In conclusion, therefore, there is a definite need for day patient treatment, but whether it is best to have day patients in a separate day patient unit or in a mixed day patient/in-patient unit is difficult to determine without follow up studies. Certainly the nursing staff would say that it is often harder for them to be as involved and therefore committed to day patients as they are to in-patients. It is certainly useful to have day patient status available as an introductory phase to in-patient treatment, or on leaving in-patient treatment, as a way of gradually re-integrating a child into his or her community.

For the future, day patient units or status may need to be considered more specifically, as the community care philosophy begins to take effect, and also as financial difficulties impinge on the National Health Service (NHS), in a similar way to the North American experience. Without adequate research, we shall not be in a position to make informed decisions about which children can best respond to day patient treatment and in what form, and which patient will need in-patient treatment. The NHS and Community Care Act (1990) has so far not addressed children's issues, but if and when it does so, consideration of joint funding of day patient units, between health, education and social work may be required, and is discussed further in Chapter 15.

Units: The National Picture

In compiling the list of in-patient and day patient units throughout the United Kingdom and Northern Ireland, it was surprising to discover that there is no central record within the NHS, either in Scotland or in England, of how many such units exist within the United Kingdom. This must make policy and planning decisions by government agencies almost impossible to decide on rational grounds, without a sound knowledge of the level of provision of services throughout the country.

The list provided in Appendix I was compiled initially in 1993 and work on it continued during 1994. The ACPP list Directory was employed together with the list in Barker's *Residential Treatment of Children*. All units within those lists designated as having in-patient or day patient units were contacted. In addition, other sources were used, for example clinical psychologists listed by specialist interest group of the British Psychological Association as having an interest in such units, as were the regional representatives of the child and adolescent section of the Royal College of Psychiatrists. Finally, information from all sources was combined, and each unit was sent a copy of the list, requested to correct it, and to add any other units known. Overall it is felt that a reasonably accurate picture of the distribution of in-patient and day patient units in the country has emerged; certainly it may be the most reliable to date.

It may be concluded that if the ACPP list was accurate, many in-patient units have closed in the last two decades. Several respondents wrote of setting up freestanding day patient units in the near future, if negotiations with their purchasers were successful. No respondent replied in terms of planning to establish an in-patient unit. Extrapolation from these trends would suggest that perhaps a gradual decrease in the in-patient units has begun, perhaps due to costs and the move towards community-based services. Much would be lost, however, if the in-patient unit were to disappear with its unique blend of therapeutic milieu and the co-ordination of multi-disciplinary inputs. It can be a haven for children who need a period of separation from overwhelming family life, amidst adults who are trained, willing and able to work as a team to help a child master his or her severe and complex difficulties, in a way that social work and educational residential establishments rarely are able to do.

References

Association of Child Psychology and Psychiatry (1990) *Directory of Psychological and Psychiatric Services for Children and their Families*. London: ACPP.

Barker, P. (1974) *The Residential Psychiatric Treatment of Children*. London: Crosby Lockwood Staples.

Bentovim, A. and Landsdown, R. (1973) 'Day hospital and centres for disturbed children in the London area.' *British Medical Journal 4*, 536–538.

Bentovim, A. and Boston, M. (1973) 'A day centre for disturbed young children and their parents.' *Journal of Child Psychotherapy 3*, 46–60.

Bierer, J. (1951) *The Day Hospital*. London: Lewis.

Connell, P.M. (1961) 'The day hospital approach in child psychiatry.' *Journal of Mental Science 107*, 969–977.

Copus, P.E. and Lumsden Walker, W.L. (1972) 'The psychiatric ward in a childrens hospital. A review of the first two years.' *British Journal of Psychiatry 121*, 323–326.

Gray, C., Chisholm, D., Smith, P., Brown, M. and McKay, C. (1992) 'The role of the child psychiatric ward in health care: experience with different types of admissions over a period of twenty one years.' *Irish Journal of Psychological Medicine 9*, 17–23.

Grizenko, N. and Sayegh, L. (1990) 'Evaluation of the effectiveness of a psychodynamically oriented day treatment program for children with behaviour problems: A pilot study.' *Canadian Journal of Psychiatry 35*, 519–525.

Grizenko, N. and Papineau, D. (1992) 'A comparison of the cost effectiveness of day treatment and residential treatment for children with severe behavioural problems.' *Canadian Journal of Psychiatry 37*, 393–400.

Hersov, L. and Bentovim, A. (1985) 'In-patient and day-hospital units.' In M. Rutter and L. Hersov (eds) *Child and Adolescent Psychiatry: Modern Approaches*. 2nd Ed. Oxford: Blackwell Scientific Publications.

National Health Service and Community Care Act (1990) London: HMSO.

Place, M., Rajah, S. and Crake, T. (1990) 'Combining day patient treatment with family work in a child psychiatric clinic.' *European Archives of Psychiatry and Neurological Sciences 239*, 6, 373–378.

Richman, M., Graham, P. and Stevenson, J. (1983) 'Long term effects of treatment in a pre-school day centre.' *British Journal of Psychiatry 142*, 71–72.

Westman, J. (1979) *Basic Handbook of Child Psychiatry*. Vol III. Joseph, D. (Editor in Chief) 288–299. New York: Basic Books Inc.

Woolacott, S., Graham, P. and Stevenson, J. (1978) 'A controlled evaluation of the therapeutic effectiveness of a psychiatric day centre for pre school children.' *British Journal of Psychiatry 132*, 349–355.

Zimet, S.G. and Farley, G.K. (1991) *Day Treatment for Children with Emotional Disorders: A Model in Action*. Vol 1. New York: USA.

CHAPTER 5

Nursing in a Child Psychiatric Unit

Royston Paice

Introduction

In this chapter the managerial and organisational considerations relating to nursing are examined, with particular reference to the Lowit Unit. It is not the intention to provide an overview of nursing care here, since Wilkinson (1983) has provided an excellent comprehensive review of nursing practice. The issues she discusses and problems considered remain as pertinent today as when first written. Regrettably since Wilkinson's contribution there has been a dearth of nursing writing on child psychiatric residential units. In addition, the author has decided not to comment regarding theoretical approaches in nursing, since McLeod, in the following chapter, provides an account, from a largely psychodynamic perspective, of a number of significant treatment issues.

The Role of the Nurse

The role of the nurse within child and family psychiatry has developed since the first residential psychiatric unit for children opened in 1947 and nurses were the major staff group therein. Since residential psychiatric units for children developed either in paediatric hospitals or mental health hospitals, the actual location determined the qualifications of registered nursing staff. Whereas in paediatric hospitals predominantly registered sick children's nurses (RSCN) would be employed, in mental health hospitals it would be registered mental nurses (RMN). Accordingly, the knowledge and skill base for child psychiatric nurses has developed from these two quite distinct fields of nursing. Interestingly, when nurses working within the specialty were recently surveyed by Hinks, 83 per cent of respondents felt that child psychiatric units should be placed under the mental health units (Hinks *et al.* 1988).

In the Lowit Unit, Royal Aberdeen Children's Hospital (RACH) the nursing staff, initially, were led by a RSCN sister and RMN charge nurse, and until 1988, registered nursing staff were predominantly RSCNs. Over the years the skills of the nursing staff have developed to the present position where 'nursing staff play a central part in multi-disciplinary teamwork having the potential to provide the essential "holistic-link" in the delivery of care' (Hinks *et al.* 1988). The philosophy of nursing care on the Lowit Unit is outlined in Appendix 5A.

The demands that children and young people put on to nurses are many and varied. Nurses must be companions in play, arbiters of fair play, protectors of the weak, providers of food, menders of toys, tellers of stories, authority figures, people with whom to argue, listeners to problems and philosophers of life. They are the adults who care enough to stay around and take whatever is hurled at them, whether it be chairs, love, abuse or jokes (Wilkinson 1983).

Equally important is the nurse's ability to create and sustain the 'right' atmosphere for children to interact. In residential units the latter should be characterised by a sense of humour and fun, feelings of caring and security, energy and activity and an awareness of limits and boundaries which are clear, yet flexible and negotiable. It is the nurse's responsibility to create and maintain the appropriate atmosphere, without which emotional growth and behavioural change would be limited (Giddey 1983). In addition, the nursing staff bring levels of expertise which can be defined as follows:

basic   that of providing a caring, emotionally satisfying, loving situation

special   in addition to above, a knowledge of the dynamics of personal problems

advanced   knowledge of the dynamics of the presenting problem but also, under guidance and supervision, providing some form of interpretive comment

consultant   advising other professionals on such matters as admission and treatment procedures. (Buchan 1973)

Nursing staff would be expected to play a central role in the assessment of the child's difficulties and from this to contribute to the planning and implementation of not just nursing care, but the whole treatment package, and then to help to evaluate its outcome. Essential to this is the nurse's ability to promote the capacity of the children to develop and maintain meaningful relationships, not least with each other, thus facilitating growth within the child.

Relationships are developed through the normal activities of daily living as well as through therapeutic activities. Working alongside other professionals, be it psychiatrist, social worker, clinical psychologist, occupational therapist, speech therapist and unit teaching staff, nurses sustain treatment both within formal settings such as family therapy, and through informal contact. Outwith the unit, nursing staff work alongside field social workers, residential social workers, educational psychologists, mainstream and special school teaching staff, and members of the children's panel. They also attend case conferences relating to the Non Accidental Injuries register. They have also a role working directly with families/carers, on a formal or informal basis.

Nurses also have to face and solve their individual and collective moral and ethical dilemmas. An important part of the role of senior nursing staff, is providing clinical supervision to assist staff in identifying their own conflicts and difficulties in working with children and their families. With reference to the supportive role that all nursing staff must play if the treatment milieu is to be therapeutic, they must first learn to care about themselves and experience being cared for, before they are capable to give care to others (Critchley 1991). Finally, nursing staff have to learn to 'survive' whatever the children bring to the treatment milieu. This may seem so basic as to hardly require saying, but the demands and stress of working intensively with children, who are often severely disturbed, needs great resilience. For many of the children, too, it is of key importance that the nurses have had the personal strength to cope with the hate and aggression they have expressed towards them without retaliation, and be there to provide nurture and containment as before (Winnicot 1968).

Staffing Issues

The recruitment, retention and training of nursing staff within the specialty are ongoing areas of concern for the Lowit Unit. These areas being inter-related affect the treatment milieu and the service that can be offered and it is, therefore, important to explore each of these areas.

Registered Nursing Staff

The Lowit Unit is the farthest north residential child psychiatric unit in the British Isles and is at some distance from other centres of population in Scotland. This may be reflected by only three of the last fourteen trained staff employed having come from outwith Aberdeen. There has been significant turnover of nursing staff too, in that six registered nurses were recruited but subsequently left the service between 1987 and 1992. Four others were recruited and remained in the service over the same period. Local policy dictates that only RSCNs or RMNs are employed as registered nurses in the Lowit Unit and all five in past or present are RMNs. It is to be noted, too, that although the unit has been running for 21 years, there is no renewable source of registered nurses within the Grampian Region, who have training or experience within the specialty.

Student Nurses

Student nurse placement has been sporadic throughout the Lowit Unit's history. There were no student nurses allocated when the unit opened. Since then there have been RSCN students placed in the Unit. It has not been possible to have any degree of accuracy, apart from human memory on this area before 1989.

Since 1989 agreement has been reached with staff from the local college of nursing that only two student nurses are placed at any time and the Unit has been approved for Project 2000 students in the child health branch programme.

As student nurses are a potential source for recruitment of staff, it is considered imperative that student nurses are regularly placed in child psychiatric units.

Nursery Nurse

There is an establishment of one nursery nurse within the unit. Turnover has inhibited the full development of the post, but it is considered that with no particular training of the nursery nurse, it should be possible for a role to be developed that makes a valuable contribution and is distinct from that of a nursery assistant.

Unqualified Staff

Nursing assistants are employed within the Unit. During the same five year period (1987–1992), three nursing assistants were recruited and subsequently left the service, with three being recruited and remaining in service. They have an important role within the Unit, supervised by registered nurses. This supervision is more direct during the day. Night staff are supervised by the night sister for the Children's Hospital.

Despite their lack of formal nursing training, nursing assistants can and do engage under supervision in all activities with children and their families, as they are able. They do so on the basis of their personal qualities and life experiences which are enhanced by the supervision and in-service training they receive.

Vacancies are advertised as for registered nurses, and there are always a large number of applicants and careful selection is required to short list for interviewing.

Retention

To retain suitably experienced and qualified nursing staff there has to be an opportunity for gaining specialist training, adequate nursing resources and a career structure within which registered nurses can progress.

For newly-qualified nurses, especially RSCNs, it can be difficult for them to progress in their career, as they are seen as being away from medical/surgical nursing and have to compete with newly qualified RSCNs even though they may have been registered for 12 to 18 months for a junior staff nurse grade. Therefore, RSCNs have to move out of the specialty after 12 months approximately.

For RMNs, it has been relatively easy to obtain higher grade staff nurse posts, such as an 'E grade', in a shorter time in the mental health unit rather than the children's hospital. Any registered nurse without any experience or training in the specialty or considerable experience working with children would only be considered for a 'D grade', which has been the unit's policy since clinical grading. This does act as a filter mechanism, as only the RMN and RSCN who are motivated sufficiently apply for posts at this grade.

Training

Child and adolescent psychiatric nursing is a recognised nursing specialty. This acknowledges the differences between nursing adults and young people. At present, basic nurse training does not fully equip nurses to work effectively with young people. Post basic courses are necessary to provide nurses with a sound theoretical base from which to practice (Wilkinson 1983).

As early as 1971 it was recognised that no present training programme can of itself adequately prepare nurses for work in psychiatric in-patient or day-patient units for children and adolescents. Indeed, even if future programmes of nurse training offer some experience in this field of nursing, it cannot be claimed that this of itself will fit nurses to take senior posts in residential and day psychiatric units for children and adolescents (Haldane, Smith, McInnes and Henderson 1971).

At this time there are limited post-basic courses for nurses in child and family psychiatry in Scotland. The only courses that at present have any relevance and would be beneficial are the Family Therapy Course Part I and Part II, run in Edinburgh by the Scottish Institute of Human Relations, which is a comprehensive training in family therapy that combines a thorough knowledge of the literature and a systematic acquisition of practice skills. This course is run over a year for each part, and comprises 30 meetings held over three terms. The other course is new – Helping Troubled Children and Young People, held in Glasgow and run by the Scottish Institute of Human Relations. This course aims to increase understanding and appreciation of children's emotional distress. This is approached from discussion, current case examples, observations of children's behaviour and a theoretical framework. Again this course is run over 30 meetings in three terms. For nursing staff to attend these courses requires not only the course fees but considerable travelling time and expense. There was, until 1993, a Professional Studies II Module caring for adolescents in a residential/day care setting, run by Lothian College of Nursing, Edinburgh. This course offered a psychodynamic and systems approach to adolescents with inputs in family and group therapy.

The English National Board Course 603 in child, adolescent and family psychiatric nursing is run in England and trains nurses within the specialty by a process of theoretical input and practical supervised experience. Between 1973 and 1988 only 254 specialist certificates have been issued (Hinks *et al.* 1988).

In the Lowit Unit, the nursing staff have had to obtain post basic training after they commenced working there. Registered nurses with an adult psychiatric or paediatric training are required to learn new theoretical concepts and develop new skills *in situ* while attempting and wishing to offer a quality service.

Until recently all new staff were expected to develop their theoretical knowledge and practical skills from observation of and supervision by experienced staff, with a great deal of time spent in discussion. All new staff need to be self-motivated to be able to develop themselves, although the amount they are able to do depends upon the individual. There is now an induction programme which is relevant to the needs of nursing staff within the Lowit Unit. This is research based as to training requirements, giving basic information about the specialty by means of identified and recorded supervision sessions with the charge nurse. There is allowance made for individual identification of needs and issues which can then be explored. Provision for placement for wider experience outwith the unit is catered for via Education Department and Social Services.

An ongoing in-service programme is provided within the Lowit Unit. This consists of one day a month, during term times, involving both nursing and teaching staff. A working party consisting of a representive from each group within the multi-disciplinary network is continually looking at and developing this programme. Nursing and teaching staff are involved in suggesting topics for this programme. Representatives of different disciplines strongly support the in-service programme and willingly give their time to help present in conjunction with the charge nurse and liaison nurse. Topics covered in recent years include eating disorders, child sexual abuse, family therapy, childhood depression, anxiety, aggression/restraint of children, behaviour therapy. The day is structured on a participative learning basis with a theoretical underpinning and its practical application. Learning methods include role-play, group exercises, group discussion. The unit in-service programme is well attended by nursing and teaching staff. Only holidays, sick leave or study leave would prevent attendance.

It must be acknowledged, however, that as the training requirements of nursing and teaching staff differ and since individuals within professions have different needs, due to their background, training and experience, it is difficult to create an in-service programme which will meet all staff requirements.

There are various conferences, workshops and seminars that occur within the area run by such organisations as the Association of Child Psychology and Psychiatry (ACPP), special schools, social work department, and the Association for Family Therapy which nursing and teaching staff are encouraged to attend, when the event appears to be of relevance. Other considerations are whether the member of staff can be spared to attend, and funding for the event. Nursing staff, also, attend events in their own time and at their own expense. In the last two year period, fourteen events outwith the Unit have been attended by nursing staff. For four of these events, only one person has attended and there have been five events when four nursing staff have attended.

The Aberdeen Royal Hospital (NHS) Trust run 'in-house' course which are open to all registered nurses and unqualified nursing staff. These tend to be relevant in general terms but not specifically geared to psychiatric nursing. Included are courses such as: 'recruitment and selection'; 'core management skills'; 'disciplinary skills'; 'standard setting'. There is usually a waiting list for attendance at these courses. All nursing staff are required to attend a resuscitation training session and fire lecture each year. Registered nurses are encouraged to attend courses at Foresterhill Nurse Training College (the local college). Courses here include professional studies and Diploma in Nursing. Attendance at these courses at times can be problematic, as clinical needs of the Unit have to take priority over personal/professional needs. If the Unit is very busy or there are acute staff shortages, the nurse may have to forego their study time and be on duty. This happened on two occasions last year when two nurses, at different times, had to miss a week of study at college and be on the Unit all week. This increases the pressures on the nurse to complete the course properly and can lead to increased feelings of anger and frustration. The nurse has still to do course work in his or her own time and the pressures of this can be seen within the clinical area.

Resources

The current nursing establishment for the Lowit Unit is one 'G' grade, five 'E' grades, and 7.98 WTE 'B' grades. Night cover is primarily by 'B' grades from the above pool. There are two members of staff on overnight, one in rotation together with one of the two part-time nurses employed specifically for this.

In considering the staffing of any ward, it is important to make adequate allowance for such inroads into numbers of staff available for maternity leave, temporary vacancies until posts are filled, annual leave, study leave and short term sickness. The extent of these effects can easily be underestimated; for example between May 1986 and December 1992 the full complement of nurses was only available for 23 months. Planned or unexpected staff shortages result in the service having to be cut, either by reducing the number of places available to children, shortening of week, or types of children admitted. The contribution of nursing staff may be reduced as regards attendance at meetings, involvement in family therapy, individual work with children and outings outwith the Unit. Individual nurses' attendance for study leave is likewise curtailed.

Recent Developments

Since the research project commenced and finished many changes have taken place at the Lowit Unit. Some of these have had an external origin and others an internal origin.

External influences have been generated by Grampian Health Board's Child and Adolescent Psychiatry Health Needs Assessment and a report by the Purchasing Strategy Group of Grampian Health Board.

Some of the recommendations were specific to the Lowit Unit, whilst others to the child and family psychiatry service in general. The recommendation with the greatest initial impact was that Grampian Health Board decided to purchase six in-patient beds instead of the ten in-patient beds they have been purchasing. The number of day places was increased to ten and it was recognised that the same budget required to be retained. The dormitory area was re-designed to create a more homely environment, which could help to eliminate some of the difficulties for children at night.

In the longer term, it was requested that written protocols be established for admission, assessment and length of stay in the Lowit Unit. The writing of these protocols was undertaken by a multi-disciplinary team, with assistance from the Child Health Directorate Business Manager. The protocols are as included and the first audit is being undertaken (see Appendix 5B).

Another recommendation was that nursing staff should have the opportunity to gain specialist qualifications in child and family psychiatric nursing, to work in different settings and to gain in other forms of specialist intervention.

Fortunately, Lothian College of Nursing and Midwifery had formulated two Professional Studies II Modules in the Mental Health of the Child and the Adolescent. These modules both ran for ten weeks each and included theoretical and practical experiences. Nursing staff in the Lowit Unit, along with nursing staff in child psychiatric settings were involved in the discussions around the planning of these modules. The Lowit Unit was designated as a clinical placement and links with Foresterhill College provided the necessary educational support for these modules.

The modules are designed to enable experienced nurses to:

(1) assess treatment settings in child, adolescent and family psychiatry

(2) choose therapeutic approaches in accordance with client needs

(3) deliver clinical care independently and competently within a multi-disciplinary team.

One staff nurse attended both modules during 1994, which resulted in them being away from the unit for two ten week periods. Also the Scottish Institute of Human Relations started a psychotherapeutically-based course 'Helping Troubled Children and Young People'. The course followed the lines of weekly reading and discussion of a theoretical nature and discussion of course members' current clinical work. The course ran for an academic year – October 1993 to June 1994 and consisted of one study day per week. It was held in Glasgow and was attended by the charge nurse. Unfortunately, due to shortages of Registered nurses, it has not been possible to continue attendance at either of these two courses at this time.

The Grampian Health Board recommendations and the finding of the research project reported in Chapter 13 led to a member of the medical staff being identified as Medical Director, with a clearer role and a greater time commitment than in the past, reporting directly to the consultant child psychiatrists group. It was envisaged the Medical Director would take over responsibility when a child was admitted to the Lowit Unit unless the nature of consultant's involvement with the case prior to admission made it preferable for him or her to maintain responsibility. The Medical Director, along with the nurse manager (the charge nurse) have jointly taken on the management of the Lowit Unit since October 1994 and are in the process of developing a clearer management structure.

As a direct response to having a greater potential number of day patients, changes were required in the daily organisation of the Unit. After discussion, it was decided to create two separate groups of children and nursing staff, with separate playrooms/bases. The aim was to create two family-type groups, with children of all ages, as it was felt that would facilitate children and staff creating and maintaining therapeutic relationships. A modified key worker system was introduced, each group having two staff nurses and nursing assistants, who organised their work within the structure of the unit philosophy.

Currently, it is felt that each group functions best with six or seven children and the registered nurses themselves have identified that each of them, with nursing assistant support, can give a quality service to three or four children and their families.

Other changes in the structure of the day and week have been made, to facilitate the medical director's role and to maximise the effectiveness and efficiency of multi-disciplinary input to the Unit.

Much effort has been put into trying to find a reliable formula for establishing nursing staff numbers in the Lowit Unit, but no national formula has been found and the nursing staff levels in other Scottish child psychiatric units vary greatly. However, the Directorate Management Team, recognising the need for a sufficient complement of staff to allow training needs to be met and the impact of leave and illness to be accommodated, have established a new 'E' grade staff nurse post and the creation of a 'D' grade bank nurse post.

Concluding Thoughts

There are many factors which make child psychiatric nursing very rewarding. These include: working with a developing human being, whose life course can be altered if the key is found; the understanding, where possible, of a child's view of the world and an acceptance of this; the use of self as the only real 'tool' we have; being oneself, and recognising the need to be open and honest in our relationships. Each child and family is a new voyage; symptoms may be similar, but are different for each child. The satisfaction is when children begin to learn new skills to help them face the world; children's satisfaction when life gets better for them, when the healing process is taking place. The joy of play, being paid to play and with a child enjoying playing – all of these make the job worthwhile.

Child psychiatric nursing is an experience of extremes from joy to sadness, from hope to frustration, from love to anger. If one child's life is changed through our relationship with them, then it has been worth it.

References

Buchan, W.J. (1973) 'Nursing and child psychiatry developments in the Nurses' function.' *Nursing Mirror*, February 9.

Critchley, D.L. (1991) 'Nursing contributions to a psychiatric in-patient treatment milieu for children and adolescents.' In R.L. Hendron and I.N. Berlin (eds) *Psychiatric In-patient Care of Children and Adolescents.* USA: Wildy.

Giddey, M. (1983) 'Home is where the heart is.' *Nursing Journal*, January 36–38.

Gray, C., Chisholm, D., Smith, P., Brown, M. and McKay, C. (1992) 'The role of the child psychiatric ward in health care.' *Irish Journal of Psychological Medicine 9*, 17–23.

Haldane, J., Smith, J., McInnes, J. and Henderson, J. (1971) 'Training nurses in child, adolescent and family psychiatry.' *Nursing Times*, March 11, 37–40.

Hinks, M., Crosbie, C., Adams, M., Skinner, A., Cooper, G. and King, M. (1988) 'Not child's play.' *Nursing Times 84*, 38, 42–44.

Wilkinson, T. (1983) *Child and Adolescent Psychiatric Nursing.* Oxford: Blackwell Scientific Publications.

Winnicot, D.W. (1968) The Family and Individual Development. London: Social Science Paperbacks.

Philosophy of Nursing Care

Children are admitted with behavioural, emotional of psychological difficulties which interfere with their normal developmental tasks. The aim of the nursing staff is to help children develop and explore different strategies to deal with their difficulties which allow the child to develop their potential as a human being.

This is hopefully facilitated by providing a warm, nurturing environment, where the child is accepted as an individual with individual needs. The opportunity is provided for all children to develop and maintain a meaningful relationship with a member of the nursing staff of their choice. Through this relationship the individual child can be helped to develop a sense of 'self-worth' and be encouraged to develop alternative methods of reacting to difficulties which they encounter.

Children learn, through consequences to their behaviour, what is desirable and what is undesirable. With much emphasis being placed on desirable behaviour.

Nursing staff will, whenever possible, remain open and truthful to the children so relationships of trust can result. Nursing staff will also strive to achieve and maintain the balance of being therapeutic and remaining in control of the group of children, thereby demonstrating an ability to tolerate extremes of behaviour and visibly display to the children that they are safe here within the Unit.

The Unit has to demonstrate a service which is able to modify itself, when desirable, to individual children and their families.

Nursing staff present with open relationships within the staff group and members of multi-disciplinary team, modelling for the children that difficulties and differences of opinions can be resolved in a safe way.

It is important to remember and recognise that each child is an individual and, whenever possible, this individuality is respected and acknowledged.

Nursing staff make themselves accessible to children's families and be willing to discuss aspects of care and assist families in making full use of this facility. It is important for parents to realise they still have responsibilities for their children while they are in the Unit and that these areas require recognition and negotiation with nursing staff.

Child Health Directorate
Lowit Unit Protocols

The Lowit Unit is a Health Care Facility for a small number of children whose psychiatric disorders are particularly complex and severe, who have not responded to other forms of treatment and require this specialist assessment/treatment. These children will commonly suffer from a combination of the following problems:

- Conduct Disorders
- Emotional Disorders
- Hyperkinetic Syndrome
- Anorexia Nervosa
- Psychosis
- Deliberate Self Harm
- Encopresis
- Specific Learning Difficulties
- Emotional/Behavioural Disorders Complicating Physical Illness.

Admission

(1) Referrals to the Lowit Unit are on the prescribed form to the Admission/Discharge Committee by:

- Consultant Psychiatrists
- Clinical Psychologists
- Hospital Social Workers

For a day or in-patient admission.

Emergency admissions are arranged by the Consultant Psychiatrists.

(2) Admission/Discharge Committee

The Committee meets monthly to discuss the cases, its membership represents the following:

- Psychiatrists
- Clinical Psychologists
- Hospital Social Workers
- Nurses
- Teachers
- Occupational Therapists

- Speech and Language Therapists
- Educational Psychologists) by invitation depending on
- Community Social Workers)

Each patient's case is presented by the referrer or their representative.

(3) Waiting Lists

Consideration is given as to whether the child's name is put on one of the following waiting lists:

(a) **Actual Waiting List** – for admission when a place becomes available.

The criterion for this admission would be for a child whose problem requires further assessment by the multi-disciplinary team.

(b) **Provisional Waiting List** – for possible admission in the future.

These would include children who through continuing treatment as an out-patient may improve and would no longer require admission.

The Actual and Provisional waiting lists are reviewed at each monthly meeting of the Admission/Discharge Committee. Each child's position on the list is reviewed in relation to their current situation.

When a child's name is put onto either waiting list a case co-ordinator is identified.

(4) In-patient Admissions

These children may exhibit any of the previous problems described, though certain disorders, Anorexia Nervosa, Deliberate Self Harm and Psychosis, almost always require such admission.

(5) Day Patients

Children are admitted as day patients whose problems require more intensive assessment/treatment than could be provided on an out-patient basis.

(6) Vacancies

Filling of vacancies depends not only on vacancies in places but also taken into consideration is the nature of the children already in the Lowit Unit.

Assessment

(1) Pre-admission meetings for each patient are convened by the case co-ordinator with members of the multi-disciplinary team and the community professionals who are involved in the management of the child. The parents also attend this meeting.

The aims and objectives of the admission are agreed for the period of assessment which in most cases is between six and ten weeks.

(2) Within two weeks of admission an internal review takes place to identify progress and any necessary changes in the child's programme.

(3) At the end of the assessment period a review meeting is held which will include hospital and community professionals and the child's parents. Decisions based on the findings presented will determine the child's future management either to continue treatment in the Lowit Unit or be discharged from the Lowit Unit with continuing work from the Out-patient Department.

For those children who remain in the Lowit Unit after assessment there will be a formal six week review of progress based on continuing assessment.

Length of Stay

(1) Every effort will be made prior to admission to plan for the discharge of each child, dependent on information available at the time.

(2) The minimum length of stay would be approximately six weeks for assessment and short-term treatment.

(3) The average length of stay, based on previous experience would be six months for children whose problems are multi-factorial.

(4) There are a small number of children whose stay is longer, up to and over one year. These are children with particularly severe and complex problems who require continuing stability and treatment from the Lowit Unit to enable them to make gradual progress.

Discharge

The child's discharge is arranged through discussion with parents, child, multi-disciplinary team and those community resources likely to be involved in the child's future management. Arrangements for follow-up are also agreed.

The child's departure from the Lowit Unit is usually phased over a period, dependent on the individual child's needs.

Work is undertaken with the child and family in preparation for discharge and they are invited to visit the Lowit Unit in the future.

General Practitioners

Children's General Practitioners are kept regularly informed by means of admission, progress and discharge summaries. Telephone discussions take place when indicated.

Involvement of Child and Family/Carers

The proposal to admit the child is discussed with the child and their parents/carers, by the referring professional, who they are already usually seeing for treatment.

Arrangements for admission are negotiated with the parents/carers and the child. Other family members may be involved in these discussions as appropriate.

Except in cases of emergency the child and their parents/carers visit the Unit prior to admission. They are shown around the Unit and necessary explanations given, together with an opportunity to ask questions. They also receive an information leaflet. A home visit by staff and the pre-admission meeting (assessment 1) are then arranged.

Throughout assessment and treatment the child and their parents/carers are being seen in various forms of therapy sessions and during these information about the child's assessment and progress is exchanged.

This information is formalised and reviewed at the six weekly review meeting (assessment 3).

The involvement of the child and parents/carers in discharge arrangements is as described in section on discharge.

Audit

These protocols will be reviewed in relation to each child on an annual basis, who has been in the unit.

CHAPTER 6

Nursing in a Child Psychiatric Unit
The Nurse–Child Relationship and Containment

David McLeod

The main aims of the chapter are:

(1) to examine aspects of children's needs and development;

(2) to outline the nursing response to those needs within the context of containment;

(3) to highlight how child psychiatric nurses can (a) facilitate and (b) obstruct the process whereby the child is 'learning from experience' (Bion 1962).

(4) to emphasise that learning from experience is a lifelong process.

Children's Needs

Kellmer Pringle (1974) has asserted that from birth onwards the child has a need for love and security which can be met by experiencing '...a stable, continuous, dependable and loving relationship with his parents (or permanent parent substitutes), who themselves enjoy a rewarding relationship with one another' (p.34). Through this experience the child is imbued with a sense of being a person of worth, having a healthy self-identity. This relationship with the parents forms the basis of all subsequent relationships which includes the capacity to respond to affection. Since approval and acceptance by others are essential for the development of self-approval and self-acceptance (Kellmer Pringle 1974) whether the child regards him or herself initially and also later others, in a positive or negative light will depend primarily on the parental attitudes towards him or her. While clearly children have other needs relating to the healthy development of personality and self-esteem, for the purposes of this chapter, the emphasis will be placed on security.

It is the stability and consistency of parental attitudes and behaviour towards the child that meets needs for security – that being considered here as a sense of continuity and predictability. Parents clearly set out expectations of the child's behaviour; the delineation of limits with the child knowing that consequences will follow if limits are exceeded.

Although needs are universal to all children, they will not inevitably be met by all parents. If this were to be the case, there would be very little need for the child psychiatric nurse. Indeed, Parker (1989) has argued that our response as nurses is, in itself, a recognition that, regardless of the reason, early childhood experiences have not permitted basic emotional needs to be met. It is an important part of the nursing response in a residential psychiatric unit to replicate aspects of parental behaviour. This includes the setting of limits, which is usually referred to as providing structure. It involves, as Balbernie (1989) has pointed out, the setting of realistic and therapeutically appropriate limits. Moreover, it is argued that '... This is something that small children demand [and] if it is not given they are driven to become increasingly beastly as their only way for getting their needs for security noticed' (p.7).

The Nurse–Child Relationship

While nursing staff may, therefore, be expected to take on the parental role for the child, Beedell (1970) cautions that they should avoid taking it over. Beedell (1970) advises that there must be a distance maintained by the caring adult so that the child does not identify with the nurse as being his real parent (or parent substitute) even though nurses are acting 'in loco parentis' and may in many ways be fulfilling parental tasks more effectively than the parents themselves. The consequences of the nurse failing to observe that distance or boundary would be one of undermining the parents in the child's eyes, which Beedell (1970) argues could be disastrous.

Nevertheless, it is vital that the nurse builds up a relationship with the child which involves a strong emotional commitment from that nurse. As Jung (1954) states 'You can exert no influence if you are not susceptible to influence'.

In many cases, the reality is that the nurse's main objective is to provide the child with his or her first experience of a 'real' relationship (Reeves 1979). However, many children who are referred to child psychiatric units are often, at least initially, wary and untrusting of adults, including nursing staff. What we encounter are the child's defence mechanisms, survival techniques which circumstances may have sadly led the child to have to resort to '... the creation of a "false self" or a flight from attachment to autism' (Balbernie 1989, p.7).

It follows that, if the child's needs for love and security are satisfied by the parents with the consequence that the child develops an integrated personality and, concomitantly, a strong sense of identity, then the inverse will also be true if needs are not met. Reeves (1979) sees the unintegrated child as unsteady, inconsistent and unreliable in dealings with people and perceives such an individual to feel no guilt and usually no grudge either, since both guilt and grudge require a continuity of experience. The assumption is that such a child is not only insecure, but that this process is a subjectively frightening experience for that child. Such a child needs to experience 'containment' which has been defined as '... not only that capacity to deal with an outburst or an explosion from the child, but also the day-to-day provision of "containing" or "holding" experiences for the child' (Parker 1989, p.15).

The essence of this concept of holding or containment is, at an emotional level, to be understood in the context of the relationship between the nurse and the child. As Balbernie (1989) states,

> 'The experience of being psychologically held by others who care enough to confront directly and not ignore or fudge painful issues and who do so time and time again, regardless of the hassles, gives the client the slow and reluctant realisation that he is valued enough for others to work with him in spite of his sense of badness.' (p.8)

There is a corresponding realisation by the child that '... its angers cannot destroy, its greed cannot empty, and its excitements cannot get out of control'. (p.8).

It may often be necessary for the nurse physically to hold and thus contain the child; such an intervention being understood within the broader context that, as mentioned earlier regarding the small child 'demanding' that limits be set to his behaviour, such a child feels unsafe and has a strong need to know that the adult is 'in control' because the child's subjective experience is of feeling very 'out of control' and vulnerable.

In addressing this question of containment, Balbernie (1989), for theoretical purposes, makes the observation that there are two strands involved – at an outer level there is structure while at an inner level there is support. These, however, are seen as overlapping with their implications of 'benevolent limits'.

Nursing: Structure and Support

In a similarly vein, acceptable limits and acceptable behaviour have been defined by Wilkinson (1983) as follows:

> **acceptable limits:** 'boundaries highlighting what behaviour will be tolerated and what behaviour is deemed unacceptable'. (p.63)

> **acceptable behaviour:** 'pro-social and... which aids personal development', with unacceptable behaviour being the converse, 'that which hinders personal and social development'. (p.63)

The ultimate goal, however, of this outer aspect of limit-setting is the complementary inner aspect whereby the child 'internalises' those limits in the sense of the development of conscience and personal boundaries. The delineation of acceptable boundaries of behaviour is, therefore, a response by nursing staff to the unintegrated child's lack of personal boundaries. Such a child is viewed by

Reeves (1983) '... Lacking a self as an autonomous "I" [an] organising centre of perceptions and experience'. Similarly, it has been observed that many children could be defined as 'damaged' because they have not developed effective boundary control or a firm identity within it. In the context of healthy development, the child is regarded as needing the establishment of a firm boundary for the self and others 'across which realistic and effective relationships and transactions can take place and within which a sense of one's own identity can be established' (Menzies Lyth 1985).

The outer aspect (structure) has little meaning if it is not complemented by the inner (support). This inner aspect may be lost sight of if nursing staff (or parents) focus unduly on the outer setting of standards of behaviour backed up by a system of punishments, rewards and 'discipline' to enforce these standards. Discipline has been defined as '... training which develops self-control and the capacity to co-operate' (Kellmer Pringle 1974, p.40) and as '... the achievement of a good and mature balance between necessary freedom and equally necessary control' (Ratcliffe 1970, p.19). The objective of discipline is, therefore, the achievement of *self-discipline* on the part of the child. Ratcliffe (1970), although acknowledging that rewards and punishments have their place, cautions that this should not be interpreted to mean that an elaborate frame of rules is needed or that children must be so closely supervised that there is no opportunity for experiment and growth. He argues that a flexible approach is needed.

Menzies Lyth (1985) goes on to suggest, however, that structure is not just a matter of outlining psychological boundaries but also concerns the physical boundaries of the unit or ward. She contends, furthermore, that an effectively bounded small unit is likely to foster 'the development of an easily identifiable and relatively integrated group within the unit with the staff as its permanent core' (p.55).

The child is, therefore, made to feel safe and 'contained' by knowing that there are clear physical boundaries to the unit. This principle is also applicable to any outside play areas. In the Lowit Unit, for example, each new child is clearly told which areas are 'out of bounds' both outwith and within the building itself. The danger exists, inevitably, that nursing staff's approach may be obstructive to the child developing stronger internal boundary control in that what is 'in' and 'out of' bounds become merely rules to be observed.

Gribble (1985), a progressive educationalist, makes the point that 'Rules in themselves do not constitute reasons; reasons dictate rules. Wherever possible children should be allowed to react to reasons, without the rules as an intermediary stage. Reasons are a consequence of reality. Rules are invented by teachers' (p.130). That last observation can equally apply to nurses. Gribble adds that '... just as adult control removes the discipline of reality, so freedom exposes you to it' (p.130).

Part of that discipline of reality within a unit might, for example, take the form of the child being rejected by peers on account of insults and sarcasm directed towards them. It is likely to be more therapeutic, in terms of the child learning from this experience, for him or her to encounter rejection, rather than adults intervening to delineate acceptable behaviour. Indeed, Wilkinson (1983) sees children's behaviour as being initially limited by adults, then by peer group pressure and finally, by internalised limits.

Turning now to the complementary inner aspect of support, it should be recognised that the concept occupies an important place in current psychoanalytic thinking. The work of Bion in the early 1960s and his development of the concepts of projective identification and maternal reverie would appear helpful in achieving greater understanding of the relationship between nurses and unit children. What would seem to bridge the gap, theoretically, between Bion's (1962) work on containment with the mother and infant, and nursing staff working with children who are sometimes in their early teens, is his emphasis on the whole projection–introjection exchange as a *communication process* between mother and infant. If this is to be transferable to the professional setting a pre-condition is that identification on the part of the child with nurses must take place. As Balbernie (1989) highlights '...the more the client is experiencing being held and cared for (without necessarily knowing it) then the greater the likelihood that he will identify with the professional' (p.11).

Projective Identification

Identification with the nurse as a role model and as someone with whom the child feels safe may lead to projective identification. The child may project onto the nurse feelings of not being in control (Parker 1989) which might well be manifested in 'acting out' behaviour, sometimes taking on the form of physical aggression towards the nurse. Such behaviour may thus be most appropriately regarded as an attempt to communicate with the nurse and make known 'felt deficiencies'. At this stage the child is unlikely to be able to conceptualise those deficiencies and thus they are projected as raw emotions, uncoded by language.

If the process of projection–reverie–introjection that constitutes containment is regarded as a learning process for the child, then the response of the nurse at this inner level of support will either be facilitative or obstructive to that learning process. This is likely to be dependent on whether he or she is able to work with these projected emotions. Copley and Forryan (1987) provide two examples of responses apparently obstructive to that learning process: (1) 'pseudo-containment' – where the nurse appears to listen to the child but is paying little attention and (2) the 'tea-towel' version where there is an apparent 'wiping away of feelings of distress', but little attention is paid to their possible meaning. A further obstructive response is where the nurse (or mother) casts herself in the role of 'sponge' to 'soak up' the child's pain.

Containment

In all the above responses, pain is not borne therapeutically, with the overall objective of modification and return to the child. By contrast, a response facilitative to self-learning is where the child is helped to acknowledge and accept ownership of unwanted feelings (through introjection). Parker (1989) points out that 'It is the capacity of the adult to hold these feelings, without attempting to deflect or suppress them, that is crucial in a therapeutic relationship' (p.17–18). Regarding the question of giving back responsibility to the child, Parker (1989) stresses the importance of staff's ability to enable residents to have doubts and uncertainties without being 'overwhelmed by them'.

Staff too, however, may have difficulties in coping with feelings and this may lead to a response which is obstructive to the process of the child internalising his or her own emotional boundaries through the ownership of his or her feelings. This can be understood in terms of nursing staff's understandable defence mechanisms against the potency of the emotions being projected on to them. Such emotions might not only be those of anger but also feelings of sadness or inadequacy of which the child wishes to be 'rid'. Menzies Lyth (1985) has highlighted one organisational defence mechanism employed by nurses, namely, 'the multiple indiscriminate caretaking by a large number of nurses which effectively prevent(s) attachment between a child and his caretakers' (p.50).

To be an effective container of the child's feelings is, in short, extremely demanding of the nurse. It is more than being a receptacle or 'dustbin', as the word container might suggest; containment can only exist in the context of attachments built on the nurse–child relationship. True containment involves not only a 'taking in' – feeling the child's pain – but also a 'giving back', allowing the child to assume greater responsibility for emotions.

The inner setting, indispensable for this process to occur, is that the child feels understood by the nurse. This creates conditions whereby 'when the imagined to be unacceptable has not only been recognised but also not condemned by a significant other, then both these processes of recognition and acceptance can be introjected as self-acceptance' (Balbernie 1989, p.13).

Self-acceptance on the part of the child would seem to be the essential, solid foundation upon which the child can begin to learn from experience. It would seem to equate with the child becoming more integrated; of having a core self and starting to learn to value and respect himself.

Dockar Drysdale (1968) has suggested that adults working with unintegrated children must be able to offer sequentially three levels of provision: (1) containment; (2) communication; and (3) conceptualisation. When feelings start to be conceptualised, this could be perceived as an indicator of greater self-acceptance; of the development of a sense of identity. It represents a progression from the frustrated communication 'acting out'. Conceptualisation of feelings represents self-expression, expression of 'the self' of which the previously unintegrated child had not been aware. The process now becomes one whereby sensations, emotions and urges can be coded, sorted and cross-referenced (Balbernie 1989).

In conclusion, as has been argued throughout this chapter, all children need to feel cared for and loved. This helps the child feel secure and meets the child's need for acceptance. If this provision is lacking, the child will *feel* the deficiency of that love and security. As a consequence, such a child is likely to be insecure, lacking a sense of self or identity and concomitantly being unaware of personal boundaries.

The nursing response to the child's need to feel secure should be aimed towards the building up of relationships which allow containment to occur. As trust is developed, the child will not initially, or perhaps never will, be able to articulate those deficiencies in words. Instead, the feelings of loss or lack are projected onto the nurse with whom the child identified.

The child lacks the boundaries or the capacity to contain and accept ownership of his/her own emotions, particularly those which relate to this perceived sense of deficiency (e.g. anger and sadness). Through feeling understood, the child can introject feelings of self-acceptance. This can serve as a platform which allows the child to confront those feelings of loss and move towards accepting greater responsibility or ownership for his or her emotions. Feeling valued and accepted is likely to help the child to internalise personal boundaries. The nursing response, while at the outer level providing structure in terms of setting limits, is at the same time at the inner level providing support, by *feeling* the child's projected emotions so as to convey understanding but without being a mere receptacle.

The child's 'learning experience' is, to be more precise, a process of the child learning to value him or herself through the experience of containing relationships. As the child develops a firmer identity and firmer personal boundaries, such security is likely to mean that there is less need to project emotions onto others.

Finally, it should be remembered that however facilitative the nursing response in providing containment, it can be no more than this – '... whether in healing or in education it is ultimately [only] the agent, in this case the child, who can bring about change for himself' (Reeves 1983, p.30).

Learning from Experience – The Nurse

If the premise is accepted that this process of learning from experience does extend into adulthood, it would seem appropriate to examine how it might be applicable to the nurse's own behaviour in the clinical setting. The work of Benner (1984) in the United States is particularly helpful in this respect. Benner, in her book *From Novice to Expert – Excellence and Power in Clinical Nursing Practice* defines experience as that which results '... when preconceived notions and expectations are challenged, refined or disconfirmed by the actual situation' (p.3). Such a conception views experience as being an active process and not '... the mere passage of time or longevity' (p.3).

Benner postulates that in the process of gaining such experience, as skills are acquired and developed, the nurse will pass through five levels of proficiency: novice, advanced beginner, competent, proficient and expert. There will also, concurrently, be certain general changes taking place, as outlined below.

(1) When faced with a particular situation, there will be a movement away from relying on abstract principles and towards relying on past concrete experience.

(2) As the nurse becomes more experienced and proficient, she or he will tend to perceive situations as 'a whole' or gestalt as opposed to a compilation of many different 'bits'. The nurse will compare past 'whole situations' with current 'whole situations'. The proficient nurse will also home in on which aspects of a situation are of greatest significance, mentally discarding other aspects.

(3) The nurse moves from the role of 'detached observer' to that of 'involved performer'. (Benner 1984)

To give a clinical example, a nurse new to child psychiatric nursing – a novice – will initially observe other nursing staff dealing with clinical situations including exclusion from class because of aggressive, acting-out behaviour on a child's part. At this stage there is a tendency to rely on principles or rules to manage the situation. Examples of such rules or principles applicable might be: 'There should be no interaction with the child during the period of exclusion' (even while holding the child if this has become necessary). A similar principle might be: 'The child should be seated quietly in a chair for a few minutes prior to returning to class'.

The novice will tend to observe such principles rigidly but in so doing will fail to be aware of the *context* of the child's behaviour; the meanings and intentions contained within the child's actions. Such rules or principles have thus major limitations in being 'context-free'.

As the nurse in the process of learning from experience becomes more proficient so he or she becomes more able to place the child's behaviour in some kind of context – to see more of the child's whole situation rather than just focusing on the child's manifest behaviour. Accordingly the nurse, with the capacity to put some kind of interpretation on the child's behaviour, is likely to respond with greater flexibility.

An example of the more experienced nurse placing the child's behaviour in a meaningful context would be of an acknowledgement that the child's Review Meeting is to occur later that morning. A combination of concrete past experiences of children in this situation, as well as knowledge arising from her relationship with this particular child, would lead the nurse to see an aggressive outburst in the context of the child's raised anxiety levels as to the outcome of the meeting and his inability to hold on to these uncertainties.

Acting on such an interpretation of the situation, once the child was settled enough to be able to be engaged in conversation, the nurse would then check out with the child if this interpretation was correct and seek to allay the child's anxieties or at least help the child to acknowledge them. Benner (1984) asserts that '... perceptual awareness is central to good nursing judgement and that this begins with vague hunches and global assessments that initially bypass critical analysis...' (p.18). This does not mean that as the nurse becomes more expert that analytical qualities are lacking. Rather more reliance is placed on synthesis, which provides a basis for effective and prompt intervention. As Benner observes '... conceptual clarity follows more often than it precedes' (p.18).

The nurse at an early stage in the development of expertise will often strictly observe that which serves, in fact, only as a guideline to practice. However, such a nurse does not necessarily possess the experience to assess the child's current state nor have developed the relationship with the child and/or the ability to help him to reduce his anxieties and thus to be more settled. One consequence of such adherence to rules or guidelines is that the nurse might unwittingly escalate the situation.

In reality, however, it is more complex than this model of nurse progression suggests. The nurse may hold on to preconceptions of the situation, even though these are not necessarily confirmed by the child's behaviour. The nurse may *not* learn from experience, as Benner acknowledges. Preconceptions and prior understanding may not be challenged or refined by each new experience; development of expertise may, thus, be inhibited. Benner (1984) has asserted that experience is '... a prerequisite for expertise' with expertise itself only developing '... when the clinician *tests* and *refines* propositions, hypotheses and principle-based expectations in actual practice situations' (p.3).

An additional factor is that the nurse may continue to refine preconceptions and expectations when faced with each new clinical situation but impose limitations or parameters on this process of refinement – and thus learning – through basing clinical practice on a particular theoretical model. It could be argued, for example, that exclusion from class represents in itself the practising of a behavioural technique, the effectiveness of which is being undermined if the nurse interacts with the child. Such interaction is giving the child social reinforcement – in behavioural terms giving the child positive attention is rewarding his unacceptable behaviour such that it is more likely to continue. Conversely, the ideal would be that the child receives no reinforcers for his unacceptable behaviour such that it is more likely therefore to be, in time, eradicated.

It would be consistent, therefore, with the behavioural standpoint for the nurse to avoid interacting with the child even while in the process of holding as this, too, could be regarded as social reinforcement. In strictly applying behavioural principles, therefore, the context of the child's current situation is not important (the meanings contained with the behaviour). The child's intentions need not concern the nurse; only the manifest behaviour is relevant.

It would seem reasonable to suggest therefore that a *rigid* adherence either to a behavioural approach or by contrast to a more psychodynamic interpretive approach could limit the nurse's capacity to learn from experience. From the point of view of the novice or advanced beginner, it is clear that it is not simply the case – as Benner (1984) would suggest it was – of the nurse gradually discarding these rules or guidelines as he or she gains in confidence and expertise from integrating new experiences.

The aforementioned 'rules' are, in fact, much more than guides to practice but rather belong to a particular ideology. The novice/advanced beginner may also find that different ideologies are prevalent within the unit which are often at variance with one another, whether being an influence on the practice of nursing or teaching staff.

There would seem to be an element, therefore, of the nurse who is willing to 'learn from experience' not only having to adopt an attitude of being open to have prior expectations of each new situation challenged, but of also being adept at negotiating this particular ideological minefield. Nurses need, there-fore, to be able to differentiate between what are, in fact, simply rules or guidelines designed to assist the beginner who has little or no experience and those which, by contrast, *appear* to be rules but which are, in fact, part of a particular theoretical approach.

According to Benner's (1984) five level typology of nursing proficiency, however, it is the very capacities to discriminate and differentiate that have not yet developed in the novice or advanced beginner.

Conclusion

Benner (1984) offers the following observation upon which it would seem fitting to conclude: 'A wealth of untapped knowledge is embedded in the practices and the "know-how" of expert nurse clinicians, but this knowledge will not expand or fully develop unless nurses systematically record what they learn from their own experience' (p. 11).

References

Balbernie, R. (1989) 'Looking at what professional carers do: the Therapeutic context and conditions of change.' *Maladjustment and Therapeutic Education 7*, 1, 4–14.

Beedell, C. (1970) *Residential Life With Children*. London: Kegan Paul.

Benner, P. (1984) *From Novice to Expert – Excellence and Power in Clinical Nursing Practice*. California: Addison Wesley.

Bion, W.R. (1962) *Learning from Experience*. London: Heinemann.

Copley, B. and Forryan, B. (1987) *Therapeutic Work With Children And Young People.* London: Robert Royce.

Dockar Drysdale, B. (1968) *Papers On Residential Work: Therapy In Child Care.* London: Longmans.

Gribble, D. (1985) *Considering Children.* London: Dorling Kindersley.

Jung, C.G. (1954) *Problems Of Modern Psychotherapy Collected works 16,* 53–75. London: Routledge and Kegan Paul.

Kellmer Pringle, M. (1974) *The Needs Of Children.* London: Hutchinson.

Menzies Lyth, I. (1985) 'The development of the self in children in institutions.' *Journal of Child Psychotherapy 11,* 2, 49–64.

Parker, C. (1989) 'Provision of a "holding" environment – care and containment in a residential setting.' *Maladjustment and Therapeutic Education 7,* 1, 15–23.

Ratcliffe, T.A. (1970) *The Child And Reality.* London: George Allen and Unwin.

Reeves, C. (1979) 'Transference in the residential treatment of children.' *Journal of Child Psychotherapy 5.* 25–37

Reeves, C. (1983) 'Maladjustment: psycho-dynamic theory and the role of therapeutic education in a residential setting.' *Maladjustment and Therapeutic Education 1,* 2, 25–31.

Wilkinson, T.R. (1983) *Child and Adolescent Psychiatric Nursing.* Oxford: Blackwell.

CHAPTER 7

The Unit School
Internal and External Relationships

Lindsey Mackie

Introduction

MacKay (1988) from his survey of educational provision in residential psychi-atric units in Scotland established that at that time there were ten units – including the Lowit Unit – in existence. They covered a wide geographical area and each appears to have developed its own unique character. Interestingly, a respondent in MacKay's survey is cited by him, as commenting that his survey was flawed, because the provisions being compared varied too widely, their quality being dependent on 'their educational and medical leadership'. In this chapter the work of one unit is described, and discussed, and in the final section specific consideration is given to the relationship between the unit and other schools within the region.

The School

The school has been an integral part of the Lowit Unit since it was first established, although it has evolved over the years. For instance the pupil teacher ratio has improved as the number of teachers has doubled from 1.5 initially to the current three full-time appointments. This improved staffing has helped to create a sense of permanence and continuity within the school, which I consider to be two of the most important elements in such educational provision. Also the number of classrooms has increased with a portacabin for a further two classrooms being acquired on the upgrading of the ward in 1989. Thus it is now possible for children to be taught in three age-grouped classes, although even now major differences in interest, aptitude and ability are found in any one group. Classes are formed by age groupings depending on the prevailing composition of the ward and hence not only may the average age of the group vary but also the range at any one time.

The difficulties the children present extend from one end of the spectrum, where there are children who show aggressive acting out behaviour, to those at the other end who are withdrawn or depressed. Some are challenging, lacking in self-discipline, unwilling to accept the authority of adults, lacking in concentration or perseverance, unable to accept competition or defeat and to relate to their peers. Others within the group may be over-compliant, anxious and prone to make very high demands of themselves. In addition, we have found that many of the children have specific learning difficulties which contribute to their behaviour problems. A common characteristic of all is low self-esteem, and therefore we aim to enhance any talents or aptitudes in the individual as a positive step towards building confidence.

It is important to note that the Unit school, administered by the Education Department of the Regional Council, is seen primarily by medical, nursing and teaching staff as a school and not as a therapy group. The teachers are employed under the same conditions of service as for teachers in all schools in the region. However, it differs in a number of respects from even a small mainstream school as can be seen from the very composition of the school day when children may be withdrawn for individual assessment or therapy on a regular basis.

Another major difference is that the school accommodation and the children's living and play rooms are all part of the same building. During school time, nursing staff are close at hand, but occupied in their own activities. Children's previous experience is often that there has not been much communication between home and school, or that communication has been distorted. At the unit, they are aware that information is shared between nurses and teachers and that both staff groups co-operate to carry out treatment plans. In addition, their own parents are kept in touch with what is happening in class, as well as at other times in discussion with nursing staff, teachers, or more formally at regular review meetings.

Child–Teacher Relationships

Obviously, good relationships are vitally important. The difficulty lies in looking into oneself and trying to delineate what it is that promotes a relationship that is friendly rather than hostile; informal, yet still preserving an element of respect for each other's point of view. In the past, relationships with teachers may not have worked out well. After all, school is the setting where family values come into contact with society's expectations and within the school community the boundaries of rules and routines are likely to be more formalised and rigid than those found in the wider community outside school. For some of the children admitted to the unit the teacher–child relationship has been disastrous, resulting in exclusion and possibly home tuition for a period before admission. Many of the children will not have come into direct conflict with teachers – their relationships may have been characterised by sympathetic and helpful teachers, who are simply unable to provide the input needed for the severe problems of one individual among the many. At the Lowit Unit this situation would seem to be reversed, with each child being the focus of the many members of the multi-disciplinary team.

As I mentioned before, it is difficult to look into oneself and to try to formalise in writing what is usually left vague and ambiguous in the phrase 'a good child–teacher relationship', but over the years it has become clear to me that an essential aspect is that pupils' good points are appreciated and highlighted but, one hopes, in a not too obvious way! Correspondingly the teacher should minimise (or try to) the things that go wrong. When the latter do occur they need to be presented as a lapse or a reversion to former ways and used to indicate that new approaches to problems have to be adopted; present difficulties reflect the fact that past strategies simply did not work. When things are 'going wrong' for a child it is very important for the teacher to attempt to unravel what is happening and why. In fact, throughout class contact time it is necessary to maintain a state of inward vigilance and careful observation while attempting to maintain an outward appearance of being relaxed and friendly.

Control, however, must not be lost if a pupil has to leave the class because of unacceptable behaviour or aggression. The teacher needs to appear sorry that the event has occurred and express regret to any other members of the class. Their help should be enlisted and a sympathetic climate created for the individual to come back into class. Sense needs to be made of the incident and the reasons for it examined. It should be remembered that over the years when things have gone awry for the child it may not have been possible to establish why such incidents have happened, not least because they are usually confusing for everyone involved. Helping children to make sense of such incidents is a vital part of a teacher's role and once children are able to do this it is a big step forward in their attaining a measure of self-control.

The fact that children are able to return to class after an incident and find that their relationship with the teacher is not destroyed nor has it become a hostile one, can be very helpful to them. Nevertheless in my opinion it is also valuable for them that there should be a consequence. For example, if a book is torn it will need to be repaired, if pencils are spilled they will need to be picked up although help is likely to be at hand from the teacher.

Also important in the work of the school is the fact that the pupil is a member of a class group (however small) though he may be withdrawn for individual work on occasions. The teacher therefore attempts to foster an atmosphere where the pupils are able to perceive each other's special needs and tolerate each other to the extent that they are able to accept that the teacher's demands on each child may be different because they have different needs. It is an only too common classroom tactic for the child to focus on any seeming injustice inherent in individualised learning programmes rather than accepting their own assignments in a positive frame of mind. A shared sense of humour is therefore often a very necessary element of the teacher–pupil relationship and may enable the teacher to stay in control without seeming too controlling.

Relationships are also made more difficult by virtue of variable lengths of stay for pupils and different entry dates. At times it seems that as soon as one cohesive class group has been formed, the balance is changed by one member leaving or a new pupil joining. Nevertheless, fostering interest and motivation, particularly in the older children remains crucial if they are to be offered a realistic chance of re-entering mainstream education. We are very aware, therefore, that it is necessary to provide as wide and varied a curriculum as possible while accepting the limitations of a small teaching staff operating within limited classroom accommodation situated in a children's hospital. In particular, we could not expect to provide the full range of subjects of a secondary school and what we provide should be seen as preparation for re-entry to mainstream education, not as a replacement for it.

Over the years we have used various strategies to extend the range of what we can offer. For example, at one time the three teachers exchanged classes once a week to offer our own special interests (sewing, baking, music). Again, at present, the two older classes are combined with two teachers in a team teaching situation. We think that this will be a more helpful experience for those about to return to mainstream classes.

In addition to this, since my appointment, we have been able to introduce a number of specialist teachers.

Specialist Teachers and Their Contribution

The first specialist teacher to be introduced was for swimming. Previously, this had occurred on a Tuesday afternoon, but only when there were enough staff available. Transport was by public bus and it was not treated as a graded learning experience. Now, with the introduction of a teacher and provision of a bus to transport us to a school/community pool with both shallow and deep ends, we are able to provide tuition for the complete non-swimmer to the most advanced. This activity remains on Tuesday afternoons and is run jointly by nursing and teaching staff on a one-to-one basis with those children that require this and in small groups for the more proficient swimmers. The swimming teacher is in overall control and it is an activity that has given great benefits all round. The physical education teacher now also provides a half hour session to each class on a Monday afternoon, though there have been difficulties first in finding accommodation and, at present, because the accommodation is cramped, with noisy acoustics. For this reason, although it is possible to cover some of the attainment targets detailed in the National Curriculum Guidelines, the emphasis in the physical education curriculum lies on improving the individual's skills and fostering his or her ability to accept competition or to aim for self-improvement. In general, the provision of specialist teachers within our school staff does help in making our educational time in the unit more 'school like' – in that the classes are taught by teachers other than the class teacher, who usually works alongside with a group of children. These teachers are also involved through the week with other schools in the city, forming a valuable link between ourselves and mainstream education.

Pupils receive specialist art and design teaching once a week in an area usually set aside as a dining room. Although this restricts the range of activities on offer, the space is adequate for most lessons. However, an area suitable for creative activity should not exclude an atmosphere of caution; artistic expression can, and sometimes should, be a messy business! This is not possible in a room set aside as a servery, with no sink area – itself a prohibitive factor when planning activities.

This negativity aside, visual arts have a high profile in the unit. Pupils directly have an effect upon and enhance their surroundings by providing work of a very high standard. Some pupils have also found that pursuing an interest or aptitude for art and design has provided a highly effective foundation for reintegrating to mainstream education.

The National Curriculum Guidelines provide a useful framework upon which to base a carefully tailored approach to art education. The subject, if delivered with enthusiasm and sensitivity, provides an interesting, joyful and productive learning environment where sensory experience is the springboard for valued self-expression. This allows pupils with limited verbal or written communication skills to interact with others by 'doing' and 'making'.

Self-esteem can be strengthened by good teaching practice. Careful profiling of pupils' needs, interests and abilities can result from a healthy pupil–teacher relationship. This allows the art teacher to devise differentiated approaches to individuals and small groups. This maximises the hugely positive potential of the artist within every child.

The choice of stimulus for activities is imperative to the process of differentiation:

(1) Using the work of a famous artist or designer whose style, approach or subject matter carries a particular significance, or whose technique is suited to the level of ability.

(2) Using images or ideas from the 'mass media' can reinforce a sense of self. The media can also be an area where pupils have a considerable expertise – well in excess of most adults.

(3) Using our immediate and local environment can deliver a sense of 'belonging' and using this as an inspiration for artwork often allows children to find the 'extraordinary' in our 'ordinary' lives.

Careful progressive programmes of study lead to exhibitions of artwork in the unit. They are recognised as highly valuable symbols of achievement, participation and enjoyment, and also provide a topical informal context for the development of critical awareness. Above all, in a small way, the work of children – displayed with pride – allows pupils, teachers, medical staff and visitors to share an experience which lifts the spirit and raises morale.

Finally, we have a drama specialist. The function of drama in a unit like ours is the development of the individual through the experience of 'acting': in both senses of the work. In dramatic action children can explore their world, themselves and their relation to others. Whether they play out the roles of mums or dads, teachers or doctors, in order to understand their everyday reality, or imaginatively explore the realms of fairy stories or myths, they are creating something of their own, out of nothing. Just as Bruno Bettleheim (1976) in *The Uses of Enchantment* suggests that a child will repeatedly ask for a fairy tale containing issues she has yet to master, so, in dramatic enactment, *Development Through Drama* (Way 1967), suggests that a definition of drama might be 'to practise living'. This would be an appropriate definition for the use of drama in the Unit, which encourages vocal and physical expression, imagination, spontaneity and resourcefulness and can contribute, one hopes, to improved balance and wellbeing for the children. Interaction with others which lies at the heart of drama can also be a crucial dimension of a child's problem. Indeed, often part of the reason for children being in the unit is their inability to relate to their peers. Drama can provide opportunities to explore relationships or problems in the 'as if' dramatic reality without any real life repercussions and gives children the chance to experiment within safe boundaries.

The drama specialist visits on Friday morning and sees all three classes, starting with the young ones and ending with the older group. Originally, classes were held in the Activity Room described previously for physical education but its distance from the unit, noisy acoustics and general cheerlessness made it inadequate provision. At present, an open carpeted space in the refurbished dormitory area is used and proving more satisfactory, providing room for activity and comfort for reflection, both requirements for drama. Initially, class teachers accompanied children to drama, but now the specialist works on her own with the class or, alternatively, at times with individual children who might specifically benefit from more focused work.

At present, a Puppet Theatre Project is underway, initiated by the specialist. In this co-operative venture between herself and the art specialist, the children are involved in the making of puppets, theatre and scenery and in the devising and performing of puppet plays based on story themes significant for their developmental needs.

Educational Visits

Another way of extending our curriculum and of adding stimulus and motivation is by providing a range of educational visits. These are normally 'whole school' outings – practically speaking, it is best to cater for all the children on any one visit because of the strictures of time and numbers. When we do go out we are very well staffed with always a generous number of nursing staff as well as teachers. In part this is necessary since some children find visits a particular difficulty, missing the structure and security of the unit. However, in terms of motivation and of awakening interest in educational topics, going out of the unit classroom is vital. Over the years we have established a framework of visits that we have found to be of value, although we remain open to any other possibilities that may be on offer. Among the regular outings are two trips to Haddo Country Park (a National Trust property and estate approximately 15 miles from Aberdeen), fitting in a nature walk in the morning and a Children's Theatre production by Haddo Arts Trust in the afternoon. For the last three years we have visited Clinterty College of Agriculture in the spring and been able to have some direct experience of the farm animals. Satrosphere, the 'hands-on' science exhibition is another regular activity and in the summer term we have had a booking on a dry ski slope where our physical education teacher instructs the children, usually in the beginning stages of ski-ing, unless they have already passed this level. I would repeat, that in terms of awakening interest and improving self-esteem, these activities are crucial. In addition, while not wishing to speak in crude terms of 'sticks' and 'carrots', nevertheless the fact that these activities are on offer for those who are coping with what is being asked of them in school makes that effort seem the more worthwhile.

Teaching Philosophy

Initially, on first coming into teaching at the Lowit Unit, I was of the opinion that a direct attack upon any deficits in academic attainments could only be beneficial. Here, for example, was a child who did not know his tables or whose handwriting or spelling was poor – with much input from the teacher in a small class now seemed the opportunity to remedy matters. However, over the years, and having dealt with a wide variety of children, my views have changed. Sometimes, in the face of the severe problems borne by the children it is necessary to prioritise the requirements of school life. Top of my list is that the pupil will manage to stay in the classroom, behaving appropriately. The exact meaning of the latter is, however, for the individual teacher to decide at each moment of time. It is my view that it may not be helpful to condone anything too unconventional, defined in terms of that which the children might expect to be allowed to do in a classroom. 'Appropriate' behaviour is likely to vary from child to child and may well not reflect the often uniformity of the mainstream classroom. For example, if I was convinced that a pupil for the time being was really not coping with maths, but could sit at a desk and colour a picture, this would be regarded as a very satisfactory way of staying in class and accepting 'the rules'. Moreover this would be seen as a significant stage in the process towards doing maths and return to 'proper school'. The latter label, while apparently derogatory to the Unit, is accepted by the pupils without comment and does help to establish and maintain the view of the Unit school as a preparation for the future.

Over the last session as one of the teaching staff has been taking the RSA Diploma Course (specific learning difficulties and assessment), my attention has been re-focused on the importance of establishing a child's specific difficulties by diagnostic testing and the provision of specific help where this can be achieved. As the expertise to test now exists among our staff it seems that we are extending our ability to help pupils with their individual learning difficulties and are better able to report to receiving schools for their future progress.

Children who it is felt may have motor or perceptual learning difficulties as well as emotional and behavioural problems are referred to the occupational therapy department for assessment. It is worthy of note that the occupational therapists have established a high level of expertise in this specialist area (see Chapter 9) and that the teachers endeavour to work closely with the therapists, responding to their suggestions and putting into practice advice given.

Some have difficulties in speech and language and here again we benefit from the expertise of the therapist who works individually with a child or when needed, works with a group of children and the class teacher (see Chapter 8).

The Multi-disciplinary Team

The multi-disciplinary team is, of course, involved in all aspects of the day to day life in the Unit and in order for the milieu to be therapeutic the team must function without friction or rivalry. Over the years it has been demonstrated that it is essential for there to be ample opportunity for both formal and informal communication. It has been found to be useful for nursing and teaching staff in particular to have time set aside for a staff support group where problems can be aired. While teachers and nurses function separately and have different roles there are obviously times when we impinge on each other and there is overlap in what we are doing. A need exists to be aware of the issues and be able to talk about them without fear of hurting feelings or jeopardising relationships. While the communication between nurses and teachers has been focused upon here, good communication is just as important between all members of the team, who need an understanding and appreciation of each other's specialities and an ability to incorporate their contribution to the whole treatment package. The wealth of expertise of the whole team is in my view our great resource.

Team membership also extends beyond working together in helping the Unit children and includes participating in relevant decision-making. At the time of writing, the author chairs the monthly Admissions/Discharge Meeting and the two-monthly Administration Meeting and is a member of the Lowit

Forum – a multi-disciplinary forum for resolving issues relating to the management of the Unit.

Liaison with Schools

When a pupil is to be admitted to the Unit the information is normally given to his school by the educational psychologist and, if possible, a visit to the school to meet with the Head Teacher, class teacher, and the pupil (if this seemed suitable) would be arranged by the Unit teacher. One or both of the above staff would be invited to the pre-intake meeting in the Unit and to the following review meetings. If the pupil's admission is anticipated to be short, school work can be continued with texts sent from the base school, and contact maintained by phone.

Contact between a former school and a Unit pupil is often variable. In some cases, teachers have paid social visits or a school friend(s) have come and, in a few instances, the whole class has written letters. In other cases, contact has been far less and it may not be appropriate for it to be at the above level. When the time comes for a pupil to leave the Unit, plans are made for the way that he will be re-integrated into school. In the case where he is returning to the original school the Head Teacher and/or class teacher will again be invited to the appropriate Review Meeting to discuss how the integration can be arranged and at what rate. Alternatively, if a new placement is required the most appropriate provision for a child's individual needs would be discussed also at a Review Meeting with the help of the educational psychologist involved. Many of the children, although they have progressed during their time in the Lowit Unit, are not yet ready for mainstream education and need the small class groupings and staff support provided by Carden School (SEBD non-residential Primary School) and Cordyce Residential School for secondary pupils. Some may be better placed in the SEN sector. Because of the large geographical area covered by the Lowit Unit, some liaison work is necessarily achieved by phone and written report, but wherever possible direct contact is made and Grampian schools have shown a great willingness to respond to invitations to attend meetings within the unit to help in the reintegration of an individual pupil.

Assessment and Reporting

If the first, obvious, part of our work as teachers in the Unit is to educate (and, in this discussion, I have tried to give a picture of what I mean by that), then the second strand is to assess and report on the child as an individual in school.

Although in a sense treatment starts for a child from the day of admission, at the same time the first six weeks are normally planned as an assessment period and appropriate tests will be carried out ranging from a medical examination to occupational therapy and speech and language assessments. Within the classroom, the teacher is observing the child, noting strengths and weaknesses, interests and motivations and trying to form a clear picture of academic attainments as well as social and emotional development. This can be exceedingly complicated as very often a child has developed a range of tactics to draw attention away from areas of difficulty and may be very reluctant to disclose weaknesses either to the adult or to his peers. Information gathered, both from direct observation and from assessments and observations of other professionals, is shared at meetings and other times and the teacher needs to be able to use it to plan an individual learning programme for each child. It is also important to be able to share information and put it across in a clear, coherent manner, in both written and spoken reports.

Staff Development and In-Service

As mentioned at the beginning of the chapter, the teachers in the Unit are employed under the same conditions as those for other teaching staff in the region and one of these conditions is the requirement for personal professional development and attendance at in-service days. This has the added difficulty that, with a limited amount of time available, not only must we keep abreast of new initiatives in education, but we also need to learn more about topics specific to our field. Attendance at mainstream in-service days is a valuable way of keeping in touch with colleagues and helps to lessen the sense of isolation that we can sometimes feel in our situation. It is also a time when we find ourselves asking about the progress of former pupils and answering questions about the service we provide. The fact of other teachers' interest in our work and the ongoing research in the Unit resulted in the School Survey described below.

The School Survey

While much is known at any one time about a particular child and his or her schooling, no-one within the Unit felt they could describe confidently the overall picture regarding regional schools' usage of the Lowit and teachers' views of it. To find out more about this, a questionnaire was designed and the main objectives of the study were:

(1) to establish the number of schools referring children to the unit or receiving them after admission over the previous 10 year period

(2) to determine the nature and extent of educational professionals' involvement prior to admission

(3) to identify the perceptions of teachers regarding the nature of children's difficulties who were admitted

(4) to discover schools' views regarding liaison with the unit and associated levels of satisfaction

(5) to attempt to establish the educational progress of children after leaving the unit school.

Our resolve to proceed with the study became the greater as on investigation it appeared that there had not been any previous attempt to explore the nature of the relationship between child psychiatric residential unit schools and those sending or receiving pupils from them.

Method

A questionnaire survey of schools was carried out in 1993 and in February 347 forms were sent to schools in the Grampian Region. These were schools listed in the Grampian Department of Education Directory of Educational Establishments (1992/93). Overall 36 academies, 275 primaries and nursery primaries were contacted in addition to 18 nursery/infant schools (NI) and 18 special schools (Sp) excluding SEN bases and units housed within other schools. Also excluded were Carden School, the primary provision for SEBD children also with learning difficulties, Cordyce Residential School (mainly secondary) and the Home Tutor Service. It was considered beyond the resources of this study to investigate these fully although they are well worthy of specific consideration.

Findings

Of the 347 schools to which a questionnaire was sent, 288 responded, giving a response rate of 83 per cent. Of these schools 75, representing over a quarter (26.6%), replied that they had a pupil or pupils who had attended the Lowit Unit during the last 10 years. In many instances, however, schools reported that they were unable to go back as far as 10 years in their recollections, often because of staff changes.

Contact with the Unit

As can be seen from Table 7.1, although Special Schools had the single highest level of contact with the Unit (50% responding positively) the numbers of Aberdeen primary schools with such contact was not significantly lower at 43.8 per cent. Worthy of note is the contrasting picture with regard to primary schools located outside the city. Perhaps contrary to expectation nearly a quarter of nursery schools (22.2%) in addition stated that their pupils transferred to or from the Unit.

The 75 'contact' schools reported in total 108 pupils as having attended the Lowit Unit. Very small numbers of schools stated that three or more of such pupils had been in attendance, as is evident from Table 7.2.

Table 7.1 School type and contact with Unit school

School Type	Nos.	Nos. reporting contact	(%)
Academy	36	9	25.0
Primary Aberdeen	64	28	43.8
Outwith City	211	25	11.9
Special School	18	9	50.0
Nursery	18	4	22.2
Total	347	75	26.6 %

Table 7.2 Number of pupils who have attended Unit by school type

| School Type | Nos of pupils | | | | | N=75 |
	1	2	3	4	5	Total
Academy	6	1	1	1	0	15
Primary Aberdeen	19	4	3	1	1	45
Outwith City	21	4	0	0	0	29
Special School	5	4	0	0	0	13
Nursery/Infant	3	0	1	0	0	6
Total Pupils	54	26	15	8	5	108

It would seem that the majority of children reported by schools as former unit pupils had attended in the recent past (see Table 7.3). However, it should be borne in mind that schools were unable to recall year of attendance of nearly a third of all pupils listed.

When schools were asked to identify those agencies involved in a child's admission to the unit, 27 cases of single agency involvement were reported, together with 32 and six instances of two and three agent involvement respectively. As would be expected, educational psychologists were referred to significantly more often than any other profession with their input being described in over half of all child attendances. Social workers were the only other additional group to be commonly mentioned. Interestingly, there were only four instances when their involvement was not together with an educational psychologist. In the light of the Unit's medical location it is worth noting

Table 7.3 Estimated year of Unit attendance

Year	Nos of Pupils
1983/84	1
84/85	3
85/86	2
86/87	6
87/88	9
88/89	10
89/90	15
90/91	16
91/92	19
92/93	8
No info	19
Total	**108**

that there were nine references to medical practitioners, with psychiatrists and school doctors each receiving three listings. Police involvement was mentioned in only one case.

Reason for Admission

Analysis of schools' perceptions of the reasons for pupils requiring treatment at the Lowit Unit revealed six main categories, as shown in Table 7.4. It should be noted, however, that many respondents indicated that their information might not be reliable and where possible this was checked against Lowit Unit records. By far the majority of cases during the period under review were boys who presented with behavioural difficulties of the disruptive/aggressive type. Only girls were reported as being treated for anorexia and boys for soiling. Approximately half of all the children included in the 'other' category were ones described as having 'medical' problems of a physical nature, such as diabetes and epilepsy. Also included were pupils seen to be autistic and suicidal. Difficulties in relating to peers was given as the main reason for admission in only two instances, as was 'assessment for hyperactivity'. Perhaps surprisingly in view of recent disclosures, in only one case, a girl under seven years of age, were family problems and possible sexual abuse mentioned. Learning difficulties were not reported at all by schools as a reason for admission. Interestingly, there was very little use of psychological/medical terminology in schools' descriptions of pupils' problems.

Table 7.4 School's perception of reason for attendance

Reason	Boys	Girls	Total
Behavioural difficulties*	45	4	49
Family problems	10	3	13
School Refusal	8	4	12
Anorexic	-	4	4
Soiler	6	-	6
Other	13	4	17
No Information	7	-	7
Total	89	19	108

* disruptive/aggressive

Mode of Attendance

It is a feature of the Lowit Unit that it provides for children across a wide age range (5 to 14 years approximately) and also for a large spectrum of problems. As a result, it offers a variety of attendance options. In Question 3 of the questionnaire respondents were required to indicate, from a variety of attendance options, the mode applicable to their pupil(s). The options were as follows:

(1) The pupil left your school for the Lowit Unit and returned to your school after treatment.

(2) The pupil left your school for the Lowit Unit but went to another placement after treatment.

(3) The pupil originally attended another school, but after treatment at the Lowit Unit was placed at your school.

(4) The pupil was excluded from your school and was a client of the Home Tutor Service for a period prior to attendance at the Lowit Unit.

As can be seen from Table 7.5 the single most common route was that a pupil returned to their original school following treatment. The high proportion in this category was unexpected in the light of experience over the years and perhaps reflects 'better memory' on the part of schools with such continuity with the pupil and in addition possibly a higher response rate from such schools. The small number of cases reported to have come to the Lowit Unit after a period of tuition with the Home Tutor Service may reflect the difficulties of keeping track of children who have had a number of changes of school and/or exclusions. The single most common reason included in the 'other' category

Table 7.5 Modes of unit attendance by school type

Attendance Options	Acad	Prim	Spec	N/I	Total
From school → L.U. → Return School	6	29	3	2	40
From school → L.U. → New School	2	22	1	2	27
From original school → L.U. → Resp. Sch.	2	13	6	-	21
Excluded sch. → Home Tutor → L.U.	1	3	-	1	5
Other	4	7	3	1	15
Total	**15**	**74**	**13**	**6**	**108**

was that a child was attending the Lowit Unit at present and thus the outcome of treatment was unknown.

Liaison with Unit Staff

For each pupil recalled, schools were asked to record whether they remembered liaison having taken place with Lowit Unit staff before, during and after admission for treatment. In a total of 99 instances, schools reported liaison as having taken place as is evident from Table 6. While nearly twice as many schools reported liaison as those indicating this did not take place, a significantly high number of respondents either did not respond to this question or were unable to provide information regarding liaison. When responses to this question were considered in relation to the pupils' year of attendance it was clear that recollections of liaison were much more frequent from 1987 onwards.

Table 7.6 Schools' Liaison with Unit Staff (per Child)

| Liaison | Admission | | | N=108 |
	Before	During	After	Total
Yes	25	39	35	99
No	20	15	17	52
D/K	18	13	10	41
No Info.	8	7	9	24

Information on the questionnaire was sought regarding contact with staff within the unit and not surprisingly this was found to be most frequently with teachers rather than others such as nurses. Contact was described as occurring most often on the basis of one or more times a month, however, many respondents were unable to provide information with regard to frequency of contact.

On examination of the schools reporting that they had never had liaison with the Lowit Unit teachers, it was found that, of the 16 instances, 10 were from schools outside the Aberdeen District, (similarly for nursing staff, seven out of the 12 cases reported were outwith Aberdeen), thus highlighting the difficulties inherent in providing liaison over such a large geographical area as Grampian Region.

Progress Following Discharge

In a final section to the questionnaire schools were invited to comment on the progress of pupils following their leaving the Lowit Unit. It appeared that of all questions this presented the greatest difficulty for respondents, especially since often pupils had subsequently moved on to new schools. Information on progress was only supplied regarding 57 cases. Of these, in 17 instances pupils were described as 'better' or progress was considered to be sustained and specifically in seven cases it was said that the child had readjusted reasonably well to mainstream education. In a further 12 cases it was reported that although the individual was coping he was still experiencing difficulties. Two and five children were attending special and residential schools respectively. In total 15 children were considered to have 'got worse'.

In conclusion, over a third of schools who had contact with the Unit chose to provide additional comments on the questionnaire. Notably, a high proportion of these related to liaison. Six commented favourably on the liaison provided by the Unit teaching and nursing staff viz: *'helpful and realistic'; 'friendly and informative'; 'helped us cater for pupil's needs on arrival'*; but an equal number also felt that there should have been closer liaison. In only one case was there any reference to the length of time between referral and admission. As this time lapse can be a very real problem the general lack of comment was surprising. Four schools, however, did refer to the difficulty of reporting on pupils over a 10-year period as is well reflected in the following comments: *'answers based on recall by long-serving members of staff'; 'I had to consult with absent or retired members of staff'*.

Final Comments on the Survey

It was very gratifying that such a high proportion of the schools in Grampian Region (83%) took the trouble to respond to the questionnaire, especially since the majority had had no previous contact with the Unit. From individual responses and the letter accompanying returned forms it would appear that the survey had generated much interest in the work of the Unit. Indeed this high level of interest was reflected in the attendance at an Open Day in the Unit in 1993 and the large numbers of teachers who came along and sought out Unit staff to discuss classroom problems and seek coping strategies. There would seem evidence that there is considerable teacher support for the Unit.

Pupil problems as identified by schools were, in fact, congruent with ward statistics. Although there is variation in reason for admission, an audit of records has revealed that for the years 1983–85 conduct disorder accounted for 42.9 per cent, and emotional disorder for 28.6 per cent of cases (Gray *et al.* 1991). In addition given that the majority of pupils are boys it can be seen that such a composition has implications for Unit teachers. Dealing with a group of children with a preponderance of disruptive and/or aggressive boys can present a serious challenge. Without doubt it would appear that in some cases schools are not fully informed or aware of children's problems, as for instance in the cases where schools were surprised to discover that a pupil was being admitted. While confidentiality must be maintained, it may result in appropriate support not being offered.

Data provided on liaison suggests that this is not always successfully managed but the differential pattern of contact between city and 'far flung' schools highlights the difficulties inherent in providing liaison over such a large geographical area.

Our attempt to ascertain outcome following discharge well illustrates the problematic nature of such a task. From our data, albeit limited, there is reason to believe that a significant minority of ex-pupils are able to return and cope in mainstream school. Since children referred to the Unit have severe difficulties this achievement should not be minimised. It needs also to be acknowledged that progress on discharge may be affected by factors outwith the Unit's control. To illustrate this point I would refer, for instance, to a teenage girl with longstanding school phobia who adjusted well to in-patient treatment and was able to be established as a pupil at an SEN base within secondary school, even on return to her home situation. However, financial problems caused the family to lose their home and to split up, the latest information being that the girl is now medically ill and school attendance has broken down again. In future life it is to be hoped that the insights gained and relationships enjoyed during admission may yet stand this individual in good stead. In other cases, too, it may be hard to determine to what degree treatment in the Unit has helped.

Perhaps it is easier to be more optimistic about children who are admitted at a younger age, especially if they fall into the group who have specific learning difficulties alongside behaviour problems and home or family problems. It is to be hoped that the assessment of their difficulties and the introduction of individual learning programmes along with family therapy should provide a better chance of success. Not all problems manifest themselves at this stage, however, and inevitably situations arise throughout childhood and adolescence where help is needed. Even though it is difficult to judge, it was good to see that 25 schools were able to record progress in their pupils at the time of completing the questionnaire. In this type of service, the results are not always clearcut but what seems important is that cases are thoroughly examined before admission to establish their need is for treatment which it is within our capabilities to offer. The family's acceptance of that treatment and their own need to make changes must also be taken into account. Having admitted children to the Unit, every effort must be made to fulfil the stated aims of their admission, if necessary adapting these aims if circumstances alter.

Finally, a difficulty for our service can often be the lack of a suitable placement for children leaving the Unit, yet schools did not comment on this in the questionnaire. Some pupils are not ready for mainstream school, yet have made sufficient gains to be ready for schooling at a placement where there is a lower staff/pupil ratio than with us. Often, on a human level, it is very frustrating for a child to see other members of the class going on to 'my new school' when he has been at the Unit longer and has made gains, and all we can say is 'you are on the waiting list, but there is no room yet'. On the other hand, it is vital that the placement selected should have a chance of success.

The pupils have already experienced failure and rejection and can only be further damaged if this is repeated. We have always appreciated the extent to which schools manage to extend a very welcoming hand to pupils; timetables have been adapted to aid reintegration and staff given time for individual contact.

In conclusion, the survey has demonstrated the importance of obtaining schools' opinion of the service provided by the Lowit Unit in general and the school in particular. Moreover, it should be repeated at appropriate periods in order to measure satisfaction. While it might be argued that the main aim of the Lowit Unit is to provide help for troubled children and their families rather than to help SEBD pupils and their schools because we aim to help children to mature, or achieve a more age-appropriate level of behaviour, we are usually helping them also to conform to school expectations. Nevertheless the schools – or the individual teachers – cannot be given the same level of support, or opportunity for insight into the reasons for a child's behaviour as a family can be.

Concluding Remarks

Forsyth and Nisbet in the late 1970s provided a detailed account of the development of alternatives to mainstream education in the city of Aberdeen. In the section entitled 'Child Guidance and Provision for the Maladjusted' the service from the appointment of the first educational psychologist in 1944 is described including the first teaching specifically designed for the 'maladjusted', which operated from the Child Guidance Clinic in 1956. The sole mention of 'classes for children in hospital' is a reference to the fact that in 1924 classes were held in the City Hospital for children with TB. However, the fact that 'Ward 7' was established in 1965 is not recorded here. It is hoped that this chapter may compensate for this omission. The responses from the questionnaire survey, moreover, would indicate that the place of the Unit within the educational system of Grampian is established. Contact with the Unit was shown to be far more extensive than has been estimated to date. Furthermore, while children are treated within a hospital and their problems may be primarily emotional and/or behavioural, they nevertheless frequently experience associated educational difficulties which require attention from a teacher and necessitate classroom work. Child psychiatric residential units cannot be regarded as facilities separate or apart from classrooms and schools.

Mackay (1988) in his survey of educational provision in residential psychiatric units in Scotland judged that those teachers who did express their satisfaction with what was being offered 'regarded their clients primarily as patients rather than pupils' and in stating this he was being critical of the teachers. In my opinion, however, it can be helpful to consider the children in this light. The parallel is clearest in cases like that of an anorexic girl who, when she fell below a 'safe' weight level, became unambiguously a patient. She did not attend school but had to stay in bed and be tube fed until she had gained sufficient weight. She was able to attend the Unit school after a period but her level of concentration and ability to produce school work at her normal standard did not return until some months later. It seems to me that during this time she was progressing in status from 'patient' to 'pupil' and that it is part of the Unit teacher's skill to recognise and cater for this progression. Children who are very anxious and or have other symptoms less easy to quantify than weight loss can similarly find difficulty with school work. Often the priority for such children for a time will be to attend a small classroom where the routines are sufficiently flexible to allow them to achieve a measure of success. One hopes that, through the range of activities provided, they will be able to become interested again and to begin to progress academically once more.

Mackay (1988) also contends that teaching staff within the multi-disciplinary team tended to have a relatively lower profile in terms of their contributions to treatment and planning for pupils admitted to units and recommends 'an increased profile of advisory and support staff in units'. In the Lowit Unit we do not regard this as necessary – liaison with staff in mainstream and special schools is maintained as it is with staff in the Department of Education of the Regional Council. Support is moreover available from colleagues within the multi-disciplinary team, who it is felt would not underestimate our work in the unit.

Few of the children admitted do not have difficulties with school work which is widely recognised by members of the team and underscores the value of our contribution. Even though the nature of our work may be different from that of teachers in mainstream schools, in that often a priority for the unit teacher may be in enabling a child to stay in a class and behave appropriately, it is nevertheless 'teachers' work' and rightly lies within an education context. While the boundaries may appear to be blurred on occasions between, for instance, nurses, therapists and teachers it should be remembered that a similar activity may be used by all three but the aims and objectives of it and expected outcomes may be significantly different.

In a sense part of the classroom process for children in the Unit consists of 'learning to learn' or learning other ways of coping with school than by aggression or avoidance. Sometimes part of this process will seem to consist of much talking amongst pupils themselves and with the teacher, rather than a strict adherence to 'school work', but this is a way of forming helpful relationships and new attitudes. The emphasis within the school as well as within the Lowit Unit itself must be on trying to help individuals, and enabling them to reach a stage where they are more able to cope with their own particular circumstances.

References

Bettleheim, B. (1976) *The Uses of Enchantment.* London: Thames and Hudson.

Forsyth, J.P. and Nisbet, J.D. (1976) *Provision for Special Education in Aberdeen 1945–1975: A Case Study in Educational Development.* Aberdeen: University of Aberdeen. Department of Education.

Gray, C., Chisholm, D., Smith, P., Brown, M. and McKay, C. (1992) 'The role of the child psychiatric ward in health care; experiences with different types of admissions over a period of twenty-one years.' *Irish Journal of Psychological Medicine 9*, 17–23.

MacKay, R.W. (1988) 'Educational provision in residential psychiatric units.' In Scottish Education Department *Alternative Approaches to Pupils with Behavioural/Emotional Problems 1986–1987.* Edinburgh: HMSO.

Way, B. (1967) *Development Through Drama.* London: Longman.

CHAPTER 8

Speech and Language Therapy in Child Psychiatry

Jane Jones

Introduction

The role of the speech and language therapist in child psychiatry has undergone major development in recent years. The findings of the research outlined in this chapter well demonstrate that evolution; evidence was found of a pattern of specific language difficulties inherent in this client group. The implications of this for speech and language therapy are considered and discussed.

Speech and Language Therapy Services in Child Psychiatry: Historical Background

In 1969, the Department of Education and Science appointed a committee, headed by Professor Randolph Quirk, to

> 'consider the need for and the role of speech therapy in the field of education and medicine, the assessment and treatment of those suffering from speech and language disorders and the training appropriate for those specially concerned in this work and to make recommendations.' (Department of Education and Science 1972, p.iv).

In 1972, when the *Quirk Report* was published, speech therapy services in Great Britain were organised in two main ways:

(1) As an education service organised as part of the school health service.

(2) As a hospital based service forming part of the NHS.

During the period between 1969 and 1972 about three times as many speech therapists were in Local Education Authority (LEA) employment as in the hospital service. In Scotland several speech and language therapy services were organised as part of the LEA Child Guidance service and the overall organiser was a psychologist responsible to the Director of Education.

The day to day running of the service was in the hands of speech and language therapists themselves and clinicians were deployed according to perceived areas of greatest need. In Aberdeen, for example, administrative responsibility lay with the principal speech therapist who co-ordinated the work in schools and hospitals in the City and reported to the Director of Education.

Quirk (DES 1972) did recommend that (cf 4.14) 'The education speech therapy service needs close working relations with a wide range of other professions... So that speech therapists are enabled to work constructively with others.' But later it is pointed out however (cf 4.15) 'There are... frequently grave defects or gaps in this system of relationships... The speech therapist has a tendency to function in a vacuum rather than in a team'. Then, as now in some areas, the team concept suffered from geographical constraints, particularly in the more education-based departments. As far as hospital-based speech thera-pists were concerned, at this time the number of posts depended largely upon the interest of a particular medical consultant and the importance attached to speech therapy. There were few distinct hospital speech therapy departments providing a service for a number of specialities.

It was one result of NHS reorganisation in 1974 that such departments came into being. In 1972 the statistics from the College of Speech Therapists showed 5.10 therapists working with the mentally ill, adults and children, out of a register of 1000 (Gravell and France 1991). A postal survey conducted by France in 1987 sought the numbers of speech and language therapists involved in psychiatry throughout the UK. Numbers were small, as only 35 therapists were found working in formal psychiatric settings, with the greatest concentra-tion in the South East of England. Most were involved solely with elderly patients. Two therapists were working in adolescent units and *only one with child psychiatric patients*. A further 40 therapists who completed France's questionnaire stated that they treated or assessed patients suffering from mental illness as part of a general clinical caseload (France, Parton and Hooker 1990).

However, although the increased risk of psychiatric problems in children with speech and language difficulties has long been acknowledged, speech therapists have never had a clear role in child psychiatry: it has taken over 20 years, since the publication of the *Quirk Report*, to identify the very specific language problems these children have, and to develop their role within the multi-disciplinary team.

Recognition of Language Disorder in Child Psychiatric Patients

It is interesting to note that, throughout the *Quirk Report*, little reference was made to child psychiatry, apart from those children with autism or known psychoses, of whom it was stated (cf 3.27) 'Both adults and children with psychotic disorders may show a wide variety of disorders of language ability. In addition we may mention an uncommon childhood disorder known as elective mutism... This is, however, a matter for the child guidance clinic, or the psychiatrist rather than the speech therapist.' Research by Wright (1968) and Kolvin and Fundudis (1981), on the other hand indicates that speech and language therapists do have a relevant role to play in elective mutism. A significant proportion of those suffering from this disorder have articulatory or language deficits. This could have direct bearing on the root of the problem and therefore careful assessment is needed before a suitable management programme can be effected.

Language problems in children associated with severe social deprivation was also noted in the *Quirk Report* (cf 3.28). The fact that the problems of such children needed close and careful unravelling was highlighted, as factors other than social deprivation may be present. That these children are at risk of later psychiatric disorder cannot be underestimated. Whilst gross deprivation would be required to affect the development of basic language skills in infants, more subtle problems influencing language use can persist in later life (Rutter and Lord 1987).

Further in the *Quirk Report* was an estimate of the actual numbers of children needing speech therapy at that time. Again, children with psychiatric disorders were not identified as a specific group but were possibly included in other categories, for example 'Special Groups'. These were defined as those children suffering from *inter alia* language disorders, autism or those in special schools – classified as Educationally Subnormal (ESN) at that time. Psychiatric units were not mentioned specifically. However, out of a population of 5000 in the 'Special Groups' category, 50 per cent were needing help. The notional caseload for a therapist dealing exclusively with this category was 10 patients, this indicating that an estimated 250 therapists were required to cope with the demand.

Since the 1980s researchers have found increasing evidence for the presence of specific language disorders in child psychiatric patients. There is concern within the speech and language therapy profession that many of these children are not adequately assessed and remain undiagnosed. This has implications for their management, including educational needs.

Child Psychiatric Disorders and Associated Communication Disorders

Over the years it has been recognised that certain types of language disability can be positively linked to specific child psychiatric disorders and a brief summary is provided below. It is important to note that the language disorders found amongst the mentally handicapped and the deaf have been omitted. Whilst it is acknowledged that psychiatric symptoms can exist in these client groups it is outwith the scope of this chapter.

Psychoses

(1) SCHIZOPHRENIA

Thought disorder reflected in disordered language.

Features
- sparse or impoverished language; children talk a great deal but make little sense. (A differential diagnosis is essential as similar symptoms are displayed as in semantic–pragmatic disorders)
- neologisms and word approximations (making up new words and articulating near approximations to the real word)
- echolalia; unintelligible speech; speaking very softly (talking to self)
- reduced quantity and quality of personal interaction resulting from the psychiatric disorder may in turn reduce or distort visual and listening skills
- disruption to communication caused by effects of medication for example slurred speech, abnormal prosodic features and lack of facial expression.

(2) CHILDHOOD DISINTEGRATIVE DISORDER

Two years of normal early language development followed by marked regression including loss of language and social skills, the features of which resemble those in autism.

(3) AUTISM

Communication impairment in verbal and non-verbal language which may be absent, immature, delayed, echolalaic or idiosyncratic.

Features
- abnormal prosodic features
- use of stereotyped phrases
- lack of / poor reciprocity in social interactions
- language comprehension difficulties.
- poor speech production
- poor eating patterns.

Anxiety and Emotional Disorders

Associated communication disorders include: stuttering; rapid breathy speech; communication avoidance; poor non-verbal skills such as lack of eye contact, few gestures; and little facial expression.

Vocal styles need to be observed, therefore, as well as language use when making a differential diagnosis.

Phobias

In themselves phobias are unlikely to affect language functioning. However it is possible for a child with a phobia to have an additional speech or language problem, which is not related to the psychiatric problem.

Obsessive–Compulsive Disorders

Obsessive recurring ideas can prevent logical thought for example the child repeats words and phrases and/or counts repetitively. A differential diagnosis is important as most children will have had normal language function before developing the psychiatric disorder.

Hysteria

While uncommon in children this is unlikely to affect language but may affect voice production.

Features
- aphonia/dysphonia
- mutism
- fluency of speech may be affected

Disruptive Behaviour/Conduct Disorders (with or without attention deficit disorder and/or hyperactivity)

Language difficulties include:

- auditory processing disorders
- semantic–pragmatic language disorder
- selective auditory attention deficit
- word-finding difficulties
- difficulties organising and structuring language into sentences
- auditory verbal comprehension problems

The above language difficulties can occur individually or a child may suffer from a combination to a greater or lesser degree. A significant number of children presenting with this psychiatric diagnosis are referred for speech and language assessment (see Lowit Unit data).

The Speech and Language Therapy Service to the Lowit Unit 1986–1992

The current level of service to the Royal Aberdeen Children's Hospital (RACH), where the research was based, is one whole time equivalent staff member. In fact two specialist speech and language therapists, each working five sessions are employed. The present postholders do not have a designated responsibility to provide speech and language therapy input to the Lowit Unit since provision is part of the overall remit for the Children's Hospital. One half-time therapist (17.5 hours per week) currently provides the input to the Lowit Unit. This has arisen because it is an area of particular personal interest, and it is felt by other members of the multi-disciplinary team that a more cohesive service may be provided by an 'identified therapist'. However, as speech and language therapy has to be available to the rest of the hospital, the amount of time devoted to child and family psychiatry is limited. It is also subject to fluctuation depending on demands from other departments.

The following study, as well as further clarifying the role of the speech and language therapist within an in-patient psychiatric unit, highlights the importance of language assessment, diagnosis and treatment of these children, and provides some recommendations for future development and service needs. An audit of the actual time spent by the speech and language therapist on the Lowit Unit was carried out during 1992 in order to evaluate the level of service provided. Over the course of one year, the time devoted to the Unit was as follows:

1	Liaison meetings*	28.5 hours
2	Patient reviews	9.0 hours
3	Therapy/patient management	34.5 hours
4	Community meetings	4.0 hours
5	Out-patient follow-up (following discharge from the Unit)	29.5 hours

Overall Total   **105.5 hours**

* *note – not exclusive to the Lowit Unit but include case presentations, discussion of current issues and new referrals to the department of Child and Family Psychiatry*

Additional time (not audited) was spent in preparation of therapy programmes and materials, report writing and occasional school visits as part of the review programme, as can be seen from Figure 8.1.

There were 131 children admitted to the Unit between 1986 and 1992, of whom 35 were referred for a speech and language assessment.

The information collected from the 35 children in the sample was as follows:

(1) Sex.

(2) Age on admission.

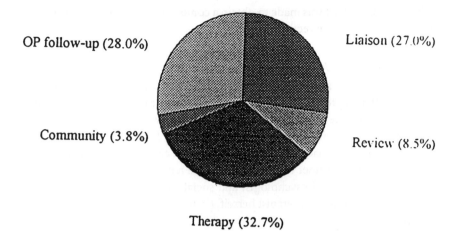

OP follow-up (28.0%)

Liaison (27.0%)

Community (3.8%)

Review (8.5%)

Therapy (32.7%)

Figure 8.1. Speech and Language Therapist's Time Spent on Lowit Unit

(3) Referral agent.

(4) Type of speech and language therapy input (assessment only; assessment and individual therapy; assessment and group therapy; assessment, individual and group therapy).

(5) Attendance at review meetings by the speech and language therapist.

(6) Whether patients had received any previous speech and language therapy.

(7) Follow up by the speech and language therapy department after discharge from the Unit.

(8) Demographic information.

The kinds of speech and language problems exhibited by these children were then studied in detail and analysed.

During the process of collating and analysing the data it was found that some records were incomplete. This was possibly due to one of several factors:

(i) Patients had been transferred out into the Community speech and language therapy service on discharge from the hospital, and contact with the hospital service had ceased.

(ii) Patients had moved to residential schools out of the area.

(iii) Changes and breaks in staffing at RACH meant that some cases were not seen consistently whilst patients on the Unit, or were not followed up after discharge and may have been re-referred elsewhere in the region.

Although every effort was made to obtain a complete data set in some instances omissions could not be rectified.

Characteristics of the Unit Children

Overall, seven girls and 28 boys had been referred with the majority of the children (28) being resident in Aberdeen – only seven came from outlying rural areas. Not unexpectedly, the children were seldom over 10 years of age (three cases only were identified); the age range extending from 4.6 to 12.9 years.

Eighteen referrals had been made by consultant child psychiatrists with unit teachers referring a further five children. Of the remaining nine cases, two had been made by a clinical psychologist and social worker and four had been at the specific request of the therapist herself. (In three instances, source of referral was unknown.)

Of the 35 children referred for assessment following admission to the Lowit, the majority, 29, were diagnosed as having speech and/or language difficulties, requiring intervention, yet only 11 had either had previous therapy or a referral for an evaluation. Five of those children had been subsequently discharged as 'satisfactory' but were referred on admission to the Unit. All were reassessed and found to have significant language difficulties.

Of the remaining 24 children who had not had a previous referral, 20 were assessed as needing therapy and four to be managed via, for example, carers/teachers. Regarding the latter group the communication problems were not regarded as being severe enough to warrant 'hands-on' therapy, but they would, nevertheless, benefit from some guidance.

Five patients received individual therapy, thirteen were included in group therapy and six were given both individual and group therapy.

The therapist's attendance at regular review meetings was rather more difficult to determine. However, it is known that for nine patients the speech and language therapist attended at least one of their review meetings. Written reports were submitted at some reviews rather than the therapist attending personally. As can be seen from Figure 8.2 the largest proportion of time was spent on assessment.

Further therapy or review is known to have been recommended in 12 out of the 29 cases of diagnosed speech/language disorders, following discharge from the unit. In ten of these cases follow-up was made and in six cases contact remains to date.

Unfortunately, for the remaining 19 children, information regarding continued management is not available as speech and language therapy records are incomplete.

It is interesting to note that of the 29 children diagnosed as having language disorders, 11 remain 'open' cases within the department of child and family psychiatry, at the time of writing.

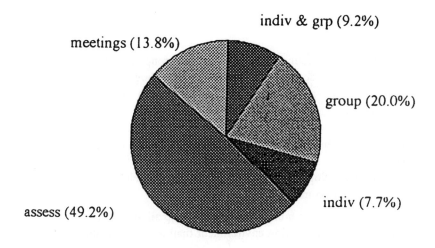

Figure 8.2. Total Time Lowit Unit Patient Input by Activity

Therapy Techniques

Individual and /or group therapy may be offered to children during their time as in-patients on the Lowit Unit. The decision is made by the speech and language therapist in consultation with other members of the multi-disciplinary team.

INDIVIDUAL THERAPY

This is seen to be an important aspect of treatment if the nature of the disorder is functional, for example errors of syntax, difficulties with certain speech sounds, voice disorders or language processing difficulties. Whilst some aspects of these disorders are dealt with as part of the educational curriculum, specific teaching on target areas is a necessary part of the programme. The speech and language therapist works closely with the teachers in order to present the programme of therapy in the most appropriate way. Setting clear objectives after the assessment process has been completed improves the efficacy of the management programme and allows a cohesive approach. As with any therapy programme there must be room for flexibility to cope with changing circumstances. This will be more relevant with child psychiatric patients than with other client groups. However, the overall goals must be clear even if the route has to be altered.

Whilst structured language programmes have a place in the treatment of children with psychiatric disorder, they cannot in themselves help a child who has difficulties with social relationships, or who is unable to use language effectively to control his or her actions and environment, or to deal with new information.

GROUP THERAPY

More children it was found were selected for group therapy than received individual sessions, as detailed previously. This underlines the importance with which we view the social aspect of language when working with child psychiatric patients.

The decision to use this method in favour of individual sessions is congruent with the overall aims of a speech and language therapy group. These are as follows:

- To help develop communication skills, giving help and guidance with specific communication situations

- To encourage communication use. A group allows for a more realistic communication environment than in a one-to-one teaching situation

- To help with development of peer relationships in a structured, non-pressured situation. A group allows children to be aware of, and tolerant towards others' limitations and difficulties. This may enhance peer relationships or raise an individual's self-esteem.

An important advantage of working in groups is that they allow further observation and assessment of patients in a variety of situations with people other than the therapist. Corkish (1990).

There needs to be a basic structure for the composition of a group if it is to function effectively and fulfill the objectives listed above. The criteria followed in this department is as follows:

(1) The group should have a maximum of six children, for the following reasons: (a) more staff would be required to maintain the smooth running of the group; (b) a larger number would make it more difficult to create any group cohesiveness and thus prevent individuals developing feelings of security and identity within the group.

(2) The group members should be of comparable age.

(3) Group members' overall ability and language competence are not necessarily crucial factors as activities take account of individual need. However there should not be too large a diversity in skills. A wide variation might necessitate the formation of two groups, or the division of the main group for selected activities.

(4) Where necessary, a child should have some individual therapy time for specific learning tasks which can then be consolidated and practised in the group. This is not, however, always possible to fit into the

programme and does not exclude a child from consideration for group therapy.

Indirect Management

There will sometimes be a proportion of children for whom indirect management is recommended. This involves working with such individuals as carers and teachers to change the child's communication environment in such a way as to help the speech or language difficulty, whilst allowing him or her to continue with normal routines. This is regarded as a valid form of therapy and is not chosen merely because the therapist's caseload prohibits a more direct form of treatment, although, unfortunately on occasions, parents of patients see it precisely that way. It is therefore vital clearly to state the reasons for choosing this form of intervention and emphasise that the situation will be carefully monitored and plans changed if necessary. The therapist needs to be sensitive to the needs of the patient's family and not to have unrealistic goals. Parents may find it difficult to understand the child's problems and to appreciate their role within the therapeutic framework. Therapists may only have a supportive role to carers who are unable to take more active participation (Gravell and France 1991). Within an in-patient unit, however, a programme of intervention involving parents may not be appropriate at that time. On the Lowit Unit at present, contact between parents and the speech and language therapist is generally only at six-weekly case reviews, unless specific appointments are made. This has been recognised as a serious gap in our service delivery and ways of improving parent-therapist contact are under discussion.

Nature and Scope of Speech and Language Problems

Of the 29 children studied on the Lowit Unit between 1986 and 1992, 27 presented with one or more of the following: difficulties with receptive language and processing of language, expressive and pragmatic language disorders. These were by far the most significant disorders to be diagnosed because they had not been previously identified and because of their probable relationship with psychiatric disorder, which will be discussed further in the chapter.

It is relevant to summarise here the psychiatric diagnoses of the children involved in this study: 17 had a conduct disorder; five had a conduct disorder with attention deficit disorder; six had a conduct disorder with attention deficit disorder and below average IQ; one was assessed as having Asperger's Syndrome; and six had anxiety disorders.

Pragmatics have a particular relevance here because it is these factors which govern our choice of language in social interaction, and the effects of our choice on others (Crystal 1988). Inappropriate use of language and its consequences are important causal factors of peer relationship problems for many of the children treated in the Lowit Unit.

Few of the children presented with articulation disorders. Those who did fell into the category of developmental delay – sound systems being immature rather than deviant. Of the 35 children originally assessed in this study only two presented with immature speech, without other diagnosed language problems, neither of whom required specific remediation. One of the two children had received therapy previously.

There were few disorders of fluency or voice amongst those children referred for speech and language assessment on the Lowit between 1986 and 1992. Four children presented with a fluency problem significant enough to impair communication. One of those children also had a moderate hearing loss and was fitted with binaural aids. Another child also suffered from a discernible voice disorder. All four of these children had additional speech and language difficulties. Since disorders of fluency and voice can have a close association with conditions such as anxiety, shy or withdrawn personalities, and hysteria the low occurrence is perhaps surprising.

It is worth noting that children with disruptive behaviour/conduct disorders frequently presented with motor learning difficulties and referrals for language assessment often come via the occupational therapist. It is also our experience that disorders of language processing, sequencing and difficulties executing a motor response to a verbal instruction are closely linked to motor learning disorders. Whilst we have no scientific data to confirm our beliefs, it is apparent from case histories that combined language and occupational therapy is beneficial to these children.

Previous Research Findings

How, then, do the types of problems encountered in our present study of child psychiatric in-patients compare with those looked at in earlier studies? There is a paucity of research into the speech and language disorders exhibited within this client group. However, the results of those studies which have been carried out provide increasing evidence for a pattern of disorders associated with children who have severe emotional and/or behavioural problems.

There is the likely hypothesis that children with speech and language handicaps are at risk of psychiatric disorders in childhood. Rutter and Lord (1987), however, found that a psychiatric disorder secondary to language delay was least likely to occur when the disorder was of articulation alone. Kotsopoulos and Boodoosingh (1987) tested 46 children referred to a Day Psychiatric programme of whom 19 had observable speech defects, none severe, and only six of those required individual therapy. Cantwell, Baker and Mattison (1980) found that only 13 per cent of their sample of psychiatrically ill children had a pure speech problem; the presence of a definable articulation disorder was significantly more common in the psychiatrically well group. Their findings concur with those of Rutter and Lord in that a child with a pure speech problem is less likely to develop secondary psychiatric disorder.

A higher incidence of speech immaturities was found by Kolvin and Fundudis (1981) in their study of elective mute children. Out of their sample of 24, 12 (50%) were found to have immaturities of speech and/or other speech difficulties. Bearing in mind the nature of the presenting symptoms and personality type of the elective mute, this higher incidence of immature speech is perhaps not surprising.

Kotsopoulos and Boodoosingh (1987) found only one child with mild voice impairment, from vocal nodules, out of their sample of 53, thus supporting the results from this study. Cantwell and Baker (1987) found a higher incidence of problems with language comprehension, expressive language, and language processing in children with behavioural and emotional disorders. Burgess and Bransby (1990) evaluated 17 children attending a unit for children with moderate emotional and behavioural problems. They found 16 of the children presented with speech and/or language problems requiring intervention. Of those 16, 13 were diagnosed as having a language disorder as opposed to language delay.

Kotsopoulos and Boodoosingh (1987) reported 71.7 per cent of their sample of 46 children presenting either speech and/or language disorder requiring individual therapy. The largest proportion of patients with severe language impairment showed a deficit in their ability to process speech sounds, for example discrimination of minimal pairs, such as t/d or r/w contrasts, or the discrimination of consonant sounds in initial, medial, or final position in words. Interestingly, only five of those 24 had articulation defects. This calls into question the long-held theory that sound processing deficit and articulation disorder are closely associated, and that 'ear-training' is a necessary part of the treatment strategy (Berry and Eisenson 1964; Renfrew 1972).

The following case histories of children included in the study illustrate the relationship between language disorder and emotional/behavioral disorder which previous researchers have highlighted.

Two Case Histories

Case 1

C. was admitted to the Unit as an in-patient at age 7.5 years, after a period of out-patient management which had limited success. C. had a history of behaviour difficulties. He had been referred to the Child Guidance Department at the age of 4.6 years. because of behaviour problems at nursery school. These continued through the first two years at primary school, during which time C. had been referred to the department of child and family psychiatry.

C. was openly defiant in class and distracted other pupils. He required considerable staff guidance and one-to-one attention. This was extremely difficult to offer in a large class and although C received some learning support, academic achievement was poor. C's behaviour also caused difficulties at home.

Although he was distractible, C. was not diagnosed as hyperactive. The educational psychologist was of the opinion that C. would choose not to listen and would ignore requests made to him. He was capable of concentrating on tasks which he wanted to do, and had chosen himself. These tended to be activities like making models and building lego.

C. was diagnosed as having a conduct disorder with attention deficit disorder and difficulty with peer relationships.

C. was referred for language assessment one month after admission to the Unit. He had no previous speech and language therapy involvement and his developmental history had not aroused cause for concern except for the behaviour difficulties. C. had no observable speech impairment. C. was assessed over several sessions using standardised tests and observation in group and class situations.

On the Sentence Comprehension Test (Wheldall, Mittler and Hobsbaum 1979), C. passed 14 of the 15 subtests. Discussion with his teacher on the Unit confirmed that C. had no particular comprehension difficulties, but that his expressive ability was limited. The teacher had noted many examples of words where C. was using approximations to the words intended for example 'masks' for maths: 'puter' for computer: 'laura' for lorry. Analysis of conversation taped during an individual session revealed that C. had difficulty organising his thoughts and expressing them verbally. This appeared to be due to specific word-finding difficulties. C. used circumlocutions, fill-in words and expressions such as 'you know', 'stuff', and 'what's it again?' On The Test of Word-Finding (German 1986) C.'s score was below the norms of the test. Word finding difficulties were evident in all subtests. During testing C. used much extra verbal behaviour and gesture as he tried to retrieve the words. Comprehension testing clearly demonstrated that he knew all the items.

The nature of C.'s language difficulty was explained to the other members of the multi-disciplinary team, including C.'s parents. C. was given individual language therapy aimed at improving listening skills and group therapy focussing on pragmatic language skills and peer relationships. A separate programme was implemented by his key workers and other members of the multi-disciplinary team on the Unit. This was aimed particularly at improving word retrieval and included specific games and projects which targeted verbal language skills along with social skills such as turn taking and co-operative play.

In early individual therapy sessions, C. would try to manipulate the activities. It appeared that the language elements in the activities were regarded as threatening by C. He therefore adopted strategies to cope with the difficulties he anticipated. Cooperation gradually improved over the following weeks, but

C. continued to exhibit oppositional behaviour, particularly in between tasks and when going from the classroom to the therapy room.

A star chart was devised by the clinical psychologist which proved successful in modifying C.'s behaviour at these times. During group therapy, C. was unaccepting of group rules, always wanting it to be his turn. Fear of failure and low self-esteem meant that C. was often unwilling to take part in a group activity which was new to him and which he felt would be difficult. He was unable to recognise the difficulties of other children in the group. If he could not retrieve the words he needed to take part in an activity he would sulk, or behave aggressively towards other children or staff.

C. received individual and group therapy for 12 months. During this time, C.'s behaviour improved to the extent that he was better able to form relationships with other children and spent time playing with them. He began to have greater success with school work and this provided sufficient reward to motivate him to try new things.

C. was gradually reintegrated into mainstream primary school with learning and auxiliary support. A language programme was planned which could be incorporated into the classroom curriculum and C. remained under review by the speech and language therapy department. Evidence suggests that C.'s inability to express his feelings verbally, engage in normal social activities with his peers, and cope with the linguistic demands of the school curriculum had a marked effect on his behaviour and self-esteem.

Case 2

D. was referred for speech and language assessment on admission to the Unit, at 5.6 years, as he was difficult to understand at times. D. had poor fine motor coordination, and received occupational therapy treatment. He exhibited behaviour problems at home and at school, distracting other pupils in class, displaying tantrums, and having poor attention control. D. found peer relationships difficult and was inclined to be aggressive.

The speech diagnosis concluded that the indistinct quality of D.'s speech was part of overall low muscle tone and should improve accordingly with general motor control. Speech therapy was not regarded as appropriate and D. was discharged.

D.'s subsequent performance observed by other professionals on the unit gave rise to further concern about his language abilities; the content of his expressive language was at times inappropriate and D. appeared to be having difficulties with language comprehension. D. was re-referred and further assessment carried out. On the British Picture Vocabulary Scale (short version) Dunn, Dunn, Whetton and Pintilie (1982), D. scored an age equivalent of 3.2 years at chronological age 5.11 years. putting him in the moderately low to extremely low range.

On the Reynell Developmental Language Scales, (Reynell 1987) achieved similarly low scores: *Verbal Comprehension* – age equivalent 4.06–4.07 years – standard score (1.9); *Expressive language* – age equivalent 4.08–4.09 years – standard score (1.0). Analysis of these tests revealed that D. had difficulty coping with complex instructions involving two or more language concepts, and organising information into syntactically correct sentence forms. The assessments demonstrated that although D. appeared to have adequate communication skills on a superficial level, he suffered from a significant language deficit. At the time his language disorder was diagnosed, D. was about to be discharged from the Unit, and reintegrated into his primary school.

He received some group therapy during his remaining time on the Unit, and therapy was continued on an individual out-patient basis following discharge. D. was given a comprehensive therapy programme aimed at improving listening skills and attention control, with carefully structured expressive language tasks. Time was also spent at D.'s school observing how he was coping in the class situation and advising his teacher about suitable language learning programmes. At the time of this research, D. was still on the speech and language therapy caseload. He maintained his place in mainstream school, but continued to need additional therapy and learning support. The psychiatrist also remained involved in D.'s management.

It was evident that as educational demands increased, D.'s language learning difficulties became more significant. He continued to experience some expressive language difficulties but the greatest area of difficulty was in reading comprehension. Mechanical reading was age appropriate, but D. was poor at deriving meaning and answering questions about reading material.

Review of Case Studies

These cases highlight some important issues concerning our referral and assessment procedures and subsequent management of this client group.

(1)   Quick 'screening' techniques do not sufficiently reveal underlying deviant language pathology; only superficial problems may be identified. Indeed, Burgess and Bransby (1990) in their study of the speech and language skills of children with emotional and behavioural problems, found that when using the checklist provided in *Guidelines for Identifying Language Disabled Children* (Beveridge and Ramsden 1987) that it *failed to identify 13 children* who were discovered to be suffering from speech and language difficulties when fully assessed. In addition they observed there were 'marked differences in the way that language competence is evaluated by different professionals'.

(2)   There are improvements which could be made in the referral procedures for children exhibiting emotional or behavioural

disorders, so that adequate evaluation of communication skills is taking place earlier in the child's management, as will be discussed in more detail later.

(3) Historically, therapists have accepted a wide variety of referrals. Now additional training and opportunities for specialisation within the profession has meant radically new working practices. This has to be to the advantage of both therapists and patients, as there is clearly a need for specialist speech and language therapists to assess and work with this client group. One immediate result of this in our own situation is that all patients admitted to the Lowit Unit would be routinely assessed.

Among a group of children Bishop and Adams (1990) identified who experienced specific language delay at age four years, and who did not catch up by the age of five and half years, 46 per cent were impaired in reading comprehension at 8.5 years of age.

Rutherford (1977), also highlights the persisting nature of specific language disorders, concluding that the child with word-finding problems 'does not outgrow his problem'. Rutherford and his team saw increasing numbers of young adults returning for help 18–25 years later where the impact of their residual disabilities on social, emotional and financial well-being was evident.

Rutherford (1977) also warns of the need to be cautious in making judgements about the extent of a child's word-finding problem based on test results obtained in a single day. In the case of C. described above it should be noted that whilst the specific measure obtained from the Test of Word Finding was useful in this particular instance, the diagnosis was supported by regular observation and examples collected by other multi-disciplinary team members.

Children with psychiatric disorders, moreover, are likely to have a greater fluctuation of word-finding abilities. Irritability and restlessness may significantly affect a child's performance. Whether the language disorder is secondary to the psychiatric disorder or its primary cause, it is reasonable to conclude that the presence of psychiatric disorder will significantly affect both the child's management and prognosis.

There needs to be a review procedure which enables these children and their carers and educators to obtain specialist advice and support, particularly at times of developmental and/or environmental change. These are the periods when the vulnerability of the child is most apparent and management programmes need to be reviewed. In our experience, children leaving the Lowit Unit to be reintegrated into either mainstream or special education at primary level, frequently need additional input from the psychiatric multi-disciplinary team as they approach secondary level.

Discussion and Conclusions

Referrals

From Lowit Unit data it is evident that the highest percentage of referrals (84%) to the speech and language therapist were made by the consultant child psychiatrists.

The patients in the study who were seen at the speech and language therapist's request had been identified 'in passing' on the unit. In each case a language deficit was diagnosed, although the disorder had not been perceived as such by other staff within the multi-disciplinary team on the unit. This clearly points to the need for all children admitted to child psychiatric units to undergo a full language evaluation. Of the 29 children on the Lowit Unit presenting with language disorder, 10 had an additional observable speech impairment which was a crucial factor influencing their referral for assessment to the speech and language therapist. It could, therefore, be hypothesised that the remaining 19 might not have been referred until relatively late in their management programme, some conceivably not at all. It is reasonable to suggest from these figures and previously quoted research results that disturbed children who appear to have normal speech could be suffering from significant communication difficulties.

Earlier researchers, notably Kotsopoulos and Boodoosingh (1987) recommended that the speech and language therapist's role should not remain limited to the assessment and treatment of those children who present clinically obvious symptoms of communication disorder, but should include 'the comprehensive language and speech assessment of every child with severe behaviour and emotional disorder'. Similarly Love and Thompson (1988) suggested that all children referred to psychiatric services should be screened by the speech therapist. Gualtieri, Koriath, Bourgondien and Saleeby (cited by Gravell and France 1991) state that 'speech and language therapists seem to be much more aware of psychiatric problems in their clients than psychiatrists and psychologists are of language disorders in theirs' (p.32).

There is a clear consensus from all the research, therefore, regarding how referrals to the speech and language therapist should be arranged. There would seem to be also an ongoing requirement for in-service training for other members of the multi-disciplinary team involved with the children. This would heighten awareness of the more subtle language problems which frequently fail to be recognised but which emerge as being crucial factors in the differential diagnosis of the child and his or her subsequent management.

There are encouraging signs in our own child and family psychiatry department that there is an increased awareness of language problems amongst children with psychiatric disorders. However, the profile of the speech and language therapy service, as a visible presence, needs to be maintained, particularly on the ward where there are more frequent changes of staff.

Resources

In April 1992, the Children's Hospital became part of the Aberdeen Royal Hospitals (NHS) Trust. Speech and Language Therapy services are part of the Therapy services Clinical Directorate (currently under review) which includes other speech and language therapists based at the Infirmary who work with an adult caseload, physiotherapists, dietitians, and non-paediatric occupational therapists.

The present arrangement of resources determines the amount of therapeutic input possible to the Lowit Unit. Demand for assessment, therapy and continued patient support for the Unit is showing a steady upward trend, highlighting the inadequacy of the current level of speech and language therapy provision. Although staffing levels for speech and language therapy services to child psychiatric patients have improved since the publication of the *Quirk Report*, the overall input is small compared with services provided to children with speech and language disorders from other client groups. The reasons for this are varied:

(1) Children with psychiatric problems have not always been identified as a clearly defined group, and therefore contact with speech and language therapists has been as part of a general caseload.

(2) The role of the speech and language therapist with children presenting with these problems has been ill-defined.

(3) Many children with psychiatric problems have not been diagnosed as having specific language difficulties. The patterns of management have not always taken the possibility of such into account.

(4) At undergraduate level, the input speech and language therapy students receive relating to child psychiatric disorders is likely to be less than 10 per cent of the total devoted to speech and language pathology. The small numbers of qualified therapists working in this field will severely restrict opportunities undergraduates will have to gain experience of this client group.

The future development of the speech and language therapy service within the child and family psychiatry department in general and the Lowit Unit in particular, depends on the level of demand, the long term objectives of both departments and the management of financial resources.

Preventive Programmes

Children with psychiatric disorders usually require long-term management. This will involve all members of the multi-disciplinary team at some stage throughout this period. In order to plan effectively we should first address some important issues arising from our own research, and studies carried out previously.

- Is there a 'critical' stage in normal language development when a child becomes at 'risk' of secondary psychiatric disorder?

- Can we therefore, improve our identification of those children who are 'at risk' by:

   (1) more accurate assessment techniques: are the assessment procedures and standardised tests available to speech and language therapists adequate to make accurate management decisions about this client group?

   (2) better communication between concerned professionals

   (3) improved patient management procedures.

Perhaps more resources should be channelled into preventive programmes aimed at identifying children, during the pre-school years, who are at risk of secondary psychiatric disorder as a result of speech and language disorder. Appropriate management strategies could be put in place, thereby reducing the communication, educational, and social difficulties which these children experience.

This might be seen as a more cost-effective method of serving this client group and of utilising the speech and language therapists' increasingly limited time. Indeed Frangouli, Sakellarapoulos, Sorokou and Dambassina-Latarjet (1989) list 'prevention of communication disorders' as one of the objectives of their Mobile Psychiatric Unit in a rural area of Greece. Preventive programmes would not in themselves eliminate the need for in-patient psychiatric care for some children, but might enable certain areas of difficulty to be addressed at a more appropriate time in the child's development.

Community Care Programmes

Much publicity has been given recently to caring in the community, and in the author's opinion, rightly so. However, there are situations in which continued care within the hospital setting is the better option and the facility for this should be provided. More particularly with regard to those emotionally vulnerable children who are treated on the Lowit Unit, links with the hospital care team should be maintained. The value of relationships already forged, and feelings of security developed within that network, cannot be underestimated.

A high percentage of children leaving the Lowit are still unable to cope with the environment of mainstream education. Special schooling, where classes are smaller with a higher teacher/pupil ratio, is a preferred option. Whilst a comprehensive speech/language evaluation has been carried out during a child's stay on the Lowit, and some therapy given, it should be the responsibility of the Unit's speech and language therapist to oversee the continuation of that management programme within the future educational setting. The speech and language therapist should act as consultant and resource person on speech and language issues, and be involved in such at all stages of education planning (Kotsopoulos and Boodoosingh 1987). Continuity of care, therefore, following discharge from the unit, should be maintained through the hospital.

Skill Mix

Muir, Baseby and Poules (1990) state that 'therapists need to be aware that the boundaries of the speech therapy role are not clear cut and may often overlap with other disciplines'. Frangouli, Sakellaropoulis, Sorokou and Dambassina-Latarjet (1989) speak of the interrelation of roles but point to the need to still retain clear cut professional responsibilities.

Certainly any degree of skill mix should be used constructively to effect a more accurate diagnosis of the child's problems and subsequent management programme. Quirk (DES 1972) saw this as increasing team effectiveness and stated (cf 6.13) 'when cooperation is close and there is mutual understanding between these experts the lines of demarcation between their different roles tend to become blurred so that speech therapists often contribute to the medical and psychological diagnosis and the doctors, psychologists, nurses, and teachers assist in the recognition and assessment of the patient's speech disorder'.

Continuing Education

Quirk reported (cf 9.05) 'the Royal College of Psychiatrists considered that at present therapists are inadequately trained in psychodynamics, family dynamics and psychotherapy'. There are now moves afoot to develop skills in psychiatric work through postgraduate training, but the availability of skilled staff and low level of funding still present problems (Muir, Baseby and Poulis 1990).

Procedural Changes: Some Thoughts for the Future

In the changing market for healthcare services our past procedures need rethinking. As was discussed earlier, relatively few speech and language thera-pists work in mental health settings. This may be partly due to established patterns of referral and liaison between the medical and allied professions. Children may be referred to either a psychiatrist or a speech and language therapist initially and the coexistence of psychiatric problems with a language disorder may go unrecognised (Lubash 1992).

Hospital, school and home for these children are not three separate envi-ronments; dealt with individually, they must be viewed as a whole. As patients will undoubtedly be followed up by child psychiatry within the hospital, the total package of care should equally involve the speech and language therapist along with other members of the multi-disciplinary team. The emphasis which child psychiatrists place on working with the family, rather than just the referred child, makes the holistic approach to therapy even more important. A child's language problem will have an affect on all members of the family which needs to be addressed along with direct work on the child's linguistic skills (Hayhow 1992). This will not only be beneficial for the child and his or her family, but will allow for more effective channels of communication between the professionals.

The cost in monetary terms is outwith the scope of this chapter. However in an age where healthcare budgets are gaining greater importance for all of us, developing such a package of care within the department of child and family psychiatry must be an attractive proposition.

Special Interest Groups

A Special Interest Group in psychiatry was set up in the early 1980s. Its purpose is to offer speech and language therapists mutual support and to exchange views and knowledge. Meetings are held at regular times during the year and study days and discussions are arranged. Membership, at the time of writing, is standing at around 50 therapists, and the group has divided into two sections, South of England and North and Midlands. Most of the therapists are largely involved with adult psychiatric patients (Muir 1992).

A small group of therapists, based in the London area, have recently started meeting to discuss issues and share information relating to their involvement with child psychiatric patients. A postal questionnaire was sent to them as part of this research. Two completed forms were returned from those therapists involved in in-patient units, which provided further evidence of the low provision of speech and language therapy input in child psychiatry, and lack of dedicated posts. However, the existence of these groups continues to raise the profile of speech and language therapy in psychiatry and marks a positive step towards improving the services. Unfortunately, geographical and financial constraints can mean difficulties for therapists attending meetings regularly.

Conclusion

The speech and language therapy service, with regard to this client group, continues to develop. As the profession becomes increasingly certain that they have a crucial role within child psychiatry, the pressures to provide the right kind of service become greater. The conclusion from this research is that a full time speech and language therapist should be a minimum requirement for an in-patient child psychiatric unit. Such a dedicated post would ensure that all children admitted to the unit would receive the necessary assessment and therapy during their stay, and a follow up service after discharge. The provision of more resources is not in itself the solution; the overall aims of the unit and how the members of the multi-disciplinary team function within that therapeutic framework is crucial to its efficacy.

References

Beveridge, H. and Ramsden, G.C. (1987) *Children with Language Disaibilites.* Buckingham: Open University Press.

Berry, M.F. and Eisenson, J. (1964) *Speech disorders: Principles and Practice of Therapy.* London: Peter Owen.

Bishop, D.V.M. and Adams, C. (1990) 'A prospective study of the relationship between specific language impairment, phonological disorders and reading retardation'. *Journal of Child Psychology and Psychiatry 31,* 1027–1050.

Burgess, J. and Bransby, G. (1990) 'An evaluation of the speech and language skills of children with emotional and behavioural problems.' *College of Speech Therapists Bulletin,* January, 2–3.

Cantwell, D., Baker, L. and Mattison, R. (1980) 'Psychiatric disorders in children with speech and language retardation.' *Archives of General Psychiatry 37,* 423–426.

Cantwell, D. and Baker, L. (1987) 'Comparison of well, emotionally disordered and behaviourally disordered children with linguistic problems.' *Journal of the American Academy of Child and Adolescent Psychiatry 26,* 2, 193–6.

Corkish, N. (1990) 'Give priority to social skills training.' *Speech Therapy in Practice,* February, iv.

Crystal, D. (1988) *Introduction to Language Pathology.* (2nd ed). London: Cole and Whurr Ltd.

Department of Education and Science (1972) *Speech Therapy Services. The Quirk Report.* London: HMSO.

Dunn, L., Dunn, L., Whetton, C. and Pintilie, D. (1982) *British Picture Vocabulary Scale.* Slough: NFER-NELSON.

France, J., Parton, J. and Hooker, H. (1990) 'Improving communication in mental institutions.' *Speech Therapy in Practice-Special Supplement,* December, iii–v.

Frangouli, A., Sakellaropoulos, P., Sorokou, T., and Dambassina-Latarjet, L. (1989) 'A mobile psychiatric unit in a rural area of Greece: The role of the speech-language pathologist.' *College of Speech Therapists Bulletin,* May, 2–3.

German, D. (1986) *Test of Word Finding.* DLM Teaching Resources: USA.

Gravell, R. and France, J. (1991) *Speech and Communication Problems in Psychiatry.* London: Chapman and Hall.

Hayhow, R. (1992) 'A family approach to developmental communication.' *Human Communication,* 18–19.

Kolvin, I. and Fundudis, T. (1981) 'Elective mute Children: Psychological development and background factors.' *Journal of Child Psychology and Psychiatry 22,* 3, 219–232.

Kotsopoulos, A. and Boodoosingh, L. (1987) 'Language and speech disorders in children attending a day psychiatric programme.' *British Journal of Disorders of Communication 22,* 227–236.

Love, A.J. and Thompson, M.G.G. (1988) 'Language disorders and attention deficit disorders in young children referred for psychiatric services.' *American Journal of Orthopsychiatry 58*, 1, 52–64.

Lubash, M. (1992) 'Rethinking the focus of our clinical work.' *The College of Speech and Language Therapy Bulletin*, November, 7–8.

Muir, N., Baseby, A., and Poules, G. (1990) 'Psychiatry, our developing role: Its challenges and rewards.' *Speech Therapy in Practice-Special supplement*, December, i–ii.

Muir, N.A. (1992) 'Busy and productive year.' *College of Speech and Language Therapists Bulletin*, June, 2.

Renfrew, C.E. (1972) 'Speech therapy.' In M. Rutter and J.A.M. Martin (eds) *The Child with Delayed Speech*. London: Heinemann.

Reynell, J.K. (1987) *Reynell Developmental Language Scales*. 2nd Rev. Slough: NFER-Nelson.

Rutherford, D. (1977) *Speech and Language Disorders and MBD. Learning Disabilities and Related disorders: Facts and Current Issues*. London: Millichap Med.Pub. Inc.

Rutter, M. and Lord, C. (1987) 'Language Disorders associated with psychiatric disturbance.' In W. Yule and M. Rutter (eds) *Language Development and Disorders*. London: MacKeith Press.

Wheldall, M., Mitler, K. and Mobsbaum, P. (1979) *Sentence Comprehension Test*. Windsor: NFER-Nelson.

Wright, H.L. (1968) 'A clinical study of children who refuse to talk at school.' *Journal of the American Academy of Child Psyciatry 17*, 603–617.

Glossary of Terms Used in the Text

Pragmatics: The study of the rules governing the relationship between language structure and language use. To have pragmatic skill means one has the ability to use language as a tool, to do what one wants it to do in terms of varying social context.

Prosody: The melody, stress and rhythm of speech.

Voice Disorder: An impairment of the voice. This may be due to vocal misuse, disease, structural abnormality, abnormality of the resonator system for example cleft palate, neuromuscular lesions, neurotic and psychogenic disorders or the effects of drug therapy.

Vocal Nodules: Non-malignant neoplasms which form on the vocal cords as a result of continuous vocal abuse.

Language Processing: The encoding, storage, retrieval and handling of linguistic information by the brain.

Echolalia: The repetition – immediate or delayed – of something heard in the speech of others. This may be a repetition word for word and frequently occurs in response to a question.

Circumlocution: Talking round a subject – often seen in stutterers as an avoidance of certain sounds or words which are perceived as difficult to say.

Elective Mutism: A condition in which the ability to speak is present, but the child elects to remain mute to certain people and in certain conditions or situations.

Syntax: The study of sentence structure.

CHAPTER 9

The Role of Occupational Therapy in Child Psychiatric Units

Jacqueline Flewker-Barker and Elizabeth Stephenson

Introduction

Although the first occupational therapist in Britain worked in adult psychiatry in the 1920s, in fact in Aberdeen, the employment of occupational therapists in child psychiatry occurred at a much later date, nearly a decade after their first appearance in child psychiatry in the USA (McRae 1992; Rockey 1987). Forward, who was clearly one of the pioneers in the field in Britain, wrote about group therapy and work with psychotic and defective children in the 1950s (Rockey 1987).

Jeffrey (1973) whose views and writings have been influential in the development of occupational therapy in Britain, saw the role created by the occupational therapist in child psychiatry as being dependent on several factors viz:

(1) The unit's overall treatment policy.

(2) The social set up within the Unit.

(3) The view of the physician.

(4) The treatment approach of the senior occupational therapist which Jeffrey described as being influenced by her training, past experience, special interests and skills, which are adjusted to meet the needs of the unit and the expectations of the other staff.

(5) The facilities available.

However, Jeffrey, who has, herself, a particular interest in play therapy, noted that in 1973 'The different roles of occupational therapists working in child psychiatry units are almost as numerous as the units of this type where occupational therapists are employed' (p.429). This 20-year-old observation appears as true today as it did when written. Similarly, Davis (1985) has argued that 'over the years the practice of occupational therapy has diversified to the extent that, although occupational therapists share a common training, the day-to-day practice of a therapist in one field can be difficult to follow by a therapist in another.' (p.266)

This, she believed, was particularly true of occupational therapists in child psychiatry, and considers that only when the occupational therapist is exposed to the speciality, does the diversity become apparent. Sholle-Martin and Alessi (1990) writing in the USA express concern and caution about the lack of a clear cut role, considering that if it persists then occupational therapy may be at risk of losing its practice with 'children hospitalised for psychiatric disturbances' (p.873). Worthy of note is the long recognised dual role of occupational therapists working with children as reflected by the inclusion of 'Instruction in the welfare of children suffering from physical and psychiatric disorders' on the American student syllabus in 1958 (Rockey 1987). At that early date too, a two year course in play therapy and play diagnosis was available for post-graduate occupational therapists.

The number of paediatric occupational therapists working in child and family psychiatry is not easy to establish. However, it is clear that in both the USA and Britain there is very limited input into child psychiatry. Jeffrey's 1980s survey found that there were 82 occupational therapists in post in child and adolescent psychiatric units (Jeffrey 1984). Ninety eight per cent of posts were filled, and 81 per cent were at senior level (including seven head posts), 38 per cent were working single handed and only 19 per cent were basic grade. Overall, 18 per cent were part time. Though a direct comparison cannot be made, McRae's later Scottish survey showed certain similarities, namely a very small number of occupational therapists (12) were employed in the five units studied; and 83 per cent were at senior level. Unlike Jeffrey's figures, however, around 50 per cent were part time (McRae 1992).

Using McRae's figures, and comparing them with the total number of occupational therapists employed in Scotland in 1992 (The Scottish Office 1994) it would appear that just under 1.5 per cent work in child and family psychiatry. This compares with a figure stated by Jeffrey, that approximately 2 per cent of occupational therapists were employed in these specialised units/clinics in 1976 (Jeffrey 1982). Currently in Grampian, however, only 0.6 per cent of the total number of occupational therapists are working in child and family psychiatry.

Currently a staffing establishment of three whole time equivalents (four staff members) cover hospital in and out-patients and the majority of school age children requiring occupational therapy in the Grampian area, Orkney and Shetland.

Characteristics of an Occupational Therapy Service

The occupational therapists at Royal Aberdeen Children's Hospital (RACH) provide a service which aims to be truly holistic and integrated. Unlike most settings where occupational therapists work either in child psychiatry or with physical disabilities, in Royal Aberdeen Children's Hospital the therapist's remit is very broad, covering a diverse range of physical conditions (congenital and acquired), developmental delay, motor-learning difficulties and emotional/behavioural problems. The result is an approach which encompasses neurodevelopmental areas as well as emotional and behavioural aspects, which is intended to address the needs of many children whose problems are multi-faceted; particularly those referred by child and family psychiatry.

This comprehensive service has developed over the past 10 years during which staff continuity and a particular interest in psychiatry has been maintained. The caseload relating to child and family psychiatry is covered by the two full-time staff members, in order to provide consistency and continuity through designated therapists. Relating to our policy of providing an integrated service via occupational therapists who can offer a variety of skills, it is preferred not to have one designated therapist solely for child and family psychiatry. However, there is a lack of training for occupational therapists in this area.

Paediatrics in itself is regarded as a specialist area in occupational therapy educational departments and only a small proportion of the occupational therapy undergraduate course is devoted to it: for example child psychiatry *per se* currently represents only six hours on the local course.

Recent statistics, collated in 1992, indicated that 28 per cent of all RACH occupational therapy referrals originate from the child and family psychiatry department. Whilst only a small proportion of these children are patients in the Lowit Unit they represent a high proportion of the time commitment, because of the complexity of their disorders and the long term involvement. This may commence prior to Lowit Unit admission and continue throughout the admission period and for many years following discharge, via review, family support and advice for the school, as is well illustrated by the case study presented later in the chapter. Due to the complex nature of the problems of these children, which often include a major 'constitutional' component, the occupational therapist's role may be in one or more of the following three key areas: motor-learning difficulties; group therapy; individual play therapy.

Motor-learning Difficulties

A high percentage of the occupational therapy referrals in Royal Aberdeen Children's Hospital, including those from child and family psychiatry, are children with motor-learning difficulties. These children can be described as 'having difficulty with movement and specific aspects of learning in the absence of cognitive impairment or obvious physical disability' (Stephenson and McKay 1986, p.1).

The service offers comprehensive assessment which includes motor, sensory and perceptual areas, education related performance and emotional/behavioural responses. A combination of standardised tests and clinical observations tapping these areas, together with the history and performance symptoms, are used to help reach a 'diagnosis'. It is felt that such comprehensive assessment is desirable in attempting to analyse the problems of this group of children. A quick, simple test is unlikely to be successful given the heterogeneity of children with motor-learning difficulties (Henderson 1987) and the subtle complexity of the disorder (McKinlay and Gordon 1986).

Assessment results in identification of specific types of dysfunction, within the 'umbrella' of motor-learning difficulties; such as problems with balance, laterality and sequence, dyspraxia and visuo-spatial problems. Frequently there is a combination of these difficulties, often linking with poor emotional and behavioural controls, that is to form a 'constitutional' problem. Research has clearly linked conduct disorders with learning difficulties and attention deficit disorders (Miller and Matthews 1988). Despite this, the literature, and experience suggest that there are few occupational therapists working with both neurological and psychiatric disorders in children, thereby encompassing motor-learning difficulties within the remit of child and family psychiatry. The experience of one of the authors in teaching Post-Graduate Courses on motor-learning difficulties throughout the UK in recent years confirms that very few course participants work in child and family psychiatry: for example, one only on a recent course which had 40 participants. Considering the fact that almost all the therapists on these courses work in paediatrics (a minority field in itself) the figure representing child psychiatry, with an interest in motor-learning difficulties, is clearly a minute percentage.

Following assessment, priorities for the child are established by the multi-disciplinary team. The child with a 'constitutional' problem may well have speech and language difficulties in addition to his motor-learning, behavioural and emotional problems. An investigative study of 31 children identified as having motor-learning problems and receiving occupational therapy at Royal Aberdeen Children's Hospital, showed that more than 50 per cent also had diagnosed speech and language difficulties (Stephenson, McKay and Chesson 1991).

All the child's problems need to be considered, and the most significant addressed. When appropriate, occupational therapy is offered. The findings of the above study suggested that an important part of therapeutic intervention is increasing the child's self-confidence and reducing tensions. Fewer behavioural problems were reported once occupational therapy had commenced.

Treatment is again holistic and attempts to address the child's emotional needs and self-esteem, as well as the more obvious sensory-motor, perceptual and specific learning problems. The approach is eclectic, using a sensory integrative base,[1] and aims to achieve enhanced, more automatic motor skills. This should reduce the child's need to 'think through' movement (inevitably inefficient) and allow more freedom to focus on aspects of learning and cognitive skills. A treatment programme is tailored to each child's needs, dependent on the specific problems identified on assessment (see Stephenson, McKay and Chesson 1991). Therapy usually commences with the provision of appropriate sensory input, working towards the production of adaptive motor responses such as enhanced balance and postural adjustments, better motor planning, improved integration of body sides.

Based on this sensory-motor foundation, we can develop more sophisticated areas; for example, fine motor control, hand-eye co-ordination and visuo-spatial skills. All these skills are thought to form the basis for appropriate behaviour and learning (Ayres 1983). Usually when a child is in the Lowit Unit, his or her key workers will be involved in therapy so that they can provide carry over between sessions.

When a child's problems in the motor-learning area are mild and thought to contribute to, but not to be a major factor in, his difficulties, appropriate therapy ideas are offered for parents or the workers to carry out with the child.

Many children referred to child and family psychiatry have motor learning problems. At any one time approximately half the children in the Lowit Unit are known to occupational therapy because of these difficulties (see later sections of this chapter). The psychiatrists have requested routine screening by occupational therapy of all the children in the Unit, but resources unfortunately do not allow this. Identification and treatment of motor learning difficulties is essential if we are to reduce further emotional and behavioural problems. In a recent study of 31 children, four of the five children referred to occupational therapy were children for whom there had been no early identification of their motor learning difficulties; and the fifth had a long gap (four years) between initial suspicions and formal identification (Stephenson, McKay and Chesson 1991). Moreover, longitudinal studies of children with motor-learning difficulties for whom no intervention was provided suggest that a considerable number experience emotional and/or behavioural difficulties in adolescence despite some spontaneous maturing of motor aspects (Gillberg, Gillberg and Groth 1989).

---

1 Sensory Integration is a child-directed therapy technique which employs appropriate sensory input aimed at achieving enhanced central nervous system integration and more automatic adaptive motor responses. Sensory input is selected and controlled in order to address the individual child's needs.

Group Therapy

According to Fergus and Buchanan (1977), traditionally, occupational therapy has used activities as the medium through which to achieve its aims; and they suggest that in order for an activity to be therapeutic it must be an 'exertion of energy in a particular direction with the aim of curing or at least contributing to the cure of disease' (p.82).

Fergus and Buchanan (1977) suggest the use of activities in a group to:

(1) provide an objective for the group

(2) establish an environment in which the child can express himself freely

(3) take the emphasis from the self and therefore be less threatening to a child

(4) act as a route through which a child can be included in a group

(5) provide a degree of structure to enable the therapist to observe a child in a less threatening setting

(6) achieve an involvement at a social level.

Fergus and Buchanan (1977) highlight the importance of the activity selected and the need to ensure that it is not too easy or difficult which may lead to the children losing interest or becoming frustrated. Group therapy has different aims and objectives and Jeffrey suggests that it is not used as a substitute for individual play therapy if that is what the child requires.

Reference is made to Forward by Fergus and Buchanan (1977) who suggested that 'the diluted therapeutic situation offered by a group is valuable for those children incapable at a particular time of facing the more intense face to face relationship: and believed that it 'offers the support of their fellows to the fearful' (Fergus and Buchanan 1977, p.82). On the other hand, in the authors' experience, group therapy can also be viewed as a progressive step for the child. That is having made substantial gains in individual play therapy, some children now need the opportunity to consolidate new skills in a safe, secure small group environment before being thrust into larger group situation such as the classroom, to try out new ways of behaving and relating to others. The groups described by both Jeffrey and Fergus and Buchanan would appear to follow the non-directive approach of Axline (1989).

However, some children, in Jeffrey's (1990) opinion, do not benefit from the group therapy experience, for example those who are severely deprived, autistic, severely neurotic, or those with some psychotic problems or brain damage.

Group therapy has been provided regularly by the occupational therapists at RACH for approximately seven years. Prior to this only one or two groups were on offer within the department of child and family psychiatry; these were mainly non-directive and run by various members of the multi-disciplinary team. There was, however, a widely recognised need for groups, and one of the occupational therapists, already experienced in individual play therapy, set up the first purely occupational therapy group. This was offered solely for children in the Lowit Unit, but because of the extreme difficulties with controls experienced by these children, it became clear that it was not possible for the group to continue in its completely non-directive form. The decision, therefore, was taken to try to provide more structure, in the form of an activity base, to enable these children to cope: the structure helping with controls, and the activity removing the focus from the child itself.

Whilst this proved more successful, it was still not an ideal situation because of the extent of the children's difficulties. The solution appeared to lie within the group itself, and once a balance was achieved between in and out-patients, and the nature of problems, the groups began to offer a much more supportive and therapeutic environment.

To date, the occupational therapy groups follow this same format; and whilst recently several other groups have emerged within the department of child and family psychiatry, the occupational therapy groups remain unique in their semi-structured, activity-based format.

Initially reservations were expressed by some of the psychiatrists around the style of the groups which had elected not to adopt a specific, traditional model. These reservations, however, now seem to have been resolved and referrals are received from many sources.

GROUP ETHOS

The occupational therapy groups, to date, have attempted to provide a setting in which children with fairly significant difficulty with controls can function. These groups are therefore slightly more structured than non-directive group sessions would be in that an activity base is used to provide a vehicle around which the group can function. The activity is very much secondary to the interaction within the group, but it does provide some structure; it may be non-directive to allow for individual expression, or when appropriate, joint working may be attempted. The therapists become part of the group, and, as far as possible, use a non-directive, reflective technique to facilitate group interaction.

'Mental and emotional health' has been described as the 'degree of freedom an individual has in choosing from among alternative types of behaviour' (Pratt and Allen 1989). The group therefore aims to help a child to choose his behavioural response. This is achieved by the therapists reflecting the situations which occur, thereby enabling the child to realise the impact of his behaviour and to begin to adapt it appropriately.

Many of these children experience problems with their peers, often contributed to by their inappropriate behavioural responses. 'Conduct disorders' are said to include 'repetitive, persistent, patterns of antisocial behaviour that violate the rights of others' (Pratt and Allen 1989). Within the safety of a group situation children can be helped to develop more acceptable options, thereby breaking these patterns by adopting alternative responses.

THE CHILDREN

The groups have been extended to include not only children who experience difficulty with controls, but also those who are anxious, withdrawn or have problems with peer relationships. In liaison with the psychiatrists, the group balance is decided. Factors such as sex, age, level of maturity, nature of problems, and in/out patient status, are considered. Experience so far suggests that children with more than a mild degree of developmental delay derive less benefit from this type of group. We suspect that this would also be the case with other populations, such as children with severe language disorders.

Usually there are two groups running concurrently:

(1) Approximately 5–6-year-olds (four children, two therapists).

(2) Approximately 8–10-year-olds (six children, two therapists).

There is flexibility at either end of the age range in order to match demand. The younger group runs for three-quarters of an hour and the older one for one hour. Children attend weekly for 10–12 weeks, and regular attendance is sought apart from in exceptional circumstances. Groups are closed rather than open-ended.

At the end of a series of sessions a decision is reached about the next step for the child. The options are varied, and include:

(1) sufficient gains made to require no further therapy

(2) a second series of groups – sometimes at a later stage – to consolidate gains

(3) more individualised help, for example play therapy

(4) more intensive assessment, for example in Lowit Unit

(5) assessment of other contributory problems for example motor learning.

THE FAMILIES

Formal feedback for parents/carers is provided at the end of each series of groups in conjunction with the appropriate psychiatrist. It is at this point that the decision is made about the child's future needs. Interim informal feedback is provided for families as appropriate. In addition, on occasion a parents'/carers' group has been offered at the same time as the children's group. This offered support and enhanced parental commitment. These groups were run by the psychiatrists and included social work or clinical psychology staff. They met with variable success, much of the variation probably being attributable to the fact that there could be no 'selection procedure' for parents, as the matching up of children was the principal criterion. However, when there has been no parents' group offered, parents have often met informally over coffee whilst their children attended the group.

THERAPISTS

Often the co-therapist is from another discipline, including members of the department of child and family psychiatry, trainees and, more recently, nursing staff from the Lowit Unit. This interdisciplinary working is a two-way learning experience, and also offers a useful opportunity for people less experienced in children's groups. In addition, it is often quite impossible for participating therapists to recall all the group dynamics fully. Therefore a scribe is often used, both enhancing the accuracy of recording and providing another opportunity for students, new staff members and others wishing to learn. The scribe is non-participant in the group itself.

SUPERVISION

Regular case supervision is offered by one of the consultant psychiatrists; though with more experienced therapists, this has adopted the format of case discussion/consultation.

Play Therapy

Play therapy is not unique to occupational therapists but it appears to be the most common and well-established role of the occupational therapist working in child psychiatry. However, Jeffrey suggests that occupational therapy has developed its own philosophy on the therapeutic medium of play to help children with behavioural and emotional disorders. This she sees as being achieved through the occupational therapy profession's three-fold approach of: (1) therapeutic relationship; (2) therapeutic techniques; and (3) therapeutic activity.

Play is indisputably a child's means of expression. Jeffrey describes young children as being unable to express their emotional needs and conflicts with the verbal ability of adults and therefore childhood has a language of its own, which is play. She goes on to say that in order to gain an understanding of those disturbed children, therapists must learn the child's 'play language'.

Jeffrey, Lyne and Redfern (1984) views 'play' as an aid to 'diagnostic, developmental and continuous assessment' and considers that it 'allows the child to regress in a socially acceptable way' since 'indulging in certain symbolic play activities releases tension, aggression and other emotions'. (p.70)

In several of her publications, Jeffrey describes the different types of play therapy, including play therapy, group therapy and family therapy. The five main individual play therapy types are identified as follows: psychoanalytically orientated; non-directive; relationship; developmental; and directed. (Jeffrey, 1990).

Though Jeffrey has published articles describing other types of play therapy and their application, most of the other literature (Copley, Forryan and O'Neill 1987) has concentrated on non-directive play therapy according to Axline principles (Axline 1989). Although Axline (1989) states that several key principles must be followed 'sincerely, consistently and intelligently to realise their possibilities', it is recognised that non-directive therapy is not a panacea but, like all things, it too has its limitations.

Copley, Forryan and O'Neill (1987) point out that that play therapy is not aimed at 'training' children to behave in more socially acceptable behaviours, but is intended to help the child gain insight, modify, replace or come to terms with his feelings.

The possible gains for the disturbed child through play therapy have been highlighted by Jeffrey (1990). These include the child being assisted in gaining insight, and altering his attitude, in order to improve relationships with adults and peers. 'The child develops new skills and uses his creativity to sublimate basic needs into a socially acceptable form. He receives praise and recognition so that his confidence and self image can improve' (p.249). By learning to understand himself, he learns to understand and accept others.

According to Jeffrey (1990) play therapy is one of the many techniques used in the field of child psychiatry and she views it as complementary to other forms of treatment proffered. She goes on to say that indiscriminate prescription of play therapy in the past has led to it being undervalued as its effectiveness has not been proved.

Individual play therapy has been provided by the occupational therapists at RACH for at least 12 years. The occupational therapists were one of several disciplines offering this type of therapy, and this remains the case. The number of children offered play therapy by occupational therapists is very small. This is due to the time commitment (therapy session, write-up, preparation, supervision) and the limited occupational therapy resources. Length of contact, however, is often considerable. Play therapy is usually provided for children who need more individual work. This may be because group therapy is not appropriate, or because the child is not yet ready or able to cope with a group situation.

Individual play therapy closely adheres to Axline's non-directive model. The room used and its contents are as similar as possible to the ideal setting described by Axline (1989). Both remain consistent throughout the duration of therapy, as does the therapist. Similarly, ideally regular days and times are adhered to. It has proved beneficial with some children to add to this consistency by providing a box of items (pens, pencils, scissors, paper, play dolls and animals) belonging specifically to that child.

Referral is always from one of the psychiatrists and, as far as possible, child and therapist are matched. Sessions last for one hour and currently children are seen weekly. The time with the therapist is the child's own 'private' time to be used as he chooses. There is therefore no direct feedback about sessions to parents/carers. Any important issues would be addressed by the referring psychiatrist in a very general way. Limit setting is minimal, and includes providing safety and discouraging of deliberate damage.

Case supervision is always available to the therapist and is provided by the referring psychiatrist. Currently, the possibility of 'group' supervision/consult-ation sessions is being considered for staff involved in play therapy. The use of therapy may be seen in the following case study.

Case study – Alan[2]

Alan was a child who required all three types of therapy; motor-learning, group and play therapy.

Alan was 7.5 years old when he was first known to occupational therapy because of his motor-learning problems. His father was a manager in the Oil Industry, and his mother, an ex-teacher, was a housewife at the time. The family lived in a suburb of Aberdeen and Alan attended the local primary school.

Initial referral from the paediatric neurologist described late motor mile-stones, general incoordination (first noted at nursery), poor concentration and some behavioural and emotional difficulties. On examination, there were no hard neurological signs; but speech was indistinct, gross motor skills poor, and he presented as a typical 'clumsy' child.

Occupational therapy assessment confirmed motor-learning difficulties, principally related to a deficit in bilateral integration, namely problems with bilateral skills, unclear hand preference, ipsilateral reach, midline crossing avoidance and the frequently associated directional and sequencing problems. In addition, balance and motor control were limited, and there were some visuo-spatial difficulties. Following feedback for parents, and liaison with educational psychology and teaching staff, regular occupational therapy for Alan's motor-learning difficulties was offered. It was also generally acknow-ledged that, in addition, he required help for the emotional/behavioural aspects. Treatment was implemented using a sensory integrative approach, and initially addressed Alan's problems with postural instability and balance. Activities were designed to provide proprioceptive and vestibular stimulation. As postural stability improved, new items were included which helped Alan to use his increased stability in varying, more demanding situations. Balance skills were developed, and work began to enhance overall motor control.

During treatment sessions the extent of Alan's emotional and behavioural problems became increasingly apparent. This concern was shared by the educational psychologist, and group therapy was suggested. Because the most

---

2 Biographical details have been changed to preserve confidentiality.

appropriate group was also run by the occupational therapists it was decided to discontinue motor-learning therapy temporarily at the end of this five month period. The group provided a setting where the nature and extent of emotional/behavioural and peer problems could be further assessed and the beginnings of remediation addressed.

Alan was included in a group of five children, all of whom had problems with peer interaction, and several of whom had considerable difficulty with behavioural controls. The group continued for 11 sessions and progressed from the early stages where children tended to work individually on their own tasks, for example, pictures, plasticine models. Latterly they were beginning to move towards co-operative working on joint projects; in this case a model classroom and a street plan incorporating their own houses. Throughout this period the nature and extent of Alan's emotional problems gave even greater cause for concern.

Alan presented initially as an immature boy who exhibited attention-seeking traits and other inappropriate behaviours, which made it difficult for him to gain the acceptance of his peers. Gradually, as he became more comfortable within the group environment, these extremes of behaviour became increasingly unacceptable to the other children, who began openly to reject and ostracise him. This led to a downwards spiral resulting in Alan being largely scapegoated by the other group members who also tended to project their own inadequacies on to him. Despite Alan's awareness of his own problems and sadness at his isolation and rejection, he was unable to alter his behaviour. Interestingly, his parents commented on similar difficulties with relationships at home and at school. Though the group was able to address some of these difficulties, it was clear that this boy required more in-depth assessment and treatment than the group alone could offer. During this time, continuing family therapy and support was ongoing – provided by the psychiatrist who had become involved following the initial suggestion of group therapy.

On completion of the group sessions, discussion took place between the psychiatrist, occupational therapists and parents. This resulted in the decision to offer a six week assessment place as an in-patient in the Lowit Unit. Following this assessment period, Alan attended the Lowit Unit for approximately one year. At the beginning of this time a motor-learning review assessment was carried out and he recommenced treatment for the persisting difficulties.

Further work was required at this stage to consolidate earlier gains. Following this phase, activities were included to enhance bilateral skills and reinforce midline crossing.

More specific tasks helped Alan with timing, force control and fine motor control. Finally activities were designed to establish hand preference more clearly, refine grasp and begin to address the problems with direction, orientation and sequence.

Carryover treatment was provided in the Unit by nursing staff who attended the occupational therapy sessions. In addition, Alan's parents encouraged him to participate in appropriate activities at home. Group therapy was not considered necessary at this stage because of the ongoing small group interaction which takes place in the Unit. However, individual play therapy was provided by a different occupational therapist from the one carrying out therapy for motor-learning difficulties. This was considered essential in order to assist Alan with role clarification.

Throughout the entire period, attendance at multi-disciplinary review meetings was necessary for the therapists and regular explanation and liaison with nursing staff, teachers and parents continued.

Occupational therapy involvement with such a child does not end on discharge from the Lowit Unit. Indeed review, and where necessary, intervention, will be provided until he reaches school-leaving age, or until such time as his problems no longer warrant occupational therapy input.

Clearly, where problems are so diverse and complex, remediation is a long process which rarely ends in complete 'cure'. Very often the sensory-motor aspects mature to an extent and respond well to occupational therapy. However, any specific learning difficulties which are present may well persist, and the emotional and behavioural problems seem to fluctuate dependent on many factors. In Alan's case there were significant gains in sensory-motor skills, but some specific education-related difficulties, such as with writing, persisted. He may require further occupational therapy to address these areas at a later date. Enhanced self-esteem, improved confidence and better coping strategies will stand him in good stead for the future and, one hopes, reduce the extent of emotional/behavioural problems.

As Alan and his family moved out of the area, it has not been possible to monitor his progress.

A Study of Occupational Therapy In-put into a Child Psychiatric Unit

Occupational therapy input has been a part of the Lowit Unit for at least 12 years. This study focuses on the nature and extent of involvement over the past five years. It also explores more recent input over a three month period in early 1993.

Five Year Study

Statistics were collated from occupational therapy case notes on children who attended the department for assessment and treatment over the five year period 1988–1992 (42 children, representing 44% of the total Lowit Unit intake). Information collected from the profiles covered a wide range of occupational therapy inputs for each child and included for example assessment/review, therapy, liaison with parents/carers, interdisciplinary liaison, meetings, duration of contact, demographic information.

The main areas covered were:

(1) Demographic information.

(2) Nature and extent of involvement.

(3) Interdisciplinary working.

(4) Resource implications.

Findings

(1) DEMOGRAPHIC INFORMATION

Only three of the 42 children (7%) children were girls despite the fact that 23 of the total Lowit Unit intake of 95 (24%) were girls. The youngest child (at point of referral to occupational therapy) was four years seven months and the eldest 14 years 10 months, the mean age being eight years five months. The age distribution of the children is shown in Figure 9.1.

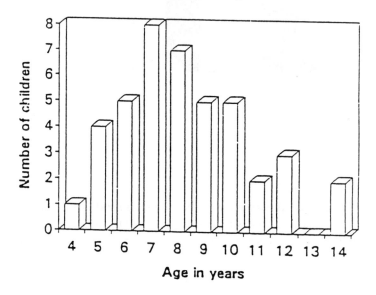

Figure 9.1

(2) NATURE OF INVOLVEMENT

As has been discussed earlier, the three main areas covered by occupational therapy are: motor learning difficulties; group therapy; and play therapy. The former includes assessment and therapy whilst group and play therapy, though essentially treatment, also contribute to the multi-disciplinary assessment process. Of the 42 children, 38 were assessed for motor learning difficulties, and of those 20 attended for regular therapy. Of the remaining 18, ideally six would have been offered therapy had resources allowed. Twelve children attended for group therapy and only four for individual play therapy. Of the total number attending occupational therapy, eight experienced two types of intervention and two children had all three. Figure 9.2 shows the number of children receiving different types of therapy.

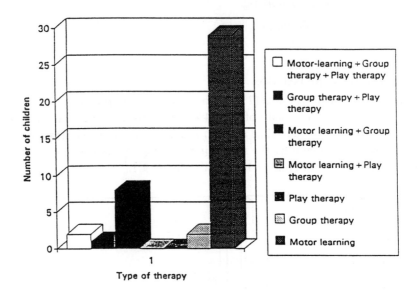

Figure 9.2

(3) EXTENT OF INVOLVEMENT

Extent can be defined as encompassing both duration and 'depth' of contact. The shortest contact period was around one month and included initial assessment, multi-disciplinary liaison and recommendations to parents and

Table 9.1 Children's Nature of Contact by Length of Involvement

Nature of Contact	Length of Involvement				
	Up to 6 months	Up to 1 year	Up to 2 years	Up to 3 years	Over 3 years
Motor Learning	19	9	3	2	5
Group Therapy	8	4	–	–	–
Play Therapy	3	–	1	–	–

members of the multi-disciplinary team. The longest period of contact with a single child extended over the entire five years and is still ongoing (see Table 9.1).

Multiplicity of input necessitated investigation into depth as well as nature of contact. For example, 'occupational therapy' encompassed: (a) assessment; (b) therapy (usually twice per week) over an extended period which in this study was up to 18 months; (c) internal and external multidisciplinary liaison; (d) explanation for parents; (e) close liaison with education throughout and following discharge from the unit; (f) continued treatment as appropriate; and regular review over several years.

(4) INTERDISCIPLINARY WORKING

Throughout the notes there was evidence of a substantial time commitment to interdisciplinary working, but it was not possible to calculate the exact figures for this five year period. This aspect of working, however, is addressed in the three month study. Nevertheless a wide spectrum of content was apparent. This varied from minimal contact for example provision of explanation for parents; and participation in multi-disciplinary review meetings at the end of assessment period, to extensive in-depth input of long duration for example over a period of approximately 18 months, fortnightly case supervision and 12 interdisciplinary unit meetings. In addition to regular informal liaison with Lowit Unit staff, there was educational and parental contact.

(5) RESOURCE IMPLICATIONS

The nature of involvement clearly had considerable resource implications. In addition to the previously mentioned children who did not receive treatment, neither review assessments, nor attendance at meetings, was as frequent as desirable.

Three Month Study

All occupational therapy contacts with the Lowit Unit over a three month period early in 1993 were logged. In addition, further information was collated from the case notes of those children who were already known to the department when logging commenced.

Of the 11 children who had occupational therapy contact during the logging period, only one was a girl, despite there being six girls out of the total Lowit Unit occupancy of 21 over the same period:

(1) This represents 52 per cent who had occupational therapy contact. Of the remainder, one of the girls and three of the boys, however, were known to occupational therapy before the logging commenced; making a total of 15 for whom there had at some time been occupational therapy intervention.

(2) The youngest child at the time of initial occupational therapy contact during the logging period was 6 years old and the oldest 12 years 8 months.

Nature of Involvement

The 11 children with whom there was direct contact during the logging period were seen for a variety of reasons, including: motor learning, group therapy and play therapy (as in the five year study). Eight children were assessed for motor-learning difficulties, and of these three were offered regular therapy. One child was already attending for treatment. (Therapy sessions for these children totalled 19, each lasting between 30 and 60 minutes.)

In addition, two children would have benefitted from treatment had resources allowed. One child attended 10 group therapy sessions, and the remaining child had his last two play therapy sessions.

During this period no child experienced more than one type of intervention, though three had previously attended for a different mode of input.

Extent of Contact

As in the five year study, extent of contact varied. Minimum contact with any one child included assessment and feedback to parents and other members of the multi-disciplinary team via Lowit Unit meetings. In contrast some children experienced much more in-depth intervention; for example assessment, regular treatment sessions (including carryover by Lowit Unit staff), regular attendance at multi-disciplinary meetings and feedback and therapy ideas for parents and appropriate staff members. For some of these children contact will be significantly longer than the three month logging period. For example, one child who was seen regularly during this period had already been known to the department for at least one year and will continue to require ongoing intervention.

Interdisciplinary Working

The time commitment to multidisciplinary meetings was substantial. Occupational therapy staff attended a total of 14 clinical meetings, including admission/discharge, community and case review. In addition, there was participation in 11 meetings concerning an open day designed to increase awareness among other professionals of the role of child and family psychiatry. Time was also spent on in-service training for unit staff. As well as the above formal meetings, there was considerable time spent in liaison with parents and other members of the multi-disciplinary team; this included treatment sessions, feedback on progress, and provision of therapy ideas.

Resource Implications

Time commitment to administrative duties was considerable and included report writing, progress notes, telephone calls.

A total of 105 hours was committed to the Lowit Unit over this three month period. However this did not allow attendance at all relevant meetings or treatment for every child requiring occupational therapy help.

Discussion

One striking feature emerging from the three month logging is the highlighting of the extent of multi-disciplinary working which goes on within the Lowit Unit. This is clearly a setting in which professionals are keenly aware of one another's roles, leading to streamlining of cross-referrals and efficient use of resources.

In relation to the client group itself, the authors had always been aware that a very small percentage of girls were referred for therapy. This feeling was borne out in both the five year and three month studies. Given that the literature generally suggests a 2:1 ratio of boys to girls with motor/learning difficulties, and the fact that approximately 50 per cent children in the Lowit Unit are assessed for these problems, one would expect a higher proportion of girls referred to occupational therapy. Potentially there are two main reasons: (1) Referral of children with motor/learning difficulties is often precipitated by the behavioural features, whereas the majority of female admissions to the Lowit Unit seem to be due to emotional or eating disorders. (2) Previous research by one of the authors found that the ratio of girls to boys with motor/learning problems referred to RACH was considerably lower than that suggested in the literature generally. Possibly some girls are being missed because they rarely present with such striking behavioural characteristics.

This study also emphasised the relatively uncommon dual role of the occupational therapists at RACH, that is working within both general paediatrics and child and family psychiatry including a holistic approach attending to both neurodevelopmental and emotional and behavioural problems. Given that the literature links emotional/behaviour factors with specific learning difficulty and attention deficit disorders, this would seem to be a logical approach. The authors would, in fact, question the wisdom of attempting to separate the psyche from the physical in any individual; particularly a child. In fact, occupational therapy is possibly unique in attending equally to psychiatric and physical conditions in its training.

Despite recognition of the need to provide children with help for both neurodevelopmental problems and emotional and behavioural ones, current therapy resources at RACH do not allow for a complete service to child and family psychiatry. Therefore, the main focus in relation to motor/learning difficulties is on assessment; resulting in early identification, one hopes, a reduction in the emotional and behavioural features in 'at risk' children. A comparatively small percentage of time is allocated to treatment of motor/learning difficulties, and group or play therapy.

In Britain over the past decades several articles on the occupational therapist's role in specific areas of paediatrics have been published. These tend, however, to focus on mainly physical conditions (Rockey 1987), and few have considered occupational therapy input into child psychiatry. Only one reference to an in-patient unit was found by the authors. Little more appears to have been published in American rather than in the British literature and, reflecting the British pattern, most concentrate on the occupational therapist's role in paediatrics in general and give only fleeting mention to the link between physical and psychological problems (Roween and Gorga 1990). Sholle-Martin and Alessi (1990), however, address the issue of occupational therapists' role definition within child psychiatry and several authors refer to the specific assessment provided by this speciality. Jeffrey (1973) addresses the need for occupational therapy in child psychiatry and throughout her writings recognises that research and evaluation are required.

Unfortunately, neither she nor the other authors supporting this view have followed this through, though Sholle-Martin and Alessi (1990) suggest how it could be done using the model of Human Occupation (Keilhofner 1985).

More recently, one of the authors of this chapter (ES), in conjunction with a child psychiatrist and one of this volume's editors (RC), undertook research and published a number of articles on children with motor learning difficulties. Although this work did not set out to consider child psychiatry, inevitably the emotional and behavioural aspects of their problems were prominent, so providing further evidence in favour of a holistic approach by occupational therapists (Stephenson, McKay and Chesson 1990; Chesson *et al.* 1990; Stephenson *et al.* 1990; Stephenson *et al.* 1991).

The Way Forward

There is clearly a need for further research into the role and value of occupational therapy in child and family psychiatry, in addition to some of the questions emerging from this study.

Specific training in child and family psychiatry currently constitutes a minute proportion of undergraduate study, and there are a very small number of post-registration courses. Further opportunities for training are obviously essential, and could be uni- or multi-disciplinary.

Current changes include introduction of Trust status and directly managed units, the move towards community care (e.g. child development teams, currently comprising paediatricians, physiotherapists, speech and language therapists and occupational therapists), GP fundholding and the need for audit. All these changes will clearly have implications for occupational therapists working within child and family psychiatry. For example, in the longer term will the child development teams extend to include meeting the multiple needs of children such as those requiring the multi-disciplinary approach of the Lowit Unit?

A 'complete' service would offer routine occupational therapy assessment for all children in in-patient units, and treatment whenever required.

References

Axline, V.M. (1989) *Play Therapy*. Edinburgh: Churchill Livingstone.

Axline, V.M. (1990) *Dibs in Search of Self*. London: Penguin Books Ltd.

Ayres, A.J. (Ed) (1983) *Sensory Intergration and the Child*. Los Angeles: Western Psychological Services.

Chesson, R., McKay, C. and Stephenson, E. (1990) 'Motor/learning difficulties and the family.' *Child; Care Health and Development 16*, 123–138.

Chesson, R., McKay, C. and Stephenson, E. (1991) 'The consequences of motor learning difficulties for school age children and their teachers; some parental views.' *Support for Learning 6*, 4, 173–177.

Copley, B., Forryan, B. and O'Neill, L. (1987) 'Play therapy and counselling work with children.' *British Journal of Occupational Therapy 50*, 12, 413–416.

Davis, S. (1985) 'The role of the occupational therapist in child psychiatry: a case illustration.' *British Journal of Occupational Therapy 40*, 9, 266–268.

Fergus, F. and Buchanan, K. (1977) 'The use of activity groups as an integral part of O.T. in child psychiatry.' *British Journal of Occupational Therapy 40*, 4, 82–83.

Gillberg, I., Gillberg, C. and Groth, J. (1989) 'Children with preschool minor neurodevelopmental disorders. V neurodevelopmental profiles at age 13.' *Developmental Medicine and Child Neurology 31*, 14–24.

Henderson, S.E. (1987) 'The assessment of "clumsy" children: old and new approaches.' *Journal of Child Psychology and Psychiatry 28*, 4, 511–527.

Jeffrey, L. (1973) 'Child Psychiatry – the need for occupational therapy.' *Occupational Therapy 36*, 8, 429–437.

Jeffrey, L. (1982) 'Occupational therapy in child and adolescent psychiatry – the future.' *British Journal of Occupational Therapy 45*, 10, 330–334.

Jeffrey, L. (1984) 'Developmental play therapy: an assessment and therapeutic technique in child psychiatry.' *British Journal of Occupational Therapy 47*, 3, 70–74.

Jeffrey, L., Kolvin, I., Robson, M., Scott, D. and Tweddle, E. (1979) 'Generic training in the psychological management of children and adolescents.' *Journal of the Association of Workers for Maladjusted Children 7*, 1, 32–43.

Jeffrey, L., Lyne, S. and Redfern, F. (1984) 'Child and adolescent psychiatry – survey 1984.' *British Journal of Occupational Therapy 47*, 12, 370–372.

Jeffrey, L. (1990) 'Play therapy.' In J. Greek (ed) *Occuptional Therapy in Mental Health: Principal Skills and Practice*. Edinburgh: Churcill Livingstone.

Kielhofner, G. (Ed) (1985) *A Model of Human Occupation*. Baltimore, M.D: Williams and Wilkins.

McKinlay, I. and Gordon, N. (1986) 'Motor learning difficulties: "clumsy children".' In N. Gordon and I. McKinlay (eds) *Neurologically Handicapped Children*. Oxford: Blackwell.

McRae, F. (1992) *Identification of the Assessments Presently used by Occupational Therapists with Emotionally and Behaviourally Disturbed Children in Child Psychiatry*. (unpublished research project – course 28).

Miller, K. and Matthews, D. (1988) 'Setting up a ward-based group therapy programme for psychiatric in-patients.' *British Journal of Occupational Therapists 51*, 1, 22–24.

Pratt, P. and Allen, A. (1989) *Occupational Therapy for Children*. St. Louis, MO: C.V. Mosby.

Rockey, J. (1987) 'Occupational therapy for children.' *British Journal of Occupational Therapists 50*, 10, 341–342.

Royeen, C.B. and Gorga, D. (1990) 'Occupational therapy in paediatric rehabilitation.' *Paediatrician 17*, 278–282.

Shapiro, M. (1992) 'Application of the Allen cognitive level test in assessing cognitive level functioning of emotionally disturbed boys.'

American Journal of Occupational Therapy 46, 6, 514–519.

Sholle-Martin, S. and Alessi, N. (1990) 'Formulating a rota for occupational therapy in child psychiatry: a clinical application.' *American Journal of Occupational Therapy 44*, 10, 871–880.

The Scottish Office (1994) Statistics of Occupational Therapists in Scotland, 1992. Edinburgh: The Scottish Office.

Stephenson, E. and McKay, C. (1986) *The Child with Motor/Learning Difficulties – A Guide for Parents and Teachers*. Aberdeen: Occupational Therapy Department, Royal Aberdeen Children's Hospital.

Stephenson, E. and McKay, C. (1989) 'A support group for parents of children with motor/learning difficulties.' *British Journal of Occupational Therapy 52*, 5, 181–183.

Stephenson, E., McKay, C. and Chesson, R. (1990) 'An investigative study of early developmental factors in children with motor/learning difficulties.' *British Journal of Occupational Therapy 53*, 1, 4–6.

Stephenson, E., McKay, C. and Chesson, R. (1991) 'The identification and treatment of motor/learning difficulties: parents' perceptions and the role of the therapist.' *Child: Care, Health and Development 17*, 91–113.

Wardle, C. (1991) 'Twentieth century influences on the development in Britain of services for child and adolescent psychiatry.' *British Journal of Psychiatry 159*, 53–68.

CHAPTER 10

Clinical Psychologists' Involvement in Child Psychiatry Units

Leonora Harding

This chapter is concerned with the work of clinical psychologists in psychiatric units for children (aged up to 14 years). There are two main parts to the chapter; the first relates to a survey of psychologists working with children and young people throughout the UK and the second describes the work of psychologists at the Royal Aberdeen Children's Hospital in the Lowit Unit.

Clinical Psychologists' Contribution to Child Psychiatry Units Throughout the UK

There are over 200 clinical psychologists who are members of a Special Interest Group of Psychologists working with Children and Young People (under the auspices of the Clinical Division of the British Psychological Society). Some of these psychologists provide a service to child psychiatric inpatient and day patient units. The management of children in such units frequently involves psychological techniques, but we have little information as to whether these are explicit within the unit, or whether they are implicit in the unit's philosophy and working structures. In addition, there is little information on the extent and nature of the psychologists' contribution in general.

Sclare, Verduyn and Dunham Survey

There have been few surveys of the work of clinical psychologists. An exception was that carried out in 1989 for the Special Interest Group of clinical psychologists working with children and young people by Irene Sclare, Chrissie Verduyn and Madeleine Dunham. This work provides us with valuable information, although it does not focus specifically on child psychiatric units. Replies from 77 per cent of district psychologists or Head of Speciality and data from a further 14 per cent of districts provides a picture of the situation in 91 per cent of districts throughout England, Wales and Scotland. Three hundred and nine child clinical psychologists (66% female, 34% male) responded to the questionnaire about their service. At that time (1988–89) there were 434 posts of which 66 (15%) were vacant.

The majority of psychologists took referrals from many sources. A hierarchy of referral sources indicated that most referrals were in descending order from: medical personnel; other NHS professionals; social services; education; the probationary service; the voluntary sector; and self-referrals. A similar pattern occurs for the psychological service based at the Royal Aberdeen Children's Hospital where on average 40 per cent referrals are from GPs, 25 per cent through Raeden (a pre-school assessment and treatment centre), 20 per cent from paediatricians and 5 per cent from the child and family psychiatry department. Most psychologists were hospital based; 24 per cent in psychiatric hospitals, 32 per cent in general hospitals and 16 per cent in health centre or other community settings.

The response to the Sclare, Verduyn and Dunham questionnaire indicated that respondents were members of more than one multi-disciplinary team including membership of out-patient psychiatric teams (53%); child development teams (28%); child psychiatry in-patient teams (21%); and child guidance units (15%). Despite this there was an indication that team-work was a small component of the work being carried out. Indeed the multi-disciplinary team model has been questioned for child psychiatry and a unidisciplinary one put forward as making for a faster and more efficient service (Silveira, Ballard, Mohan and MacGibbon 1992). In addition, psychologists were asked to rank-order six activities in priority of involvement. The top rank was assigned to individual intervention (63%), family intervention providing a close second (62%). Other activities such as assessment and consultation were assigned lower status. The report indicated that there was a wide variety of work being undertaken in a variety of settings and no one model of service delivery was paramount. Derek Bolton's work in an adolescent psychiatry unit (Bolton 1986) also reflects this division into assessment and various therapies, with multi-disciplinary team work being emphasised in this context.

The Sclare, Verduyn and Dunham questionnaire indicated that most district services were supplied by one child psychologist only (37%), whilst 24 per cent had two psychologists, and only 23 per cent had three or more psychologists. Sixteen per cent of districts had no child clinical psychology service at the time of the survey (1987–88). The number of psychologists in post is well below the recommended level (British Psychological Society (BPS) 1993) of one per 150,000 of the population for most districts, or one per consultant psychiatrist or consultant paediatrician (Jellema 1990).

Although the Sclare, Verduyn and Dunham survey was never intended to provide data on in-patient units specifically, it highlighted the need for further knowledge in this area. It was evident, moreover, that an investigation of clinical psychologists input into units would be of considerable interest, especially since even the number working in such facilities was not known.

1992 Survey

A survey was carried out by the author in 1992. Its main aims to

(1) identify units where there was a service from clinical psychologists

(2) calculate the proportion of clinical psychologists providing a service to such units

(3) delineate the nature and extent of clinical psychology input

(4) enable comparison of the role of the Lowit Unit psychologist with that in general.

SURVEY METHODS

All members of the Special Interest Group of Clinical Psychologists working with Children and Young People were circulated with a questionnaire regarding their input to residential or day units; this included the psychologist working in the Lowit Unit. A further 20 questionnaires were sent to known child clinical psychologists in Scotland and four other known child psychiatric units. This yielded 122 replies representing a 52 per cent response rate.

Subsequently, a further letter and brief response sheet was circulated to psychologists who had not responded and a second questionnaire was forwarded on request. A further 74 replies were elicited following reminders to non-respondents, providing a 84 per cent overall response rate. The percentage response rate was 100 per cent for Scotland and 81 per cent for England and Wales. Replies from psychologists not working in child or child/adolescent psychiatric units were disregarded. For the purposes of this survey a child or child/adolescent unit was defined as one in which children and young people (aged within the range 4–14 years) attended on at least a daily basis (seven or more hours per day) or a residential basis. Where two or more psychologists replied for more than one unit, replies for the unit as a whole were considered. If there was a slight disagreement then the reply of the main worker (who spent the most time in the unit) was used.

SURVEY RESPONSE

Overall, the questionnaires indicated that there were 20 psychologists who worked in 17 child or child/adolescent psychiatric units (including the Lowit Unit). This represents a small percentage of the number of possible units (as indicated by Brown – see Appendix 1). In addition, there were replies from 18 psychologists who worked in 16 adolescent units (10–18 years) and three psychologists who made a contribution to paediatric units. Two other psychologists indicated that they occasionally had children with psychological problems admitted to medical wards. Three psychologists completed the questionnaire but it was clear that the 'unit' was an out-patient appointment-based department, so these replies were not included in this survey. There was also a reply from a psychologist where the unit had recently closed and, although it was hoped that it would re-open, this was not included either. Even though few psychologists work in units, the responses give us some interesting information regarding their role and contribution to such units.

The Nature of British Units
STATUS AND HOURS

Of the 17 units surveyed only three were purely residential and seven had both in-patients and day patients, the others (seven) were a day patient facility only (see Table 10.1). The majority were open all year, except bank holidays. The day units function from mainly 9am to 5pm, or 8am to 4 pm, five days a week, with a break for weekends. Of the 10 residential or day/residential units, four opened at weekends, four opened Monday to Friday and the other two opened Monday to Thursday. These are distributed throughout the UK.

Table 10.1. Child Psychiatric Units – Level of Service

Unit No	Type	Open Days per week	Hours	Numbers Day	Attending Residential	Ages
1	Day	5	24	NR		10–16
2	Day	5	9–5	NR		0–16
3	Day	5	9–5	10		4–12
4	Day	5	9–5	12		3–16
5	Day	5	Day	3/16		3–16
6	Day	5	8.30–3.30	8		6–16
7	Day	5	Day	Varies		<5–11
8	Day/Res	7	24	3–4	<18	Pre-school -13 $\frac{1}{2}$
9	Day/Res	7	24	Expansion Likely	12	0–12
10	Day/Res	5	24	6	6	3–14
11	Day/Res	5	24	8	8	0–13
12	Day/Res	5	24	2 variable	10	5–14
13	Day/Res	4	24	5 or 6	2	18 months upwards
14	Day/Res	5	24	20	15	0–18
15	Res	7	24	–	9	4–12
16	Res	5	24	–	8	8–15
17	Res	7	24	Occ 1 or 2	6	3–15

The ages of those attending ranged from 0 to 18 years and the numbers attending ranged from five or six up to 18 (see Table 10.1).

STAFFING

For about half the units, a child psychiatrist took overall responsibility for the unit and there were other consultant psychiatrists involved. There are a variety of other workers involved including nursing staff, teachers (at least 15 units), occupational therapists (at least 12 units), speech therapists (at least four units), and others. The 'other' category included social workers (at least 10 units), specialist teachers (for art, music and PE), nursery nurses (at least six units), psychotherapists (at least two units).

Most units surveyed had at least one psychologist involved in the unit, although many gave a part-time service (see Table 10.2)

CHILD MANAGEMENT TECHNIQUES

As can be seen from the accompanying table (Table 10.3), a variety of psychological techniques are used in the units. The most frequently described were positive reward systems incorporating star charts and rewards of staff time or material rewards (money being used as a reward only rarely). Social reward systems were also linked to systems where there was a withdrawal of attention or privilege. No unit used a token economy. Most psychologists indicated that although these techniques were used, programmes were usually designed and tailored to the individual child.

Other management techniques which were used included withdrawal of privileges such as trips to the swimming pool or outings. Incident-based problem solving approaches where particular events and their management are discussed as a team was also mentioned by two psychologists. An associated and innovative technique was the utilisation of TV recording and playback to parents and staff for discussion of management of particular children and events. Other approaches which are not strictly management approaches are also mentioned. These include: social skills training, cognitive behaviour therapy, relaxation, and psychopharmacology.

With regard to time-out and exclusion techniques, psychologists indicated that their unit had guidelines regarding their use. One psychologist mentioned that exclusion or time-out could also be removal of the child to a bed in the corridor at night time. However, the child was not left unsupervised although they might be ignored.

In linking these responses to those given, it would seem that many psychological-based management principles are utilised in these units, and in most cases (12 out of 17), the psychologist has been involved in the planning of the management policy (see Table 10.4). However, it may be (as commented on by two psychologists), that in the majority of cases, the management policy has been set by the multi-disciplinary team in general.

Table 10.2 – Unit Staffing

Unit	Day	Nursing staff Qualified	Auxiliary	Teachers	Psych-iatrists	Psycho-ologists	Nursery Nurses	Occupational Therapists	Speech & Language Therapists	Social Workers	Additional Teachers	Other
1	Day	–	–	–	1	1	–	–		1		
2	Day	–	–	–	2	1	1	–		3		CPT[1]
3	Day	6	–	1	2	2	2	1				
4	Day	4	–	1	2	2	1	3				SHOs SR
5	Day	3	–	2	3	2	–					
6	Day	2		1	2	2		1		1		
7	Day	?	?	2	1	0.5		1	0.5			
8	Day/Res	12	4	4	1	1	3	2(p/t)		1	Art/Music	
9	Day/Res	9	4	2	2	1		1		1	Yes	
10	Day/Res	6	2	1	1		1	1	little			
11	Day/Res	'lots'		4	8	1.5	1	2	2	Yes		
12	Day/Res			4	3.5	1		2	0.5	1	Art/PE	
13	Day/Res	6	–	2	2	1	2	0.5		1	Music	
14	Day/Res	20	10	3	3	2		3				
15	Res	20	1	5	4	2		1		1		
16	Res	8	4	1	3	1				1		
17	Res	8		2	6	1		–		1		Psy.T[2]

[1] Child Psycho Therapist   [2] Psycho Therapist

Table 10.3. Utilisation of Child Management Techniques

Nos of Units using Technique

	Often	Sometimes	Frequency Rarely/ Never	No Reply	Don't Know
Time out, using a time out room	–	8	5	4	–
Exclusion from the classroom	–	8	5	4	–
Exclusion or time out to a chair or place in same room	2	9	1	4	1
Exclusion or time out to a chair or place in a separate room or corridor	1	8	4	4	–
Therapeutic holding	–	9	3	5	–
Physical restraint	–	6	6	4	1
Star charts	5	8	–	4	–
Reward of time or trips with a member of staff	3	7	2	4	1
Material rewards eg sticker book, pens, badges etc	3	7	2	4	1
Monetary rewards	–	2	10	4	1
Withholding of rewards	–	6	6	4	1
Response shaping	4	5	2	5	1

UNIT PHILOSOPHY

Some units (eight of those replying) had a guiding philosophy which was outlined as incorporating some, or all of the principles outlined below. Seven psychologists did not complete this section, one indicated that the philosophy was under 'major review' and another commented that there was no agreed ethos as the two teams have quite different approaches. Although many units might have been able to give a brief clear aim had they been asked, only one unit gave a clear succinct summary of its aim that is the unit is for the short-term assessment and treatment of emotional disturbance within families.

Table 10.4. Principles Incorporated in the Unit Philosophy

(Numbers in brackets indicate numbers of respondents)

1. **Eclectic Multi-disciplinary Approach** (9)

    Holistic care, team approach, multi-disciplinary (4)

    Eclectic approach drawing in behavioural, cognitive and psychodynamic techniques (3)

    Nursing care can only be brought about within the context of a staff team where different abilities and skills are accorded with and valued (1)

    Using all possible resources (1)

2. **Environment of the Unit** (5)

    Homely atmosphere (2); A flexible and objective setting (1); Therapeutic ambience (1);

    Atmosphere of trust and confidence (1)

3. **Parenting** (5)

    Clear communication to empower parents and families to move forward (3)

    Give them parenting skills(1)

    Commitment to the family; Child seen in the context of the family (1)

4. **Family Therapy** (3)

    Incorporating Systems Approach to Treatment (2); Family Therapy (1)

5. **Clear and Consistent Care** (4)

    Individualised tailored programmes of care (2); Giving clear limits (1);

    Nursing care should be consistent (1)

6. **Developmental Context** (3)

    Within a developmental framework (1)

    Within developmental context of the family (1)

    Supportive environment for growth (1)

    Past and present life events updated facilitating change (1)

7. **Wider Context** (1)

    The unit is part of a treatment system including out-patient and community work.

Table 10.4. (continued)

8. **Emphasis on Children's Thoughts** (2)

    Human beings have a right to a loving and trusting relationship which will form a basis for them to realise their own potential (1)

    Child has own individuality and right to self expression (1)

    Child must be valued in his/her own right (1)

9. **Emphasis on Other Theoretical Approach** (1)

    Social Learning Theory

THERAPEUTIC MILIEU

The therapeutic milieu when it existed was thought to contain/encompass the features summarised in Table 10.5. This is based on nine psychologists completing this section and they referred to these features when describing the therapeutic milieu. Several made comments at times, such as 'it depends so much on individual staff' indicating that the milieu, if it existed it was not a permanent feature. This was reiterated by one other psychologist who commented that a difficult and demanding mix (of children) combined with staff shortages can render the milieu less than therapeutic. Another psychologist indicated that the milieu existed for patients but was 'not ideal for staff support'.

Table 10.5. Main features of Therapeutic Milieu identified

Feature	Numbers
Structure	4
Communication/shared experience	5
Children's interactions; children/staff or peer group support	3
Staff	5
Approaches used	8
Special groups	2
Liaison external agencies/parental involvement	2

CLINICAL PSYCHOLOGISTS CONTRIBUTION TO THE MANAGEMENT OF THE UNIT

From the responses most of the 17 units covered had some clinical psychology input as is evident from Table 10.2.

The amount of psychology service given, however, varied from close to nil right through to 100 per cent (see Table 10.6). Clinical psychologists are involved in the organisation and running of the unit in the majority of cases, although they are not usually involved in the management of all patients (see Table 10.7).

Table 10.6. Psychologists' Involvement in the Units

Unit No	Type	Nos of Psychologists	% WTE
1	Day	1	100
2	Day	1	50
3	Day	2	10
4	Day	2	10
5	Day	2	30
6	Day	2	10
7	Day	1	50
8	Day/Res	1	10
9	Day/Res	1	20
10	Day/Res	1	Consultation Only
11	Day/Res	2	50
12	Day/Res	1	30
13	Day/Res	1	Minimal
14	Day/Res	2	60
15	Res	2	30
16	Res	1	50
17	Res	1	25

Many psychologists recognised that their input was minimal and expressed the view that they would like (and others would like) it to be more. Many said that they could not complete parts of the questionnaire because of lack of knowledge through minimal involvement. There are in addition several known units where there was no response from a clinical psychologist. We do not know the level of psychological service to these units.

Two psychologists indicated that they (as well as other professionals including nurses) might be principal case holder and that (although working with others) they would be professionally responsible for the care. With regard to psychometric assessment, several psychologists commented that they only carried out such assessments occasionally. Similarly, behavioural observations were often carried out by trainees. Six psychologists made general comments to the effect that the unit was run by a multi-disciplinary team, of which they were a member and which was run democratically, both with regard to management and with regard to therapy. Psychological principles of management are discussed in general in such meetings and also with regard to specific children, treatment being tailored to fit each child in many cases. Although psychologists are actively involved in devising behavioural treatment pro-

Table 10.7. Clinical Psychologists' Contribution to Running of Unit

Contribution	Yes	No	No reply	Other
Attend management meetings	15	1	1	
Attend admissions/discharge meetings	14	1	1	1
Attend case reviews for *all* patients	6	8	3	
Attend case reviews for some patients	12	1	4	
Observe and review behaviour of individual children	14	1	2	
Devise (in consultation with nursing and other staff) individual programmes for behavioural management	13	1	1	
Carry out psychometric assessments	13	1	1	
Engage in family therapy meetings	14	3		
Engage in individual play therapy	10	6	1	
Contribute to staff development through teaching	14	0	3	
Involvement in planning general ward management policy	12	4	0	1 (very occasionally)

grammes, unit managers supervise their implementation and nurses in general implement them. Psychologists are largely involved in teaching programmes and behavioural workshops.

In the area of therapy, one psychologist commented that they contributed to the development of any psychotherapeutic procedures not just behavioural ones. In the 'other' category, psychologists responded that they were involved in children's groups, the supervision of groups, staff/children community meetings, assessments for admission, case management, liaison with other agencies and family therapy within the unit.

PROBLEMS IN SUPPLYING A PSYCHOLOGICAL SERVICE TO THE UNIT

Only replies from three units indicated that there were no problems. The main problem cited involved resources. Time and pressure of work was mentioned in eight cases and this included the distance a person had to travel to the unit from the usual place of work, preventing 'popping in'. Staffing problems in general were mentioned by five psychologists, finance in general by one and level of psychology staffing by one. One mentioned that there was no established post for the unit, time was 'borrowed from out-patient work'. Grouping all these categories together as a general resource deficit, psychologists from twelve units mentioned this as a problem.

The second general problem which was mentioned by eight psychologists involved working relationships between staff. This was mainly expressed as certain people dictating a policy which was sometimes said to have been in existence too long, or certain people not communicating well or being in competition. The people identified in these cases were: psychiatrist (four times), and the charge nurse (three times). Two psychologists expressed this problem more generally as 'the usual multi-disciplinary team tensions', or 'problem in the relationship with different professionals'.

One psychologist indicated a slightly different problem which was that he/she felt that pressure of time led to an over-emphasis on individual work with children rather than emphasis on the team and training them in psychological principles. This respondent also indicated that the questionnaire had prompted a re-thinking of the psychological input to the unit with perhaps a re-orientation towards behavioural technique training.

OTHER COMMENTS

There were few other comments in response to the questionnaire although two people indicated that they had given a poor quality response for reasons beyond their control (for example the maternity leave of a key worker). Other comments came from psychologists working in four units, and these were: mention of involvement of other agencies (e.g. 'educational psychology', regular discussions with members of other agencies attending); importance of the school and school staff; psychology input.

The following comment typifies the replies in this section: *'Less psychology input than formerly – not a good use of psychologist's time. Only able to provide a token service, would like to provide more.'*

It is also relevant to comment here that one respondent who was not supplying a service said that they had pulled out of the unit for various reasons. On the other hand, three people, who were not supplying a service, indicated that there was local interest in such provision and they might have input in the future.

Although clinical psychologists do not have overall responsibility for the running of units or day to day decision making, they do make a contribution as part of the multi-disciplinary team to the total organisation. In the main they see themselves as providing specific input (mainly of a therapeutic nature) to the management of individual cases.

However, psychology as a theoretical discipline pervades the units through child management principles, therapeutic techniques and the philosophy/guiding principles used in the units.

Clinical Psychology Contribution to the Lowit Unit

Fluctuating staff levels in the psychology department of the Royal Aberdeen Children's Hospital and in the Lowit Unit have meant that the contribution of clinical psychology has varied from year to year (see Table 10. 8).

Although clinical psychology input has varied between 5 per cent and 50 per cent of one psychologist in terms of time commitment, the number of children seen accounts for a small percentage of referrals to clinical psychology services for children and young people, based at the Royal Aberdeen Children's Hospital. It is difficult to determine the extent to which the contribution of psychology will be affected by the developments of trust status for the Aberdeen Royal Hospitals and together with increasing accountability of staff, the costing of services, and the development of service level agreements. At the time of writing there is no service level agreement to Child and Family Psychiatry and it seems likely that development here will be responsive to our work load in other areas.

At present there are about 12 to 20 children referred a year from the Lowit Unit, which represents 3–5 per cent of all referrals to the Psychology Department (see Table 10.9a). Two or three children per year are referred in the reverse direction, that is, from Psychology to the Lowit Unit. The problems presented by these children are varied although there remains a majority of children with behavioural difficulties (see Table 10.9b).

Psychologists have always attended all relevant unit meetings and one psychologist has taken over the role of main liaison person for this. Relevant meetings include the Admissions/Discharge Meeting, the Administration Meeting, Community Meeting, In-Service Planning Meeting and the Lowit Forum. Psychologists have also made contributions to small working groups from time to time, for example a working group for the time-out policy; working group for revision of the Community Meeting; working group on the revision of the Admission/Discharge Meeting. Psychologists are also involved in all case review meetings for children with whom they are involved. Our national survey indicated in fact that 75 per cent of psychologists were involved in ward planning and management (see Table 10.7).

The psychology staff have made a major contribution to teaching two or three day workshops per year for unit staff with topics ranging from behavioural methods to play and child development. This reflects again in part the national survey, where most psychologists contributed to teaching.

Table 10.8 – Clinical Psychology Input to the Lowit Unit – January 1987 – January 1993

Date Starting	Overall Staffing	Psychologists Involved	Number of Psychologists Involved	% of one Psychologist's time (one WTE)	Referral System	Physical Presence
Jan 1987	4.1 WTE	All potentially involved	5	60%	By request or previous involvement in the case	Two offices in Unit
July 1988	4.1 WTE	All potentially involved	5	50%	By request or previous involvement in the case	One office
Late 1988/ Early 1989	4.1 WTE	Two psychologists involved	2	60%	Potential input to all cases psychologist attended pre-intake meeting for each case	One office (not of psychologist involved in Unit)
Dec 1990	3.0 WTE	One psychologist involved	1	30%	Potential input to all cases. Psychologist attended pre-intake meeting for each case	One office (not of psychologist involved in Unit)
April 1991	3.0 WTE	One psychologist involved (loss of psychology staff in general led to reduced input)	1	5%	By consultation only (Lowit Unit Day Status much of the time)	No offices in Unit
Sept 1991	4.4 WTE	Two psychologists	2	40%	Potential input to all cases	No offices in Unit
Sept 1992	4.1 WTE	One psychologist involved (loss of staff and rationalisation of department)	1	40%	Potential input to all cases	No offices in Unit

Table 10.9a. Psychological Involvement in Lowit Unit Cases

Year	Nos in Unit	Nos seen	Nos of clinical psychologists with unit input
1987	14	10	4
1988	17	13	5
1989	18	14	2
1990	24	21	2
1991	17	14	2

Table 10.9b. Type of Problem Involving Clinical Psychologist
(Main Problem Recorded)

Year	Anorexic	Behaviour Problem	School Phobia/ Anxiety	Enuresis/ Encopresis	Hyper- activity	Other* or DK	Total
1987	1	6	–	–	2	1	10
1988	–	6	1	3	2	1	13
1989	–	7	2	3	–	2	14
1990	–	12	1	1	–	7	21
1991	1	8	–	1	2	2	14
Total	2	39	4	8	6	13	72

* ('other' category includes sexual abuse; panic attacks; ? psychotic; parent/child problem; depression; learning difficulty)

The Role of the Clinical Psychologist in the Lowit Unit
The psychologist's contribution to the unit's work is threefold:

(1) assessment

(2) behavioural management

(3) family and individual work.

which are considered in more detail below.

ASSESSMENT

(a) *Behavioural observations both general and for specific behaviours*

Direct observations are seen as particularly useful in the assessment of hyperactivity, where the sampling approach is used but they might also be carried out for other behaviours and interactions. Behavioural check-lists, such as those of Rutter (Rutter 1967; Rutter, Tizard and Whitmore 1970), Conners (Goyette, Conners and Ulrich 1978) and observation charts which other team members might be asked to complete, would also fall under this category.

(b) *Psychometric assessment*

This includes the range from intellectual assessment and attainment in reading, writing and number/maths to the assessment of specific learning difficulties, for example visual motor deficits; memory and distractibility. The psychologist is likely to liaise with other people (for example class teacher, educational psychologist) in this area.

(c) *Other possible assessments*

These include assessing family relations, personality, anxiety and attachment assessment.

BEHAVIOURAL MANAGEMENT

This is usually based on the assessments referred to previously. Individual programmes are devised either following a review meeting or in consultation with the staff (or both). Programmes include: management of tantrums; non-compliance and other undesirable behaviour; programmes for eating disorders; management of encopresis; desensitisation programmes for anxiety problems (for example school phobia). The programmes are usually changed over time to encourage shaping of the child's behaviour.

Of course behavioural management occurs as part of daily ward management (e.g. eating and other routines) and there are specific techniques used here (e.g. exclusion, time-out, restraint, therapeutic holding). As a department there has been some input to the time-out policy, but we have not, so far, been involved in discussion on other management techniques.

FAMILY AND INDIVIDUAL WORK

Since it is part of our role to empower parents, we are occasionally involved in task-related family therapy and behavioural management work with parents. However, this direct work with families and parents is less pronounced than in our out-patients work (see Table 10.10). Similarly, children are sometimes seen by a psychologist in their own right for individual therapy. This can be counselling, management of anxiety, cognitive therapy, individual social skills or other work.

Comparison with Other Units

These interventions are very similar to those carried out by clinical psychologists in the units covered by the survey (see Table 10.7). Assessment was infrequently carried out by most psychologists, yet it is a fairly frequent part of the work in the Lowit Unit. However, although the types of psychological intervention carried out in the Lowit unit are similar to those carried out by psychologists in other parts of the country, many units (possibly up to 88%) have no psychologist attached and therefore the Lowit Unit is atypical in this respect.

Table 10.10 gives an indication of the number and types of intervention entered into by psychologists through the years 1987–1992. In effect, one child may have several types of treatment, including several interventions by the child psychologist. One type of intervention may lead to another, for example observations lead to behaviour management programmes, assessments lead to teaching methods, family or personality assessment lead to family therapy sessions.

Table 10.10. Type of Psychological Intervention

	1987	1988	1989	1990	1991
Case co-ordination	2	1	3	1	1
Psychometric assessment	1	3	3	3	4
Family or personality assessment	3	2	2	2	–
Observations	6	7	9	1	5
Behavioural programme	6	8	10	6	4
Individual work	2	–	1	–	–
Consultation only	1	1	2	2	3
Other*	1	–	1	3	2
Total	22	22	31	25	19

* ('other' category includes involvement in family therapy meetings; behavioural work with parents; parent–child relationship sessions; social skills group)

The work carried out in the Lowit Unit is limited when compared with the role psychologists have when treating children referred as out-patients. Professional autonomy is also reduced by this restriction of our role and in its place we have a multi-disciplinary therapeutic team. The multi-disciplinary team versus a unidisciplinary approach has been much discussed of late and the future of the multi-disciplinary approach has been linked with the necessity for psychiatrists to give up their leadership positions (Cottrell 1993). The multi-disciplinary approach can be difficult, for example, in developing a therapeutic behavioural programme many nursing staff, teachers, psychologists and psychiatrists may have different viewpoints. Obtaining a consensus or compromise is very difficult to achieve because of the potential numbers of members of the multi-disciplinary team and their intraprofessional conflicts.

Case Studies Relating to Psychological Intervention

The type of work the psychologist may undertake is given by two case examples (given in Boxes 10.1 and 10.2). It should be noted that these are hypothetical cases based on two or three children per case. Names and other personal details have been changed in order to maintain the anonymity of the client. The cases illustrate the sequence of activities that take place in an individual child's treatment and the extent to which psychological interventions are linked to interventions by other members of the team.

Box 10.1

Julie Mitchell Aged 9 years 6 months

Background

Julie was first seen by the paediatrician as she was admitted to one of the medical wards with specific pains. She was extremely anxious and screamed and cried a lot about the pains and being separated from her mother.

Psychological intervention	**(Interventions by others in the team)**
1. Relaxation training) } 2. Observations)	Programme for separation from mother and reducing crying
3. Assessment of family relations	Family therapy by other members of the team
4. Individual play and work aimed at exploring and diminishing anxieties	
5. Assessment of intelligence and attainments	Communication with unit teachers
6. Following up contacts with home, school and educational psychologist	

Julie's problems had been precipitated by the move of her older brother to secondary school. Always inclined to be off school for minor illnesses, it seems likely that the new loss of security meant that Julie could only feel a bit secure when ill. Yet she could not be ill for any length of time – hence her escape into the illness behaviour of severe aches and pains. Similar to school phobia, Julie had intense separation anxiety when away from her mother and this link was used to assist Julie to reduce her screaming and crying (if Julie managed to use the relaxation tape and not cry for a period of time, then she could see her mother). This was carried out by ward staff in the main. Assessment of the family relations was carried out using the Family Relations Test (Bene-Anthony 1965) by the psychologist and family dynamics were assessed by the psychiatrist.

There were indications that this was a family whose members were considerably involved with each other and who did not acknowledge conflicts and bad feelings. In the longer term, family therapy helped to change the family dynamics and enable Julie to express her feelings more directly within the family. This was paralleled with individual play therapy for Julie to encourage the expression and acceptance of anxieties and aggression as being normal and acceptable feelings.

Throughout this period Julie had been attending the ward school and the teachers indicated that possibly Julie was not as able as other members of her family and that parental expectations might be too high (one parent is a teacher and the other a high ranking civil servant). Psychometric assessment did indeed indicate that this was the case and this information was given to the parents by the psychiatrist, who also discussed Julie's strengths and problems of acceptance.

As Julie's self-esteem and independence developed she became ready for discharge into the community. As is normal practice in the unit, Julie was reintegrated gradually into school with considerable liaison with the educational psychologist, between Lowit teacher and teacher at school and support and continuing treatment was given to the child on an out-patient basis (social worker and psychiatrist).

Stephen is the youngest child in a family of three and has two older sisters, both of whom were doing very well at school. Stephen was known to the psychiatrist who thought him an unusual child in many ways. The main problem for which he was referred was severe behavioural problems both at home and at school, including kicking and hitting others. He also appeared to be rather clumsy and boisterous. Initial psychometric assessments were carried out by the clinical psychologist and occupational therapist and indicated that Stephen had gross motor difficulties (occupational therapy assessment) but that also his attainments (especially reading and writing) were well below what one could expect from his IQ (which was well above average). Further assessment of his reading difficulty indicated that he had largely visual-motor problems and the best approach to reading for Stephen might be through a phonics or multi-sensory approach. Discussion with the teacher involved with Stephen enabled this approach to be put into practice. The occupational therapist also followed up assessment with a motor programme, carried out by her in conjunction with nursing staff.

Simultaneously with these assessments, Stephen had been observed by ward staff and after an initial 'honeymoon period' some of his behavioural difficulties began to show, although the kicking and hitting behaviours were no longer in evidence (possibly because the structured nature of the ward with strict behavioural limits was unlike that of home). Observations showed that Stephen often swore at people when asked to do something (although he complied) and at other children when they were working near him. He wanted to do well and especially to please his teacher, and this motivation was utilised in a reward schedule incorporating a star-chart for periods of time when little swearing was seen (two minor swears allowed per time period), and exclusion from the classroom (when swearing became excessive and continued to occur despite three warnings). If Stephen had three good time periods in a day he obtained a reward of a visit to the Activity Room with a member of the nursing staff in the evening.

Throughout this time the family had been seen by the psychiatrist and one member of the nursing staff and they requested a family assessment. It was thought that Stephen was rather a precocious child, but assessment also showed that he had little regard for his mother although he had high positive regard for his father who was away a great deal. Stephen's mother had not acknowledged her problem with Stephen initially, but the family therapy enabled her to express her difficulties. She accepted help in the form of relationship play therapy with Stephen with use of video camera and 'bug in ear' (the parent–child game) and management advice directly to Stephen's mother. This helped them to develop a stronger bond.

As Stephen's behaviour improved, the programme was amended so that Stephen had to not swear at all during designated time periods and had to obtain more successful time periods per day to get his reward (this is in accordance with the principle of response shaping).

Over the period of time on the unit, Stephen's behaviour improved, he had a better relationship with his mother and other members of the family and he had made progress in school. He was a more confident child with high self-esteem. He was integrated back into his school very gradually with much liaison between the teaching staff on the unit and those at school.

Commentary on Case Studies
These cases are by no means typical, nor are they atypical. Each child brings with him or her many potentials and problems. It is through the work of the

Box 10.2

Stephen Elliot Aged 7 years 6 months

Background

Stephen had severe behavioural problems which included kicking and hitting other people (both adults and children) and frequent swearing and shouting. He was behind in school work and was thought to have other learning difficulties.

Psychological Intervention	Interventions by others in the team
1. Assessment of level of intelligence and attainment	linked with assessment and treatment by OTs
2. Further assessment of reading difficulty	linked with teaching methods
3. Observations of swearing behaviour	linked with reward schedule for good behaviour and exclusion schedule for swearing (nursing staff)
4. Family relations assessment	linked with family therapy (other team members)
5. Amendments to programme	Carried out by nursing staff
6. Relationship play therapy with mother	
7. Programme terminated	
– discharged	

team in the Lowit Unit that we hope to enhance the child's development, potential and adjustment. In coming to the Lowit Unit the child is, to some extent, taken from their normal environment of family, school and friends. This enables us to help the child whilst working with the parents and other family members (if appropriate) in order to facilitate better relationships for the child in the future.

Final Conclusions

The clinical psychologist has a significant contribution to make to child psychiatric in-patient units. Psychologists are able to offer a wide range of assessment procedures and therapies, and as behavioural principles are endemic in the role of the unit they have an important role in the organisation and management of the unit.

However, our survey reported earlier would indicate that, in most units, the contribution of the psychologist is absent or partial. When this occurs, therefore, the behavioural input may be either missing or lack in detailed theoretical knowledge. Partial input from psychologists may well mean that they are not able to function fully as part of the multi-disciplinary team. Communication may become more difficult and, as a consequence, interpersonal conflict is more likely and concomitantly the therapeutic milieu will suffer. The reasons why the psychologist's input is partial or lacking may be many and varied, but three main difficulties seem paramount.

First, the psychologists are independent professionals, who have their own professional working practices and case load. The contribution to the child psychiatric in-patient unit is only a part and a relatively small part of this case load. Psychologists may feel that their main priority is for patients who have no other professional involvement and for whom they are the *only* therapist. Children in in-patient units are well endowed with therapists, including a psychiatrist; therefore, psychologists may regard unit children as less of a priority than out-patient or other (for example paediatric) in-patient services. As resources become increasingly stretched, these arguments may become reinforced by managerial decision-making.

Second, a child psychologist is an autonomous professional in other spheres of life. He/she is likely to carry out a variety of assessment and therapeutic techniques with an individual child/child and their family. As we have seen, the professional input to a child psychiatry unit is often limited to assessment and behavioural management with the other therapeutic work being undertaken by other professionals. Behavioural psychologists do not usually have the main professional responsibility to the case, this being undertaken by the psychiatrist involved. Hence professional autonomy is limited or absent in this setting and this may be a strong reason why psychologists are not willing to be more involved in the work.

Finally, communication between people in behavioural and family issues is always difficult. People, even professionals, bring with them their own history as well as professional expertise from different theoretical stances. When many people are involved in the case of a child, it is difficult for all to meet, and even more difficult for them to gain a consensus viewpoint. Compromises may be inadequate because a half-way stage may be inappropriate treatment for a child. One or another treatment from the different theoretical viewpoint may have a better chance of being successful. It may be that psychologists do not wish to muddy the already not very clear waters of the treatment plans for the children on these units. A case of 'too many cooks spoil the broth'.

Despite the problematic nature of the psychologist's input, it would seem desirable that there is clinical psychology involvement in a unit. Clearly the need thus exists for the clarification of the role and the development of appropriate working practices. It would be useful if future research could identify units where models of good practice exist and evaluate their transferability.

References

Bene, E. and Anthony, J. (1965) *Family Relations Test* (children's version). Slough: NFER/Nelson.

Bolton, D. (1986) 'The clinical psychologist in adolescent psychiatry.' In D. Steinberg. *The Adolescent Unit.* Chichester: Wiley.

The British Psychological Society (1993) *Purchasing Clinical Psychology Services.* Briefing Paper No 1. Services for children, young people and their families. Leicester: The British Psychological Society.

Cottrell, D. (1993) 'In defence of multi-disciplinary teams in child and adolescent psychiatry.' *Psychiatric Bulletin 17,* 733–735.

Goyette, C.H., Conners, C.K. and Ulrich, R.F. (1978) 'Normative data on revised Conners parent and teacher rating scales.' *Journal of Abnormal Clinical Psychology 6,* 221–236.

Jellema, M. (1990) 'Clinical psychology forum.' No 26, 29. Leicester: The *British Psychological Society.*

Rutter, M. (1967) 'A children's behaviour questionaire for completion by teachers: preliminary findings.' *Journal of Child Psychology and Psychiatry 8,* 1–11.

Rutter, M., Tizard, J. and Whitmore, K. (eds) (1970) *Education, Health and Behaviour.* London: Longmans.

Sclare, I., Verduyn, C. and Dunham, M. (1989) *Preliminary Report Concerning Child Clinical Psychology Services in Great Britain.* Report of the Special Interest Group of Clinical Psychologists working with children and young people. (available from I Sclare, Guys Hospital, London).

Silveira, W.R., Ballard, C.G., Mohan, R.N.C. and MacGibbon, L. (1992) 'Is there a case for unidisciplinary working in child psychiatry?' *Psychiatric Bulletin 16,* 34–35.

CHAPTER 11

Social Work – Child and Family Psychiatry – The Lowit Unit

Nan Riddell and Ronnie Wilson

In 1959 a psychiatrist and a psychiatric social worker, with the backing and encouragement of the then Professor of Mental Health, persuaded the management of the Royal Aberdeen Sick Children's Hospital that it would be a worthwhile project to develop a psychiatric service for children. This male psychiatrist and female social worker had worked and trained together in adult psychiatry in Edinburgh and Aberdeen.

Initially, the department of child psychiatry offered a very part-time service, two days per week. The psychiatrist saw a child, while the social worker worked with the parent, usually the mother. This conjoint working, with the psychiatrist undertaking the psychotherapeutic work with the child and the social worker counselling and advising the parent, very quickly became established and expanded. Other agencies and disciplines became involved. Links were developed with child care agencies, the Local Authority Children's Department and voluntary agencies. Clinical psychology was beginning also to become established within the hospital.

Expertise, based on experience, and incorporating strands of a psychodynamic approach and the behaviourist theories from psychology was developed.

The department became firmly established with the opening of the out-patient block in the early 1960s and was further expanded a few years later.

At the time of writing, when financial restraints, cutbacks and perceived threats to services seem all pervasive, it is hard to imagine the enthusiasm, optimism and service expansion of that period. With the opening of the in-patient ward and the inclusion of a 'school', teaching became another profession involved, joining the multi-disciplinary group, which included occupational therapy, clinical psychology and speech therapy.

From the start, the ward had been established as a five day in-patient unit, operating from Sunday afternoon/evening through to Friday afternoon. The bridging/linking role of the social worker between the family and the ward was established from the start. The social worker would frequently be there to welcome parents with their children when they were returning after the weekend. Any problems or difficulties could therefore be dealt with at a time when feelings were still fresh. This involvement also enabled staff to develop insights into how the family coped or survived with the child that they then had to work with for the rest of the week. The social work role has always been to provide a broad perspective on the child who is in the ward considering him or her in relation to school, family and community. This stemmed from the belief that children cannot be treated in isolation from their social situation. For the child receiving in-patient treatment this necessarily includes both the ward environment and the social context he came from and to which he will return.

From these early days more than 30 years ago, social work itself has undergone considerable changes in its structure and practice, and approach to providing a service. Initially, the 'psychiatric' social workers worked within the department of child psychiatry (later child and family psychiatry) while an 'almoner' still operated within the other parts of the hospital. Services developed in child and family psychiatry in the first place because of the multi-disciplinary approach there. As a result of the social work commitment to the concept of a co-ordinated approach throughout the whole hospital, the balance became more equitable over recent years and may have swung more in favour of providing a service to children and families with a greater emphasis on welfare and counselling, acknowledging the stresses and anxieties experienced by many families as a result of the child's admission and illness.

Practice and structural links have been established also between the hospital and a nearby pre-school assessment centre. Similar links were established with the more recently founded young people's department located within adult psychiatry on a separate site. Additional practice links are also acknowledged between the adjacent maternity hospital, particularly the neo-natal unit.

Social work linkages, however, reflect the multi-disciplinary approach developed which involves psychiatrists, paediatricians, psychologists, physiotherapists, speech and language therapists and teachers.

When a psychiatric service was being developed within the hospital, social work training was still very much in its infancy and the profession not perceived as a homogeneous group. With the advent of the Kilbrandon Report (1966) recommending generic, all purpose social work departments, the social work training together with the development of qualification based education started to take off. The 1968 Social Work (Scotland) Act gave the profession the legal footing it required to work constructively with children and families using compulsory measures as necessary. This act, through the development of the Hearing System, was a watershed in the treatment of children and young people who were in trouble or requiring care and protection. The welfare principle was also given primacy, including in the management of offenders, in that any decisions taken at children's hearings relating to children had to be seen to be in their best interests.

Another significant milestone for the development of social work in a hospital setting occurred in 1975. In May of that year, local government was re-organised to establish very large regional authorities which were mandated to provide major services such as education and social work. Prior to that time, social workers within hospitals were directly employed by the hospital/Health Authority. From then on all hospital-based social workers were incorporated into the management structures of these very large local authority departments.

This had a very significant affect on the structures and practices of the social workers involved. A much more clearly defined hierarchical system developed. The social work service became independent of the other disciplines within the hospital setting. There were significant new statutory child care responsibilities to be assumed by these social workers. As part of the wider social work department, social workers now had a direct responsibility to deal with all non-accidental injury, child abuse and child protection situations. They also had a direct responsibility to deal directly with the Hearing System, and thus compulsory measures of care became an additional therapeutic tool in dealing with some children and families over the wide range of grounds of referral to the Hearing System.

These developments clearly enabled the social work team based within the Children's Hospital to forge more direct links between the hospital and their colleagues in the community. The social work team within the children's hospital has, therefore, been spending a considerable amount of energy in developing and attempting to maintain links across a number of directions, both within and outwith the hospital. Tensions and stresses involved in trying to maintain some kind of balance while acknowledging the need to prioritise has inevitably led to a situation where the balance is never quite right; the demand or perceived need to provide a service in one area inevitably has led to the diminution of a service in another area. This is considered unavoidable in any 'dynamic' system.

As part of the process of review it was recognised that the approach to working within the ward (latterly the Lowit Unit) was leading to a significantly poorer quality of service therein. As a result, in 1988, a social worker was identified to have a specific remit in the unit. The inevitable changes, due to fluctuating pressures, however, have meant that this worker has never been exclusively dedicated: nevertheless, very close links have been maintained. The same approach of providing practice links between the ward, the child, the family and the outside community as was established at the very early days of the ward was seen still as a significant role of social work in this setting.

Over the years social work practice has had a direct influence on practices within the ward. In line with social work practice of involving parents and children in child care reviews, it eventually became accepted that parents should be at all review meetings concerning their child's assessment and future care. Children may also be involved. It is arguable that the systems of admissions and developing care plans with clear purposes can be traced to the influence of the same child care review systems. There was little doubt that such fundamental changes were necessary and were inevitably to occur. Each child was the responsibility of a psychiatrist who developed his or her own care plan. Although systems theories were being widely used to help families change and function more effectively the 'family' of the ward could appear to be somewhat ignored.

Over time many of these issues have been slowly and, at times, painfully addressed (and for an account of current developments see Chapter 5). It is, perhaps, in the nature of things that change comes about slowly and is resisted. Given that it can be seen in the families that we deal with, why should we be surprised when we, too, are resistant? It is to be hoped, however, that the advice given to families when they seek help prevails – to maintain a focus on the child, and to consider that which is in the child's best interest.

While the future must lie in all the various child care systems becoming much more integrated as parts of an overall child care strategy, it is at times very hard to envisage this occurring. Numerous barriers appear to exist within, and between, systems. Although different agencies are at different stages of development, there are common features in that all are feeling pre-occupied with and overwhelmed by the task in hand. It is, therefore, difficult to achieve a broader perspective of the scene.

It is acknowledged that often there is a random element in the way in which some children and families end up seeking services from one agency as opposed to another. There are differences in detail but the commonality of difficulty and reasons for looking for, or being sent for, help is substantial. The reasons behind an admission to the Lowit Unit or into care can broadly be similar in a large number of cases, as can even the purpose for an admission. The resources available to the Lowit Unit are potentially greater than most children's homes can have at hand, both in terms of assessing need and difficulty, and developing therapeutic plans. Child care resources are generally quite scarce. There is a distinct perception of crises and general low morale across the board. Many workers within units and teams, especially in the residential setting, can feel deskilled and isolated. It is, therefore, vitally important that these groups can be able to link up more effectively to provide a service to the common client. Those responsible for planning the provision of services must be able to lift their eyes away from the apparently omnipresent crisis to broader horizons.

In the following case study, social work involvement with the family is highlighted, as is also the interaction between the child's and parent's difficulties.

A Case Study

Children admitted to the Lowit Unit are generally those whose behaviour poses a fairly immediate threat to their safety or wellbeing or, more usually, those where the behaviour has persisted over a long period and remained resistant to outpatient treatment or community-based intervention. By the time a child comes into the unit parents have often become just as 'stuck' as the children and an admission offers the opportunity for all members of the family to break the patterns of interaction which may have been contributing to or maintaining the child's difficulty. Successful treatment outcomes depend not only on change in the behaviour of the child but also in parents' ability to accommodate this change. In some cases, however, admission to the Lowit Unit can establish that such changes are not possible for a family and that a child's interests may be best served by him being cared for in a situation other than at home with his parents. The following is an example of such a case.

Mike was 13 years old when first admitted to the Lowit Unit. At the time of admission he had been unable to attend school for several months and was also presenting considerable management problems for his parents. Mike was the younger of the two sons of Mr and Mrs S. and lived with them and his elder brother, Peter (then aged 15 years) in an area of the city fairly deprived in terms of social and recreational facilities, but where there was a strong sense of community. The S. family were well known and well integrated in the neighbourhood.

At the time of admission to the unit, a social worker had been working with the family over a long period, at times with professionals from other disciplines. When Mike was admitted to the Unit, I (NR) assumed responsibility for his case and for the Compulsory Domiciliary Supervision Requirement of which he was subject, and which included a condition that Mike should remain in the Lowit Unit from Monday to Friday each week and return to his parents' care each weekend.

Mike in the Lowit Unit

Somewhat to the surprise of everyone concerned with Mike and his family, there was not the difficulty that had been anticipated in effecting his separation from home nor, for the first few weeks of his admission, were there any problems in getting him to return to the unit after his weekends at home. After a prolonged absence which began six weeks after his admission, due initially to a legitimate medical condition, the pattern of Mike managing to return to the unit each week appeared to have been broken and, following this, there was never any certainty that he would return when expected each week. Although Mr and Mrs S. were committed to his being in the unit, there were often times when their efforts were not enough to ensure his return.

When in the unit, Mike presented for the most part as an agreeable and likeable boy with a good sense of humour who entered into the activities of the unit with enthusiasm. It was soon recognised, however, that despite his appearance of bravado, Mike was a fairly anxious boy who was functioning in many areas – educationally, socially and emotionally – at the level of a much younger child. It was soon evident, too, that he was a boy who did not like to be thwarted and at times he resorted to various strategies, from sulking to running off from the unit or threatening to do himself harm in his attempts to have his demands met. Over time Mike became more able to accept what was required of him by staff when clear and firm guidelines were given. Despite this Mike's difficulty in returning to the unit continued throughout the time of his admission. Members of the team who were working directly with Mike and his family found it difficult to sort out how much his difficulty was due to a basic anxiety, perhaps in relation to his worry about what might be happening at home in his absence, and how much it was due to Mike's well entrenched pattern of resisting anything with which he was not in agreement.

Work with Parents

Throughout the time of Mike's admission, his parents remained supportive of his placement in the unit although, as mentioned previously, they were unable at times to ensure his return. Work done with parents involved looking with them in some detail at their families of origin and at how their own experiences of parenting were contributing to some of the difficulties they were experiencing with Mike.

Since Mike's difficulty in managing to attend and remain in the unit, just as it had been in school, seemed to be fairly directly related to his need to be at home with parents it seemed reasonable to try to establish why this family's system made it difficult for Mike to manage anything that required him to be separated from his home.

Parental Histories

Mrs S. presented as a warm and caring person whose concern for others extended well beyond her immediate family. She appeared to be the unofficial babysitter for the area in which the family lived and admitted with pride that she would 'never say no' if she could help someone in any way, especially where children were concerned. While there was undoubtedly a genuine desire to help others in what she did, Mrs S.'s 'never' saying no' may have had origins in her own harsh upbringing.

When Mrs S. was about eight years old her mother began to suffer recurring mental illness which required her to be hospitalised for long periods and during these times Mrs S. had taken on a major responsibility for her younger siblings. Though Mrs S. was able to talk easily and at length about most aspects of her life, her relationship with her father was a subject which she found hard to discuss except to say that she hated him. She could instance memories which still caused her hurt, for example how her father would give her sister money for bus fares to school while she was required to walk. She could also recall how her father would require her to rise very early to attend to domestic chores. Though Mrs S. would state simply that she 'loved kids and would do anything for them', it seemed likely that her inability to say no, especially where children were concerned, stemmed in part at least from her own feelings of hurt and rejection. When this hypothesis was transferred to her own children, it was not difficult to understand the great difficulty she had in imposing limits on them, or indeed in denying any of their demands.

Mr S.'s background, too, was not one that had equipped him well for the requirements of parenthood. An only child, with a father who went to sea, Mr S. appeared to have been very close to and very influenced by his mother. Even after his marriage when he was in his early forties, Mr S. had continued to visit his mother daily before going to work and Mrs S. could recall her resentment of the intrusion by her mother-in-law in the early years of the couple's marriage and which had continued until her death when Mike was three years old.

Shortly after his mother's death, Mr S. had become unemployed and had begun to drink heavily, his drinking habits eventually leading to a separation between the couple with Mr S. moving to live with his mother-in-law. The family then appear to have settled into a routine where Mr S. would spend the daytime in the family home before returning each evening to sleep at the home of his mother-in-law. When going over this part of the family history, Mrs S. had described how her mother lived in a house very near and identical in design to the one which Mr S.'s mother had lived, speculating that 'maybe he felt he was going home'. This pattern continued for several years although at the time of Mike's admission to the Lowit Unit the couple had become reconciled. However, Mr S. had never been able to resume employment.

Although Mr S. appeared to be committed to his wife and family it was a commitment that was restricted by his own limitations, particularly his pressing need for attention. When thwarted in any way or feeling aggrieved by real or imagined slights by family or neighbours, Mr S. could become very abusive or physically violent, to the point where furniture and fittings in the family home were often damaged. Though the behaviour could be understood in terms of Mr S. not having managed the maturational process for sound adult functioning, it was further complicated by the fact that he would still drink heavily at times and had required neurosurgical intervention after a fall (in the year prior to Mike's admission) which could have left him with a degree of intellectual impairment. Taken together, these factors mitigated against Mr S. being able to present Mike with an appropriate role model or to engage, with any consistency, or, at times, with much interest, in the work being undertaken with the family.

Work Undertaken with Family

That there was warmth and commitment in the S. household could not be doubted, nor could the fact that there were standards of behaviour which were expected of Mike and his brother, neither of whom had been in any trouble in the community. It was apparent, however, that the positive features of the family had not been enough to enable Mike to manage the requirement of school attendance or to ensure his regular return to the unit after weekends at home. Work done with the family during the months of Mike's stay in the unit focused on the need for parents to present him with a consistent and united front. A major difficulty in this was Mrs S.'s ambivalence, understandable in terms of Mr S.'s very varying moods, that her husband might go 'over the top' when a firm response was needed. This would leave Mr S. feeling frustrated and impotent at his lack of success in affecting the situation and at times would result in him abdicating any responsibility, preferring to 'leave it to you folks'.

Throughout the months of Mike's admission, work was continued with parents and although their warmth and commitment remained much in evidence so, too, did the fact that they were unable to affect much change in Mike's behaviour. After Mike had been in the unit for six months it was decided that he was unlikely to manage a return to mainstream education from the Lowit Unit and with parents' agreement, an application was made for a place in a local residential school. It was considered that, for a boy who, prior to the Lowit Unit, had not been managing any school attendance nor much by way of social interaction outwith his home, the gains Mike had made in the Lowit Unit were considerable and the hope was that these could be maintained and consolidated by his placement at C. school which had been identified as the one most suited to his needs.

The plan was that Mike would make the transition to this school in a planned and gradual way from a base in the Lowit Unit in the expectation that, as he became familiar with the school, his anxiety about being there would decrease. Unfortunately, at this very crucial time for Mike, staff shortage required that the Unit operate on a day basis only and Mike was unable, even with considerable support, to manage even initial limited attendance with any consistency. As with the Lowit Unit, Mike presented no difficulties on the occasions he did manage to attend the school, where he was seen to be working to the best of his ability. However, the continuing difficulty in separating from home made it unlikely that Mike was going to be able to achieve the kind of consistent attendance which would be necessary for him to gain from his placement at the school. The question then was whether Mike's attendance at C. school, where attendance was voluntary, should be ensured by his removal from home or whether consideration should be given to placing him in a residential school where his attendance would be compulsory. On balance, it was agreed that, because C. school had been identified as the one more suited to his particular needs, he should be taken into care. From the knowledge gained about Mike during his time in the Lowit Unit it seemed that he operated best when limits and expectations were clear and consistent. It was hoped, therefore, that from a base in a children's home where this could happen for him, Mike would manage the requirements of regular school attendance and also develop further the age appropriate social skills which he had begun to show in the Lowit Unit.

A Children's Hearing agreed the recommendation that Mike should be received into care and varied his compulsory Supervision Requirement to state that he should reside in B. House, a Children's Home on the outskirts of the city. Though Mr and Mrs S. were upset at Mike's departure from the family home, both gave their support to the plan. They could acknowledge that Mike would never manage school attendance from home and Mrs S. was also able to foresee difficulty for him in the future in managing a work situation or anything that required him to function independently of home. Not surprisingly, Mike did not give his support to the plan and his move to the Children's Home was effected with considerable resistance on his part. Once there, however, Mike settled well and was quickly established in a routine of attendance at C. school. Regular contact was maintained with home. No overnight stays were considered until Mike was well practised in making visits home and returning without difficulty to B. House.

Work with the family continued on a regular basis in sessions held at the Children's Home, though parents enjoyed the 'social' rather than the 'work' aspect of these visits. The focus, as before, was in helping parents become firmer in their handling of Mike and though Mrs S. did become somewhat more able to resist some of his demands, she could acknowledge that there continued to be 'lapses'. The other continuing difficulty was that even when Mrs S. did remain firm in her resolve, it was not always guaranteed that Mr S. would not accede to Mike's demands. Mr S. could acknowledge that the 'hassle' of it all was more than his indifferent health could manage.

Over the months he remained at B. House, Mike made considerable progress in all areas. As well as managing an exemplary school attendance, he made considerable progress in all areas of personal and social functioning. During one family session it was heartening, when Mr S. had digressed on to one of his favourite topics – films and film stars – that Mike was the one who pointed out to him that was not the purpose of the sessions.

The original plan had been that Mike would be phased in from B. House to become resident at C. School. However, the structure of the Children's Home and the relationships which he had built up there appeared to be working so well for him that the 'means' became an 'end' in itself. There was an acknowledgement, even by Mike, that the compulsory nature of his placement there had contributed significantly to its success.

For 18 months Mike continued in this situation, living at B. House, attending C. school daily and becoming a valued member of both communities. Overnight stays at home had been introduced when it was felt that Mike was able to return to B. House without difficulty. There were concerns that Mike's standard of self-care was less on these visits and worries, too, that on these occasions he was indulging in some substance abuse with friends in the neighbourhood of his home. While aware that Mike continued to need a firm safe structure, staff working with him at the time had to balance the need for his safety with his exposure to the inevitable temptations that most young people face. As his sixteenth birthday approached, Mike was making it clear that his plan was to return home when he reached school leaving age. He would not consider moving on to a residential unit designed to help young people move from care towards independent living. Parents were acknowledging that Mike had managed better what was required of him when living outwith the family and would have preferred it if Mike had availed himself of a placement in the unit. Mike, however, remained optimistically convinced that he would manage at home. Just prior to his sixteenth birthday, Mike began, for the first time in the 18 months he had been at B. House, to absent himself or not return when expected, clearly posting his intention to leave care. Though it would have been possible to continue his Supervision Requirement and enforce his residence at B. House, it was felt that this would undo much of the work that had been done with Mike towards taking responsibility for his actions and choices. Instead, Mike was discharged from care with the clear message that further help was available to him if and when he wished to avail himself of it.

Mike returned home and fears that the gain he had made in B. House and C. school would be lost appeared to be confirmed as he settled back in the family, living off handouts from parents who received no state benefit for him. Mike had no eligibility for benefit in his own right and had difficulty in managing the regular attendance at the local Careers Office which was necessary for him to be eligible for payment of a hardship allowance.

Within a year of his discharge from care, Mike was charged, with others, with housebreaking offences and made subject of a probation order at which time responsibility for his case transferred to a social worker in the adult services team.

Conclusion

Mike's case history is an interesting one in the light of current thinking and legislation which places considerable emphasis on children's rights and parental rights and responsibilities (as discussed in Chapter 14). Agencies involved in promoting the welfare of children (particularly social work because of its statutory responsibility) stand where these interface, an uncomfortable place to be when decisions have to be made about whether parents' rights to bring up their children in their own way, appear not to be meeting the child's rights to a standard of care that will meet his developmental needs in ways that will prepare him best for sound adult functioning. Residential staff in the Lowit Unit and in B. House temporarily assumed parental responsibility for Mike providing for him the safe and consistent structure within which children are considered most likely to develop their maximum potential.

Relating to the progress Mike made in both these places, there was a feeling of disappointment within the professional group involved with him when he opted to return home on reaching his sixteenth birthday and a questioning of whether the intervention had served any useful purpose. In the present political and economic climate when outcomes, even in the provision of social services must be seen to be cost effective, how can the usefulness of what was offered Mike be measured? At its simplest what was offered him when he was placed away from home was an exposure to adults who exercised their 'parental responsibilities' towards him in ways that helped him mature and manage more age-appropriate behaviour. If these experiences have given Mike additional and useful terms of reference on which to draw in his adult life, particularly if and when he becomes a parent, then the intervention will have been worthwhile. Indeed, as the medical director was quoted saying in Chapter 13 'it's important that the children take away a little bit of that relationship forged (in the Unit)'.

CHAPTER 12

The Role of the Psychiatrist

Douglas Chisholm

Introduction

Much of the value of a child psychiatric unit stems from the intensive, co-ordinated, multi-disciplinary work that can take place there. For this to occur most effectively it is crucial that the roles of the different professions be clarified, yet, as Parry-Jones (1986) points out, regarding mental health there has tended to be difficulty in differentiating their appropriate contributions. In considering this it should be recognised that there are relevant skills and knowledge common to all, or at least some of the professions involved, while each also has its own more specific areas (Cox and Wolkind 1990). Although all workers in a child psychiatric unit may well spend the larger proportion of their time utilising skills that members of other professions share, they will do so in ways influenced by training, experience, skills and knowledge specific to their own professions; certainly their contributions to discussions will be influenced by these factors. Both the specific skills and knowledge and the shared areas are essential to the fulfilment of professional roles.

The areas specific to child psychiatrists stem from their basic medical training, their training in other medical specialities, such as neurology and paediatrics, and their general psychiatric and child and adolescent psychiatric training (Cox and Wolkind 1990). In addition, consultant psychiatrists have the final medical and legal responsibility for the diagnosis and treatment of all the children in the unit and medical responsibility for the management of the unit overall. They will also be bound by their responsibilities as regards confidentiality, ethical issues, note-keeping and communication with the child's family doctor. Child and adolescent psychiatrists also have certain duties and responsibilities in relation to the Mental Health legislation as is discussed at more length in Chapter 14, but this is rarely involved in child psychiatric in-patient practice although the detention of a child as young as nine years has occurred (Morton and McEwan 1994).

In this chapter I will consider the role of the child psychiatrist regarding the more specific areas outlined above and then consider areas of overlap. It is to be noted that in dealing with more specific areas the psychiatrist has to take into full account the comments of non-medical colleagues who may well have information that will help to clarify a diagnosis or influence a choice of treatment. This particularly applies to nursing staff whose observations of the children can provide information about them not otherwise available, and it applies to areas as traditionally 'the doctor's' as the prescription of medication.

This account of how the psychiatrist's role is fulfilled is based primarily on the author's experience in the Lowit Unit and knowledge of other centres, although it is acknowledged that differences in practice are found between units.

The psychiatrist's role is considered as follows:

(1) Medical Responsibilities

(2) Psychiatric Responsibilities

(3) Role as Consultant in Charge

(4) Shared Areas

(5) Role as Medical Director

(6) The Role of the Psychiatrist in a Changing Scene.

Nevertheless this differentiation must be regarded as artificial, as considerable overlap between areas exists.

(1) Medical Responsibilities

(a) Physical illness

Although the medical care of the child with physical illness will often require the involvement of a paediatrician or paediatric surgeon, a psychiatrist is usually the first doctor to see a child who develops an intercurrent physical illness while in the child psychiatric unit. On the basis of the psychiatrist's assessment: the child will be treated and nursed in the unit; sent home to be looked after by his or her family doctor; or referred to a paediatrician or paediatric surgeon. In all cases the psychiatrist will have responsibility for communicating with the family doctor or other consultant as appropriate. It is, of course, also essential that the parents are involved in whatever decisions are made. In the decision on whether the child should be looked after at home or in the unit the psychiatrist will consider not only which setting is best for treatment of the child's physical illness but also which will be most helpful with regard to the child's psychiatric disorder. For example, the opportunity to provide nurturing for their child when he or she is sick, is often one which allows parents to begin to involve themselves with their child, in a constructive way, and allows the child to accept parental help.

(b) 'Routine' Physical Examination

The term 'routine' is used here to distinguish these physical examinations from ones carried out because it is thought the child may have some intercurrent physical illness. It is 'routine' in the sense that it regularly takes place but there is no implication that it is less than thorough or that aspects relevant to the child's psychiatric disorder are not particularly covered. Such examinations are carried out at the time of the child's admission to check the child's physical health and to identify any physical contribution to his or her problems.

In the Lowit Unit, although a paediatric neurologist or paediatrician is subsequently involved, the initial examination is undertaken by a psychiatrist. Consideration of the physical contribution to the child's psychiatric problems has been included in the section on 'Medical Responsibilities' but is, of course, equally a psychiatric responsibility – thus reflecting the artificial nature of the division. The physical assessment for completion of a Record of Need in Scotland ('statementing' of a child in England under the Education Act of 1981 is the corresponding process) can also be carried out by a psychiatrist. This need not be the case, however, even when the child is a psychiatric in-patient and, indeed, in the Lowit Unit it is normally undertaken by the child's school doctor.

The importance of the 'routine' physical examination is underlined by the finding of Gray *et al.* (1992) that 19.2 per cent of child psychiatric in-patients and day patients had physical disorders. Bailey (1994) also found a high incidence of physical disorder among child and adolescent offenders assessed, even though they often had had previous contact with a number of agencies, including medical and psychiatric ones. In the view of the author, too, as investigations of brain function become more advanced relevant physical factors will be more frequently identified. A higher prevalence of these among in-patients may be expected than among the larger number of disturbed children treated as out-patients, or the very much still greater number never referred, since children referred to in-patient units tend to include those with the most severe, complex or puzzling disorders.

(2) Psychiatric Responsibilities

(a) Assessment of the Child

By the time a child is admitted to a child psychiatric unit, at least a provisional assessment will have been made of the nature and extent of his or her difficulties. If the admission has been an emergency or urgent one, the depth and scope of this assessment may well be less than it would be with a routine admission. The form and content of the assessment will also be very much influenced by the philosophy of the unit, and the views of the senior staff as to what it should contain. With this diversity, no single approach would cover all units but it is felt there would be wide agreement that, as in the Lowit Unit, a comprehensive assessment of a child has to cover biological, psychological and social aspects, as well as having a developmental perspective. In addition, it will include assessment of parents and family. As part of this assessment, the psychiatrist will have undertaken a psychiatric interview or interviews of the child and parents or family, including an assessment of the child's mental state.

The need for further investigations may have become apparent through physical examination, from the psychiatric interviews, or from other information available, for example the observations of nursing staff. Possible relevant neuro-biological investigations include blood, CSF, urine analysis, EEG's (including 24-hour recordings), X-rays, NMR's and CAT scans. Ophthalmological, audiological and otological examination are also relevant since it is known that physical problems in these areas are more common in certain groups of child and adolescent psychiatric patients. Genetic investigation is becoming increasingly relevant. If a paediatrician or paediatric neurologist is involved in the unit, the decision about investigations may well be made by him or her, or be based on consultation.

Other investigations/assessments fall into the areas of other disciplines involved in the unit and the choice of tests will be their responsibility. It is no longer considered acceptable practice to make a referral, for example, to a clinical psychologist, in terms of a request for a particular test. However, it will normally be the psychiatrist (in consultation with other staff) who makes the initial referral, and indicates the area of concern, unless other professionals have had a high level of involvement.

On the basis of all the information available, the psychiatrist will come to a decision as to the child's psychiatric disorder and its severity. A statement concerning how the disorder has come about, and is maintained, will be made and strengths of the child and family will be identified. Thus a diagnostic appraisal will be reached including a diagnostic classification and formulation. Cox and Rutter (1985) and others have highlighted the value of this process. Such a diagnostic appraisal may well be revised throughout the child's stay. Indeed, for many children a major reason for admission is to obtain a thorough and detailed assessment. Such an assessment requires a pooling of the observations and assessments from the different disciplines, and for the child in a child psychiatric unit, these have to be considered in relation to the psychiatric diagnostic appraisal. This is not because the non-psychiatric observations and assessment are any less important or valid, but because, in addition to the psychiatrist's medical responsibility, it would not be justified to admit a child to a child psychiatric ward if it were not for issues concerning the diagnosis, assessment, exclusion and/or treatment of psychiatric disorder. It is the view of the psychiatrists working in the Lowit Unit that this statement, despite the flavour of a traditional disease model, is not incompatible with understanding of the child's and family's problems from many different approaches, including psycho-dynamic, behavioural or in systemic terms, and linking both individual and family perspectives. Indeed, they would agree with the view that the willingness to use a whole range of conceptual models is central to the medical approach to psychiatric problems (Steinberg 1986).

(b) Assessment of Parents and Other Family Members

Although the child is the designated patient, assessment of the parents is also essential. Primarily this assessment focuses on their parenting role but a full understanding of the factors affecting the child can often only be obtained by a wider assessment of the parents. Other areas of assessment include their physical and mental health, their personalities and their marital relationship. The parents' childhood experience will usually be covered, including their relationships with their own parents who may, of course, still be actively involved. The parents' right to set limits on how far these areas are investigated for the purpose of the assessment need to be respected and the depth and scope of the enquiries should be no further than is necessary for the best management of the child.

Although other professionals will often be involved in initial assessment, the psychiatrist has a key role with regard to the parents' physical and mental health. For assessment of the parents' physical health (in addition to their own account of this) he or she is likely to rely on information from the family doctor and perhaps other consultants. This may well be the case, too, regarding the parents' mental health. Sometimes, however, the sensitive issue may arise that the child and adolescent psychiatrist may consider that a parent is suffering from a psychiatric disorder that has not previously been diagnosed. This may be because the parent has not sought help in the past or not revealed his or her difficulties, or the disorder has only recently arisen. In these circumstances, the child and adolescent psychiatrist will have a responsibility to decide in consultation with the family doctor and other colleagues, who of those involved should undertake treatment if the parent is agreeable – or whether referral to an adult psychiatrist is appropriate. It is important, too, that this is clarified with the parent since the doctor–parent relationship differs from the doctor–patient one in many respects. With more serious disorders, involvement of an adult psychiatrist, either to take over the treatment or to provide consultation, would be good practice.

In some cases identifying the parent as having a psychiatric disorder may not be helpful or acceptable to the parent and it may be more constructive to continue to work with the family without doing so.

Similar considerations apply to other family members. However, the central role of parents in the family means that assessment of their functioning is of particular importance, and there is often less choice as to whether or not to actively address their difficulties. Nonetheless, it is a frequent occurrence that a psychiatrist will become aware that another family member may also have a psychiatric disorder. When that occurs a decision has to be made as to whether they should be assessed and treated in their own right. Sometimes such intervention may not be necessary, at least immediately, particularly if there is reason to expect that it will clear up in response to family intervention.

Many of these situations underline the importance of the child psychiatrist having adult psychiatric training. There are occasions, too, when the child psychiatrist needs both his child and his adult psychiatric training for the treatment of a parent in the child's interests. For example, there was described recently the treatment of a parent with stimulants for a previously undiagnosed attention deficit disorder, so that the parent would be able to manage a child with the same disorder more effectively (Evans, Vallano and Pelham 1994).

(c) Treatment

Although the psychiatrist will have responsibility for the treatment the child and family receive, much of it will not fall into his or her specific area of expertise. Some will belong to the shared area, while other treatments such as speech and language therapy or occupational therapy require the specific skills of other professionals. Deciding on much of the treatment is, therefore, a shared process, although there are limitations on this regarding the use of, and selection of medication.

It is also the psychiatrist's responsibility to ensure that information on medication is provided for the child, parents and other professionals. They should be informed regarding reasons for prescription, possible side effects and how it is expected to help. Once medication is started, monitoring response and change in dosage depend not only on information from the child and parent but also on the observations of nursing staff and other professionals. For example, in the author's experience, the comments of the ward teachers about the response of hyperkinetic children to stimulant medication has been the most valuable indication of the drug's effectiveness. Systematic time-sampling obser-vations under the direction of the psychologist and information from question-naires given by them to teachers and parents are also important sources of information. Wilkinson (1978) in addition has shown how nursing staff in a child psychiatric ward can carry out systematic observations.

Both as regards medication and other forms of treatment, the psychiatrist has a responsibility to obtain the informed consent of parents and child. If the child were to refuse to give consent and it was felt the implications of the refusal were understood, and reasonable judgement had been exercised, then the treatment could not proceed. This is equally applicable in the case of use of any form of restraint. Refusal in the 'heat of the moment' to accept the latter as part of treatment would not necessarily lead to abandoning its use since considera-tions such as the safety of the child and others would need to be taken into account. It would clearly be important in such circumstances that there was full parental support and agreement.

Circumstances also can arise when the use of Mental Health legislation is necessary for treatment to continue.

(3) Consultant-in-Charge

Any case admitted to a child psychiatric unit has a consultant child psychiatrist identified as in clinical charge. This means that he or she will have the responsibility with regard to the decision to admit, to discharge and as to forms of treatment subject to the agreement of the child and parents. However, despite responsibility for these decisions, there are considerable limitations to independent decision making. The extent of these limitations is likely to vary considerably between units. It will be influenced by the philosophy of the unit, the types of patient admitted and the approaches to assessment and treatment used.

For example, the greater the extent to which the unit is influenced by the philosophy of the therapeutic community the more likely it is that decisions will be reached by the multi-disciplinary team although, as Morrice (1965) points out, even in a therapeutic community there are circumstances in which the psychiatrist must exercise authority. However, for the majority of children admitted to child psychiatric units the relationships between children and staff are of central importance and it is arguable that this means that it is therefore important that they take a major part in decision-making. If the therapeutic milieu is viewed as a key treatment tool it is essential that the multi-disciplinary team have a major part in that decision-making.

In the Lowit Unit, where the milieu aims to facilitate other treatment measures in some cases, and is the main treatment tool in others, decision-making is by consensus when possible, but by the consultant-in-charge (or occasionally by another professional when the authority has been delegated) in certain circumstances. These include when an urgent decision is required; when a consensus cannot be reached; when the decision depends on some psychiatric or medical judgement that only the psychiatrist is trained to provide; or, an infrequent occurrence, when the consensus of the group, perhaps due to some unresolved conflict in the group dynamics, favours a decision unacceptable in the professional judgement of the consultant-in-charge.

As consultant-in-charge, too, the psychiatrist will have a responsibility to ensure that there is good communication with community agencies, including health, education and social work. This will apply in preparation for admission, during the child's stay in the unit and in preparation for and, in many cases, after discharge. However, for these children with a longer stay in the unit, it may be realistic for the emphasis on communication with community agencies to be less intensive during a substantial part of their stay than around admission and discharge. Nonetheless, keeping schools abreast of developments, is helpful when it comes to planning for discharge and return to school. It does not imply that it will be the psychiatrist who personally maintains these links as it may well be more appropriate for other members of the team to do so, for example with members of their own profession. Much of the maintenance of community links in the Lowit Unit takes place through pre-intake meetings and regular review meetings of each child admitted. One or more of these meetings would undertake planning for discharge and, as well as more informal contacts, additional meetings are arranged when required. Information including all agreed decisions are also conveyed by written reports. Communication after discharge may well be restricted to specific professionals and is decided on an individual case basis.

(4) Shared Areas

Many of the therapeutic approaches utilised to help children and their families may be equally well carried out by, for example, nurses, social workers, or psychologists as by a psychiatrist. Indeed, although the Joint Committee on Higher Psychiatric Training (1990) identifies treatments in which trainee child and adolescent psychiatrists should have received training, it is likely that they will proceed to make consistent use of only a limited number of these approaches. Two psychiatrists may show less similarity in their approaches to treatment than a psychiatrist and a member of another discipline. This is not to deny that his or her psychiatric training may well influence a psychiatrist to undertake a treatment such as family therapy in a different way in some respects from members of other professions.

It can easily occur, therefore, that although a psychiatrist is the consultant-in-charge of a particular case, he may have, when he or she undertakes therapy with that child or family, less experience, skill or training than another professional involved. In practice, too, it is likely that it will often be the case that it is not possible or appropriate for the most skilled professional in a particular treatment to undertake it because of practical considerations. These may include demands on the time of the therapist, or factors relating to relationships between psychiatrist, the child and family. It is likely, too, that group supervision for therapists will be multi-disciplinary. In the Lowit Unit therapies which psychiatrists may undertake falling into this shared area include child psychotherapy and play therapy, family therapy, marital therapy, group therapy for children or parents, behaviour therapy, and counselling of child and parents.

Traditionally, psychiatrists are much more likely to ask a psychologist to undertake behaviour therapy or cognitive therapy but it is recognised that psychiatrists with different training might well undertake these themselves more frequently. While such traditions do not imply that therapies are in some sense 'the property' of the profession that carries them out, such traditions are helpful in enabling professionals to acquire particular experience in certain areas, facilitating the allocation of pieces of work and making inter-disciplinary rivalry less likely. That therapists from other disciplines do not view particular therapies as their 'property' is demonstrated by their willingness to offer training to psychiatrists, especially in training grades, and to other professionals.

(5) As Medical Director

(a) The Need for a Co-ordinator with an Overall View

This has been included as part of the role of the psychiatrist since in the UK, whether or not the actual title is used, each unit has usually identified a psychiatrist to fulfil the role. It is generally agreed that there are advantages in having someone taking particular responsibility for having an overall view of the functioning of the unit, although it would not be impossible for most of the duties to be carried out by some professional other than a psychiatrist and indeed, they may well be shared by a number of people. Since the primary task of the unit, however, is to provide psychiatric assessment and treatment it would seem appropriate for that person to be a psychiatrist.

The central importance of the role of the Medical Director has long been recognised. For example, Shaw in 1966 described the Medical Director as controlling staff, environment, programme and tone of the unit, but Harper and Geraty (1987) comment that it is not usual for all staff to be responsible to one person in a single hierarchical line. Moreover, as Barker (1974) points out, the role of the Director in the UK differs considerably from the situation in the USA as described by Shaw (1966). In the UK, nursing and other disciplines belong to different organisational hierarchies. Indeed, in the Lowit Unit, as Chesson points out in Chapter 13, no fewer than six management pathways were identified and somewhat similar situations are believed to apply in other child psychiatry in-patient units. Furthermore, if more than one consultant has patients in a unit, then the Medical Director will not have clinical responsibility for all the patients. This adds complexity to the running of the unit since issues will arise about choice of patients for admission, length of stay, the impact of the problems of the patients and their management plans about which different consultants may have different views. These issues are more likely to be problematic when there is pressure on places or staff are feeling under stress in managing the children. In the Lowit Unit, these issues have been addressed by discussion at the multi-disciplinary monthly Admission and Discharge Meetings, at weekly Community Meetings and in *ad hoc* discussions. To all of these the Medical Director has been able to contribute an overview of the Unit, so allowing informed decision making and co-ordination of treatment.

Over the years with psychiatrists sharing broadly similar philosophies and views about treatment priorities, these arrangements have worked relatively smoothly. They also have the advantages of allowing consultants to have a realistic view of what the unit can achieve; allowing continuity of psychiatric care of patients before, during and after admission; facilitating in-depth discussion of cases; ensuring that all consultants have some understanding of current ward dynamics when on call; and making it more possible for consultants other than the director to contribute to developments and innovations in the way the unit operates. However, the instituting of the Purchaser–Provider split with the devolution of budgets as part of NHS re-organisation, and reduced availability of places in schools for seriously emotionally and behaviourally disturbed children and in social work care has meant that the arrangements are having to be re-examined. The findings, too, of the study by Chesson reported in Chapter 13 pointed to the need for this to be reviewed.

(b) Partnership and the Therapeutic Milieu

Despite the limits to the power invested in the Medical Director, Barker (1975) argued that it was part of his or her role to provide leadership and direction to the multi-disciplinary staff group. In practice, the responsibilities of the Medical Director are discharged through partnerships with other professionals and, particularly, with their senior members. The most central of these partnerships is with the senior nurse of the unit. In a setting such as the Lowit Unit where the Charge Nurse is the most senior nurse with close day-to-day involvement and with both clinical and managerial responsibilities, the partnership requires to be primarily with the Charge Nurse with the support of the senior nursing administrator. In another setting, the nursing administrator might be equally or more involved. The central importance of this partnership reflects the key role of the nursing staff in units in the UK, which has been recognised from the opening of the first unit (Cameron 1949). Cameron (1949) describes the management of the children as initially by psychiatrists and nurses only, but the involvement of other disciplines, as is now standard, has not changed the fact that nurses are the professionals with by far most contact with the children. Indeed, for many of the children it will be the relationships formed with the nursing staff that will be the biggest determinant of how beneficial admission proves to be.

Since the senior nurse is the line manager for the nursing staff in the unit, it is only through partnership with him or her that the Medical Director is likely to be able to establish and maintain a therapeutic milieu, that is to establish and maintain 'a ward structure, organisation and setting which can help to reduce the emotional and behavioural disorders of the children' (Hersov and Bentovim 1985, p.768). The same partnership is of central importance too as regards staff training and development. The emphasis on this partnership is not to devalue other professional relationships, since co-operation will be required to address aspects of the functioning of the milieu. For example, the involvement of a clinical psychologist is essential if a behavioural dimension is to be incorporated in staff training and development.

(c) Training and Staff Development

Although each professional group has a responsibility for the training and experience of its own members, there are advantages in the Medical Director taking a central role regarding staff development. This is appropriate because the capacity of the child psychiatric in-patient unit to carry out its work effectively will depend on the staff having received adequate training and being able to apply what they have learned in the day-to-day work of the unit. With regard to helping nursing staff in their work Wilkinson (1983) states that there must be a continuing development of skills combined with space to explore relationships with particular emphasis on counter-transference. This has clearly to be an ongoing process and will be largely undertaken by senior nursing staff in the unit.

However, the Medical Director will wish to ensure that what is being taught can be translated into a form consistent with the overall philosophy of the unit, or that the inconsistencies are recognised and their implications explored. Gaps in training will need to be recognised, together with difficulties and areas where staff feel in the need of input. The Medical Director can arrange to have these addressed through contributions from colleagues involved in the unit, or, indeed, from other agencies. Some of the training events are likely to be primarily for one discipline while others will be multi-disciplinary.

The Medical Director may also arrange for supervision to be available when appropriate for members of staff carrying out specific therapies such as family therapy, play therapy, cognitive therapy and relaxation therapy. This supervision may take place in an individual or group setting. In the Lowit Unit, where nursing staff have not usually had post basic training in Child and Adolescent Psychiatric Nursing, the Medical Director has had to have a particularly active role as regards this, especially at periods where there has been a higher staff turnover with new, often inexperienced, staff being appointed.

To a considerable extent, the Medical Director has discharged this function through multi-disciplinary meetings which examine the training needs of nursing staff and consider how these can best be met. This has been combined, however, with the use of ward rounds and a weekly nursing support meeting to link theory and practice and to promote staff development. This input is in addition to supervision provided by the Charge Nurse and senior nurses where staff development is also addressed. Teachers have usually participated in training days and events as well but they have also had their own professional development days and training courses. Other professionals have joined part or the whole of Lowit Unit training days when the topic has been of particular interest.

(d) The Unit and the Wider Community

Another key area of concern for the Medical Director is the relationship of the unit as a whole with the wider community. A major objective is to ensure that the work of the unit is understood by other professionals involved in caring for children and their families. These would include general practitioners, social workers, members of the legal system, educational psychologists and educational administrators. Both for this to occur and to ensure that admissions, discharges and follow-ups are undertaken as constructively as possible, links with these other professionals will need to be fostered.

(e) The Relationship of the Medical Director to the Multi-Disciplinary Group

Hersov and Bentovim (1985) state that an in-patient unit requires sensitive and thoughtful leadership so that 'blending together of medical care, educational practice, occupational and psychological therapies, social case work and administrative efficiency' can occur (Hersov and Bentovim, p.767). They suggest that the leadership requires to be able to resolve disputes over roles and organisation, which clearly is necessary if the staff is to be an effective team.

In discussing multi-disciplinary work, both Parry-Jones (1986) and Trowell (1990) refer to the distinction between a team in which the members work regularly together and develop shared working relationships, and a network where there is no one permanent and definite face-to-face group but members of different disciplines form temporary teams for particular purposes. Parry-Jones describes how at Highfield, the Oxford Regional Psychiatric Adolescent Unit, many of the problems of permanent teamwork were avoided by recognising that the staff associated with the Unit formed a multi-disciplinary network from which temporary teams would undertake particular pieces of work.

In contrast, in the Lowit Unit, with its smaller size and more variable length of stay, it has been considered necessary for the nurses, at least, to function as a team. The 'multi-disciplinary' team, therefore, in the sense described above is constituted by the nurses and teachers (see Chesson, Chapter 13). While there is clearly scope for conflicts to occur, for instance through the mirroring of children's difficulties, through unqualified nursing assistants being sometimes more experienced and, in some respects, more skilled than often relatively inexperienced qualified staff, and through personality factors, the scope for inter-disciplinary rivalry within the team is much reduced. It is to be noted that Trowell (1990) considered inter-disciplinary rivalry to be more often a major problem than personality clashes. While inter-disciplinary rivalries in the wider network can and indeed almost inevitably do at times occur, their intensity is less and, provided measures are taken to address them, serious upset to the children can be avoided.

The working of the nurses and teachers as a team has been facilitated through a weekly staff support meeting with an outside facilitator. Although the Medical Director will probably always be situated on the boundary, to what extent he or she should be considered as part of the team and take part in such meetings is clearly an issue. This view of the functioning of the Lowit Unit is illustrated in Figure 12.1.

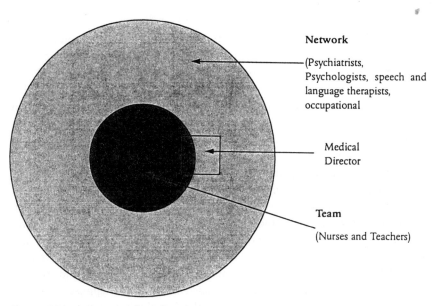

Network

(Psychiatrists, Psychologists, speech and language therapists, occupational

Medical Director

Team

(Nurses and Teachers)

Figure 12.1. Multi-disciplinary network and team (Lowit Unit)

(f) Relationship of the Director to the Psychotherapist

An issue concerning the running of child psychiatric in-patient units that has been discussed – particularly in the past, at considerable length in the USA – has been the place of individual psychotherapy within in-patient treatment. One aspect of this has been the role of the therapist and Irwin (1982) writes of the 'traditional' model where the core of the programme is individual psychotherapy and consequently 'it is natural that the therapist becomes the team leader, formulating, co-ordinating and directing the management of the child's case' (p.13). Other models have included the therapist having no communication with the in-patient setting (Robinson 1947); a therapist–administrator split where the Director shapes the milieu treatment plan and acts as the link between the therapist and the milieu staff; team-oriented administration, where the case management is a collaborative effort but the child's therapist is an important contributor; and the approach used by Irwin himself, where the child's therapist is also the family's therapist, and decisions are arrived at through consensus after open discussion. However, in Irwin's model, if a consensus cannot be achieved, or the Director strongly disagrees with the predominant opinion, he or she can unilaterally decide on the child's management. In more recent years, both in the USA and in this country, the emphasis on individual therapy as the key treatment modality has markedly receded so that the so-called 'traditional' model is no longer relevant but the Medical Director would still require to be sensitive to the issues around the place of individual therapy and of the therapist discussed above.

(g) Psychiatric Administration

Harper and Geraty (1987), describing the situation in the USA in more recent years, state that most clinicians find themselves poorly prepared to function well in administrative positions, and identified psychiatric administration as a developing field related to the larger field of management. They argue for the value of addressing organisational problems through a systems analysis rather than considering them 'in terms of the parties' feelings, motivations and characterology'. They consider that for any problem in an in-patient setting a 'differential diagnosis' is required; this should include a systems analysis and attend to biological and psychological factors.

In addition to considering systemic aspects such as the permeability or rigidity of its boundaries, the effectiveness of communication, and the pattern of decision-making, the author would argue that such concepts as Bion's 'workgroup' and 'basic assumption groups', Ezriel's 'avoided relationship' and fear of 'the calamity', the ideas of Winnicot, Docker-Drysdale, Menzies-Lyth and others on holding and containment and issues of transference and countertransference are valuable in arriving at such differential diagnoses. While it would be inappropriate, too, to look at the functioning of individual staff members as if they were patients, it would be equally inappropriate for the Medical Director to ignore the feelings of members of staff and not to use skills possessed in understanding people in trying to understand how a problem has arisen and may be resolved. Some training in administration and management is now widely recognised as an important part of the training of a psychiatrist but is still generally inadequate fully to equip a psychiatrist for the greater demands of acting as Medical Director for a child psychiatry unit.

(6) The Role of the Psychiatrist in a Changing Scene

It is likely to be as Medical Director that the role of the psychiatrist in the in-patient unit will be most affected by the changing scene in the NHS. Re-organisation of the NHS has meant that the Trust or Directly Managed Unit has become answerable to the purchasers for the services it provides. The management of the Trust or Directly Managed Unit is likely to look to the Medical Director in turn to ensure that the child psychiatric in-patient unit provides the service as contracted. This will entail the Medical Director being involved with the content of contracts, of protocols associated with them, and with issues of quality control within the unit by for example initiating regular audits of aspects of its functioning.

At least periodically, too, the Medical Director is likely to be involved in arguing for continuing funding of the unit. To some extent the evidence, albeit limited, available from research studies carried out in other centres may be used, but it is likely that, despite the difficulties in proving the efficiency of child psychiatric in-patient units, descriptive local data will be valuable in supporting the case for further funding. The Medical Director will have a responsibility to ensure that such information is available, that a sound case is put and that audits take place regularly.

He or she will also have a role in keeping purchasers informed regarding the part child psychiatric in-patient units can play including, on occasion, about the feasibility of extending the unit's remit. For example, if the purchasers want the unit to make other forms of provision, say, for admitting children with learning disabilities, the Medical Director in collaboration with colleagues will decide not only whether the unit can make such provisions, but also whether it should do so in the light of what is known about the psychiatric needs of children and families in the community. It is likely, indeed, that the Medical Director will, at times, feel very much caught between the pressures of market forces on the one hand and those deriving from Needs Assessments on the other (see Chapter 14).

With budgets being devolved to units, too, the Medical Director will have to be involved in financial decision making. While he or she will share with other professionals a recognition of the need to meet the costs for adequate multi-disciplinary staffing, other demands on money are likely to be recognised such as the need to budget for investigations, which are likely to become more expensive as scientific and technological progress continues. In addition, the cost of drugs must be met, taking into account the high costs which may be associated with new products; clozapine is a current example.

These changes may raise again the issue of whether a child and adolescent psychiatrist is the most appropriate person to be Director of a Child Psychiatric In-Patient Unit. As has previously been said, it would be possible for many of the responsibilities of the Medical Director to be undertaken by another member of the multi-disciplinary group and, indeed, such issues as budgeting and contracting have not been medical responsibilities in the past. However, it remains the case that child and adolescent psychiatrists are particularly well fitted by training and experience to take a holistic view of the difficulties of the child and family and to understand and co-ordinate the contributions of the other disciplines involved. It must be acknowledged, however, that increasingly this view is challenged but there is little clear evidence emerging regarding who is taking on such responsibilities. The importance of close co-operation between clinicians and managers is well recognised (The Scottish Office Audit Unit 1994). It seems likely, therefore, that the role of the child and adolescent psychiatrist as Medical Director will continue, reinforced by recent developments which have created important additional areas of responsibility.

References

Bailey, S. (1994) *Serious Young Offenders – What Has Psychiatry to Offer?* Paper at Autumn Meeting of The Royal College of Psychiatrists (Scottish Division, Stirling).

Barker, P. (1974) *The Residential Psychiatric Treatment of Children.* Crosby London: Lockwood Staples.

Cameron, K.A. (1949) 'A psychiatric in-patient department for children.' *Journal of Mental Science 95,* 560–566.

Cox, A. and Wolkind, S. (1990) 'Role of the child and adolescent psychiatrist.' In Occasional Papers No 8. *Child and Adolescent Psychiatry: Into the 1990s.* London: Royal College of Psychiatrists.

Evans, S.W., Vallano, G. and Pelham, W. (1994) 'Treatment of parenting behavior with a psychostimulant: a case study of an adult with attention-deficit hyperactivity disorder.' *Journal of Child and Adolescent Psychopharmacology 4,* 1, 63–69.

Gray, C., Chisholm, D., Smith, P., Brown, M. and McKay, C. (1992) 'The role of the child psychiatric ward in health care: experiences with different types of admission over a period of 21 years.' *Irish Journal of Psychological Medicine 9,* 17–23.

Harper, G. and Geraty, R. (1987) 'Hospital and residential treatment.' In R. Michels and J. Cavenor and Jr (eds) *Psychiatry, Vol 2.* New York: Basic Books.

Hersov, L. and Bentovim, A. (1985) 'In-patient and day patient units.' In M. Rutter and L. Hersov (eds) *Child and Adolescent Psychiatry: Modern Approaches* (2nd ed). Oxford: Blackwell.

Irwin, M. (1982) 'Literature review.' In J.L. Schulman and M. Irwin (eds) *Psychiatric Hospitalisation of Children.* Springfield, USA: Charles C Thomas.

Joint Committee on Higher Psychiatric Training (1990) *Requirements for Appeal of Higher Training Schemes in Child and Adolescent Psychiatry Handbook.* London: Royal College of Psychiatrists.

Morrice, J.K.V. (1965) 'Permissiveness.' *British Journal of Medical Psychology 38,* 247–251.

Morton, M. and McEwan, T. (1994) 'Psychosis in a 9 year old child.' Paper at Academic Meeting of Child and Adolescent Psychiatry Section of Royal College of Psychiatrists (Scottish Division, Inverness).

Parry-Jones, W. (1986) 'Multi-disciplinary teamwork: help or hindrance.' In G. Steinberg. *The Adolescent Unit.* Chichester: Wiley.

Robinson, J.F. (1947) 'Resident psychiatric treatment of children.' *American Journal of Orthopsychiatry 17,* 484–487.

The Scottish Office Audit Unit (1994) *Caring for Sick Children: A Study of Hospital Services in Scotland.* Edinburgh: Scottish Office.

Shaw, C.R. (1966) *The Psychiatric Disorders of Childhood.* New York: Appleton Century-Crofts.

Steinberg, D. (1986) 'The psychiatrist and the adolescent unit.' In D. Steinberg. *The Adolescent Unit.* Chichester: Wiley.

Trowell, J. (1990) 'Sustaining multi-disciplinary work in the Royal College of
    Psychiatrists.' Occasional Papers No 8 *Child and Adolescent Psychiatry: Into the
    1990s.* London: Royal College of Psychiatrists.

Wilkinson, T. (1978) 'The problems and values of objective nursing observations
    in psychiatric nursing care.' *Journal of Advanced Nursing 4,* 151–159.

Wilkinson, T. (1983) *Child and Adolescent Psychiatric Nursing.* Oxford: Blackwell
    Scientific Publications.

CHAPTER 13

Dimensions of Therapeutic Input
A Research Study

Rosemary Chesson

Introduction

Although the first psychiatric ward for children in Britain was established nearly 50 years ago (Gray *et al.* 1992) there has been little systematic investigation of units and the nature and extent of therapeutic input therein, as has been highlighted in previous chapters. This is despite the fact that both in Britain and the USA the need for such research has been recognised. Pfeiffer and Strzelecki (1990), for example, following a review of 34 articles on in-patient psychiatric treatment of children and adolescents, concluded that 'much of the complexity of what constitutes the in-patient psychiatric treatment environment has not been adequately examined empirically' (p.851). Although the foundations for such research were laid in the 1960s and 1970s through the work of Adler (1968) and Redl (1959) in particular, researchers appear reluctant to grapple with problems relating to the critical dimensions of the therapeutic milieu. Recent work in the USA has tended to focus on characteristics of patients and their families and notably the application of systems theory (Blotcky, Dimperio, Blotcky and Looney 1987). In Britain the growing emphasis placed on clinical audit, while leading to renewed research interest in units, has tended to focus on outcome. Yet as long ago as 1988, Canfield, Muller and Clarkin were pointing to the need to capture the social-developmental context of the hospital setting and ward atmosphere. Clearly little is known regarding the *processes* occurring within units and the factors affecting the interaction between staff and children.

Given that the role of child psychiatric residential units is being examined within the NHS and that financial, political and ideological objections to their continued existence are being voiced, more needs to be known about their work and what they can offer the child. Indeed this has been acknowledged for some time by the Royal College of Psychiatrists (Research Committee of the Royal College of Psychiatrists 1991).

Background to the Research

Two major factors were instrumental in leading to this research:

(1) In 1990 the Unit had been in existence for 21 years and it appeared timely to analyse new admissions over this period (Gray *et al.* 1991). This review underscored the view that the value of in-patient psychiatric provision may lie, in part, in allowing flexible multi-faceted and intensive treatment to be arranged which facilitates the co-ordination of medical, social, educational and psychiatric approaches (Wolkind and Gent 1987).

(2) In 1991, because of the temporary unavailability of staff, the Unit was unable to offer residential care. This led to staff reviewing the functions of the Unit and examining the main differences between treatment input for day and in-patients. This consequently resulted in the recognition of the need to identify the main features of treatment in a residential setting.

The main aim of this research therefore was to establish a database regarding therapeutic input to a child psychiatric ward and to seek greater understanding of the on-going processes and influences on practice. It is worthy of note that few studies of units have been carried out by researchers not members of the psychology or psychiatry professions. To the best of the author's knowledge this research was unique in being carried out by a sociologist. However, it should be remembered that over thirty years ago a British sociologist – Rapoport (1960) – contributed to our understanding of the dynamics of a therapeutic milieu.

This work seeks to describe as many aspects of the Lowit Unit as possible, however insignificant at first they might appear. Thus it was considered inevitable that negative as well as positive aspects of ward life would emerge from such an account. In this chapter an emphasis has been placed on letting staff 'speak for themselves' and hence a high number of quotations are used.

Research Design

It was acknowledged from the start that it would be difficult to encapsulate on-going processes and the study would have to be descriptive. Choice of research methods was restricted given: the characteristics of the unit; its limited number of patients; the flexibility of treatment; and number of staff involved with varying time commitments. Thus a fine-grained (Pfeiffer and Strzelecki 1990) research method was adopted. It was accepted by unit staff that the study would depend heavily on observational data and would be qualitative rather than quantitative. It was carried out by the author, who had had no previous direct contact with the unit and possessed few, if any, preconceived ideas regarding the dynamics of child psychiatric in-patient units.

Initial contact with the Unit revealed that the research might be considerably more difficult to carry out than anticipated. This was because of the complexity of the Unit itself; the multi-disciplinary nature of input; the fact that unit involvement by staff necessitated both direct and indirect commitments; and the difficulties of establishing unit – and therefore research – boundaries in the light of extensive contact with external agencies. It was apparent also that although it had been intended to use pre-existing records and notes these would be of limited value as they had not been collected for research purposes and therefore were not sufficiently comprehensive. In addition, there was variation between staff and discipline regarding the extent and scope of record keeping. It was clear that of necessity data would have to be gathered specifically for the project but this would then be advantageous in enabling purposive data gathering in an appropriate format. Also, it became increasingly evident that data would have to be obtained by a variety of methods to reflect the multi-faceted nature of the unit's work. Such an approach would inevitably be labour intensive. A high level of co-operation from all the staff would be required and the author had little prior knowledge on which to be confident that this would be forthcoming.

Early on, staff's interest was clearly visible and a willingness to take on a more participatory role was expressed. As the research progressed the design evolved so that, as a consequence, by the end of this investigation it was merely one of several studies on-going in the Unit; the multi-disciplinary nature of therapeutic input was well reflected in the multi-disciplinary teamwork on the research enterprise (as evident from this volume). The work carried out by Unit staff proved invaluable in complementing this study.

Finally, it is worthy of note that, although the paucity of previous research made this project more daunting, at the same time it created opportunities. Our thinking, for example, was less likely to be circumscribed and we were free to develop our own frameworks for analysis.

Methods

Data were collected over a 12 month period from April 1992 and was carried out over two decades after the Lowit Unit first opened. It is relevant to the study to bear in mind that at this time the unit had 10 beds and catered for up to 16 children (including day patients) at any one time. The main elements of the research were as follows:

(1) A QUESTIONNAIRE SURVEY OF ALL STAFF

A questionnaire was distributed to all staff in May 1992 and respondents were asked to complete this with as little consultation as possible with colleagues. All of the 18 questions were open-ended and a generous amount of space was available for comment. The main areas covered were: input into the Unit; training qualifications and previous experience; views of Unit philosophy and child management techniques; and influences on professional practice. In addition, staff were asked to indicate if they were prepared to be interviewed.

(2) AN INTERVIEW SURVEY OF STAFF

Twenty-nine members of staff were interviewed during the summer of 1992. Interviews were semi-structured and lasted on average for 45 minutes (range 20 minutes to two and a half hours). The interviews were used to expand on written comments as well as gathering new information on, for example, multi-disciplinary teamwork and characteristics of treatment. The interviews focused on the following concerns: previous experience; functions and roles; factors facilitating and inhibiting relationships; effects of hospitalisation on children and their families; features of the ward environment.

(3) THE OBSERVATION OF WARD ROUTINES

(a) Observation by the author took place for the duration of the study and encompassed meetings, including those relating to admission and discharge. Ninety per cent of community meetings were attended together with a small sample of children's review meetings. Notes were kept during observations through the recording of key words.

(b) *Ad hoc* observation of the unit, including meal times and bedtimes, also some school classes.

(c) Maintenance of ward logs regarding ward traffic. On designated days all visitors (including staff) to the unit were logged as were all telephone calls.

(d) Shadowing of the unit ward charge nurse throughout the working day by the author.

(e) Attendance at one-off events such as in-service days, open-days and the Christmas Party!

(4) CONTENT ANALYSIS OF UNIT DOCUMENTS

Reports on the ward, minutes of meetings, policy statements and other written material was collected and analysed.

Data-analysis

Data were analysed by progressive focusing and the generation of categories. Validity was pursued through establishing internal validity and triangulation.

Study Findings

The data reported here relates to staff responses to questions asked either in the questionnaire (91% response rate) or at interview. The main criterion for reporting is 'goodness of fit' between interview/questionnaire comment and material collected via, for example, meeting attendance, logs and other unit documentation. It should be borne in mind that in the time period between the questionnaire and interview surveys some staff changes occurred relating to registrars being on rotation, and resignations among nursing and occupational therapy staff. Wherever possible replacement staff were interviewed and, in fact, all agreed to participate. Thus when the two surveys are taken into account 15 nursing staff were included and six medical practitioners (including three consultants and one associate specialist) as well as a clinical psychologist, social worker and speech and language therapist and four occupational therapists. In addition, six teachers, three of whom were full-time (one of whom was the school head teacher), participated. The remaining school staff were visiting specialists (art and physical education) and a relief teacher.

Staff Profile

Key characteristics were as follows:

(1) The majority of staff including the Medical Director were women but four psychiatrists and four nurses including the Charge Nurse were men.

(2) Despite difficulties in recruiting nurses and the scarcity of suitably qualified therapy staff there was stability within the group. Worthy of note is that nearly half (45.2%) of all staff had worked in the unit between two and five years. Details are given in Table 13.1.

Table 13.1 Period of Unit Input by Profession

Profession	<2	*Time in years* 2–5	6–10	10+	Total
Nurses	2	8	2	–	12
Teachers	2	2	1	1	6
Doctors	2	1	1	2	6
OT	1	2	1	–	4
ST/SW/CP*	1	1	–	1	3
Total	**8**	**14**	**5**	**4**	**31**

* *Speech and language therapist; social worker; clinical psychologist*

(3) At the time of the study the charge nurse had joined the Unit in the previous five years transferring from adult psychiatry. Several of the longer serving members of staff saw the appointment as a watershed, with more professionalism in the work of nursing staff from this time.

(4) Staff possessed a wide range of qualifications. As was to be expected, all the senior medical staff had higher qualifications, as did the clinical psychologist (D Phil) and the head teacher, (M Phil). Less predictably, although only one nurse had a certificate in Child and Family Psychiatry Nursing, two were graduates and a number had or were pursuing relevant qualifications. Of six qualified nurses, three had trained as registered sick children's nurses and three as registered mental nurses. Although the majority of staff had trained partly or wholly locally all the senior medical staff had periods of training elsewhere including in Cambridge, Dublin, Edinburgh, Ottawa and Toronto, and approximately one third of non-medical staff were awarded qualifications from outwith Aberdeen.

Previous and Relevant Experience

Very few of the staff had worked in Child and Family Psychiatric residential settings other than the Lowit Unit, the exceptions being four medical staff (although two were short term placements): one nurse and one therapist. However, several staff had worked in a range of child care facilities. For example, one of the therapists had worked at a residential school for children with cerebral palsy and another as a nursery nurse in a child assessment and development unit. Four of the teachers had worked in special needs schools and two staff members had worked for periods in the local Camphill/Steiner community. As would be expected, all of the doctors had experience of adult psychiatry as did a number of non-medical staff. The latter tended, however, to hold somewhat ambivalent views of its value, as the following comment illustrates: 'All aspects of adult psychiatry have had some relevance but it doesn't adequately prepare for this speciality' (charge nurse). By contrast a registered children's nurse remarked 'this is a totally different job from working as a sick children's nurse' (staff nurse).

Interestingly, a nursing assistant, when questioned regarding training, felt that 'nothing prepares for this except parenthood'. Yet when all staff were asked to identify the main influences on their professional practice (as discussed in more detail later) only two made explicit reference to their own families. Both were women (one doctor and one nurse). In addition, in response to a question requiring the identification of relevant experience, one consultant and one social worker listed the 'years at home with my own children'. Twenty-two of the 29 interviewees were parents and in some cases, grandparents. Reference to staff's own children often occurred in the context of discussing ward practices regarding child management. For example, a teacher reflecting on the consistency shown towards children on the ward said

> 'my own childhood punishments were repressive and I've avoided this with my own children. This was my approach here initially but have decided with the children in the unit there have to be consequences for their actions. Contrary to my own beliefs I am adapting to the situation.'

Table 13. 2 shows the age range of staff's children and the extensive nature of the experience is evident.

Table 13.2 Ages of Staff's Children (in years)

			N=22			
		Age				
	<4	5–11	12–16	17–20	21+	N/I
Number	1	9	3	10	8	3

When asked explicitly at interview whether being a parent affected their practice, 14 felt that this was the case and only two said that it has no influence. Advantages of parenthood were seen to be twofold: (1) children could be used as an indicator of 'normal' development; (2) parenthood enabled staff to empathise with parents. Comments included:

> 'It's much easier to work with children and do the developmental bit when you've had you own... better perception of "normal": very easy to get out of the mode of what normal children do.'

> 'Invaluable – if didn't have own, would be less accepting of some aspects of these children's behaviour... they're not that different!.'

> 'Some children have more problems than others – knowing it has worked for you means that you are able to feedback positively – I had a soiler'. 'Knowing they can come through it, you can come through it and come through the other side OK.'

Nonetheless several staff emphasised that in their opinion it was not essential to be a parent to do the job.

> 'Useful but not essential. Helps understand how frustrated parents can feel if children giving hell!.'

> *(Responses given by clinical psychologist, doctor, nurse and therapists.)*

Finally the comments of a registrar should be noted: 'I don't have any children, but I was a child!'.

Other influences on professional practice ranged from: restrictions on practice related to pressure of work; limited facilities; lack of role clarity; the nature of the children on the unit; to: factors with regard to experience; personal convictions acquired over the years; values; and colleagues' support, supervision and practice. The latter was, in fact, the single most frequently cited influence and, surprisingly, there were few explicit references to professional training and theoretical perspectives, although both of the latter were identified by medical staff. Teachers' answers in particular tended to be the most child centred. The two views below, although atypical in their comprehensiveness, are indicative of the influences described.

> 'Drawing on the experience of other staff and reading "Journal of Maladjustment and Therapeutic Education"; (The Medical Director's) meetings helpful to give a perspective on a situation; Wilkinson's book *Child and Adolescent Psychiatric Nursing* is also helpful...' (*staff nurse*)

> 'An accumulation over many years of several specific techniques and considerable experience which have resulted in the use of an integrated approach to therapy, rather than the use of any one isolated skill. I hope this offers the child the best option.' (*head occupational therapist*)

The very few references to theoretical influences is interesting in the light of the comment of a nursing assistant who had recently joined the unit:

> 'I do need some theory... sometimes I feel inadequate because no one trained me to work with the child... if I had a reference book it would be fine... people have to learn what works and what doesn't.'

Clearly some staff feel that recent work experience had been of greater value than initial professional training as reflected in the following:

> 'Part of the job is learning, knowing how much to say to whom. You need to work through experience – no one can tell you.' (*teacher*)

Reasons for Working in the Unit

Staff at interview indicated that, in general, they had chosen to work in the Unit. Two major reasons for application were: (1) interest in working with children and; (2) the opportunity to work with families. Concomitantly, an interest in psychology, psychiatry or psychotherapy was articulated. Nurses, however, who had previous employment in adult psychiatry spoke of their growing dissatisfaction with such nursing:

> 'became disillusioned in adult psychiatry. I was attracted to the job here because drugs were not used;'

'The more I got involved in psychiatry the more interested I got in psychotherapeutic and not medical model.'

Frequently staff's answers revealed a strong motivation:

'I liked the idea of developing people and being able to facilitate normal development.' (*therapist*)

Potentialities of the work were, in fact, emphasised by a wide range of professions.

While very few staff were not committed to psychiatry from the start, an exception was an occupational therapist who discovered that input to child and family psychiatry 'came with the job'. She commented

'I came here with no special interest in child and family psychiatry. It's now probably the area I'm most interested in because of the multi-disciplinary team – and the psychiatrists value what we do'.

Unit Philosophy

Staff were asked on the questionnaire to outline the main aspects of the Unit's philosophy. Responses revealed that this was described in terms of applied principles and related to everyday routines. References to abstract concepts or linkages to wider philosophical thought were rare. Close consistency was evident between nurses' and teachers' responses, and very much reflected the ward document on the philosophy of nursing care (see Chapter 5). The three main elements of unit philosophy identified were: (1) provision of a safe/caring environment; (2) enablement of children to develop relationships; and (3) provision of strategies to parents to help them cope. The variation in response can be gauged from the comments below:

'Understand and respect children, enable them to confide in caring adults and have their confidentiality respected; enable carers to look at children's needs and redefine own as parents, to enable children to grow emotionally, promote integration and co-operation of all agencies involved with children.' (*Medical Director*)

'Child seen as a unit in a "wider system", needing not only individual help but also working in the context of the family.' (*charge nurse*)

'The philosophy of the unit is to take children in the hope of getting to change things.' (*social worker*)

Five staff however did not respond to this question or expressed ignorance of a ward philosophy 'I haven't the faintest idea' (*therapist*). Undoubtedly the most succinct response – from the clinical psychologist – was 'provide a therapeutic milieu'.

Child Management and Theoretical Perspectives

Compared with describing the Unit's philosophy, staff were more confident when describing the child management techniques used. There was widespread agreement regarding the main methods. The response of the Medical Director, may be regarded as representative:

(1) Clear and as far as possible consistent setting of limits combined with attention to the more nurturing aspects of the relationship.

(2) Attention and praise for desirable behaviour, withdrawal of attention for undesirable.

(3) Discussion of problem areas and efforts to improve child's self awareness and insight.

(4) Behavioural programme often involving rewards and sometimes consequences.

(5) Interventions to relieve circumstances or tensions which gave rise to the problem behaviour whether in the Lowit Unit or in the family.

Responses to the child are based on understanding of his/her individual needs while keeping perspective of the group and the individual.'

Table 13.3 Main Child Management Techniques Described by Staff

	N = 27*
Behavioural programme	13
Attention/praise/reward	8
Structure/Therapeutic milieu	8
Time out/exclusion	7
Positive relationships	3
Setting of limits/consequences	6
Other	4
Don't know	2

* more than one technique described

Despite behavioural programmes being so frequently mentioned, as evident from Table 13.3, there is very little evidence to suggest that the overriding theoretical base of the Unit was behavioural. Most commonly used approaches

were seen to be eclectic and there were many systems theory adherents among
Unit staff, few who would have disagreed with the social worker who said:

> '(main theoretical approach) systems theory – I feel strongly that the
> behaviour of all children who come into the unit can only be fully
> understood (and therefore addressed) if it is considered in terms of the
> wider system in which it is occurring, for example home,
> neighbourhood, school etc. For this reason it is vital that this total
> system is understood... if any improvement in the child's behaviour
> (while in the unit) is to be sustained on their return home.'

The eclecticism of the current and former director is demonstrated in their
responses, viz:

> 'Attachment theory, systems theory. Behaviour therapy approaches,
> learning theory, psychoanalytic theory (especially Anna Freud, Melanie
> Klein), maturational model.' (*Medical Director*)

> 'Psychodynamic – particularly the work of Winnicot, therapeutic
> community concepts, behaviour therapy, systems theory,
> developmental perspectives.' (*former Medical Director*)

Interestingly, two nurses (both staff grade) tended to lean heavily in the
direction of psychodynamic theory as, for instance, reflected in Chapter 6.

Functions of the Unit

Similarly, staff had little difficulty in identifying the main functions of the Unit;
the four main ones given were as follows:

- help children overcome problems (27)
- comprehensive assessment (17)
- support parents/work with families (15)
- offer secure environment (14).

In the words of the Medical Director the unit provided for 'assessment;
treatment; integration of other therapeutic inputs to give an overview of a case;
placement for the future; training of staff...'.

Staff Status and Role

Staff were asked on the questionnaire to calculate the number of hours spent
on the Unit. From their responses a marked difference emerged between
full-time nurses and teachers, whose work was based exclusively on the Unit
and other staff whose ward commitments were but part of a wider set of
responsibilities. An exception among the nurses was a liaison sister who was
based on the ward but who worked mainly with out-patients, some of whom
became in-patients. Also in recent years the school head teacher had accepted

responsibilities for patients' education throughout the hospital. Only one of the nursing day staff worked part-time, although this applied to all of the night staff. However, teaching and nursing hours were seen to differ significantly in that the former were not required to work shifts, had shorter working hours (a 32 hour working week compared with the nurses' 37.5 hours) and longer holidays.

Non-nursing / non-teaching staff stressed the extent to which their involvement with the ward could vary month by month, year by year relating to the number of patients with which they were involved and the nature of their difficulties. Therapists, together with both the clinical psychologist and social worker, drew attention to the seeming invisibility of 'non-hands-on' work which included case reviews, report writing, telephone calls and informal meetings, all of which they felt tended to be underestimated. All non-nursing/non-teaching staff had wider responsibilities such as those associated with outreach and out-patient work, and membership of other hospital based multi-disciplinary teams.

It is also relevant to note that staff within the unit were members of different organisational hierarchies, as can be seen from Figure 13.1. Not only did part of the core ward staff (the teachers) report to Grampian Regional Council rather than the NHS Trust but also a hospital employee (the speech and language therapist) was not part of the Child Health Directorate. No fewer than seven different management pathways existed regarding staff who had an input on the ward.

On the questionnaire staff were asked to describe their own role and Table 13.4 summarises the descriptions provided. 'Unique descriptors' as given in the third column indicate those functions which *solely* were presented by members of the professional group themselves and were not forwarded by any other discipline. As a result an interesting profile of staff contribution emerged. Only three disciplines – psychiatry, therapy and clinical psychology – included in their role descriptions reference to membership of the multi-disciplinary team. The overwhelming majority of staff, regardless of profession, felt that their own role had not been clear on starting work in the unit; clarity was reported by merely five staff members. Commonly, staff commented on how their role within the unit differed from previous roles, the charge nurse in fact viewing himself as 'de-skilled' on taking up the post. A teacher highlighting the novel features of teaching in the ward said 'got to get used to the culture shock... no staff room. Very much on one's own. Only times all the teachers get together alone is on the four in-service teaching days'. Other views expressed reflected uncertainty: 'Very different to other children's wards where children got better and went home – here not so clear cut' (staff nurse); 'Difficult to get hold of structures' (doctor).

Two major issues emerged from opinions expressed (1) the number of staff involved with children was initially problematic – 'I didn't know who everyone

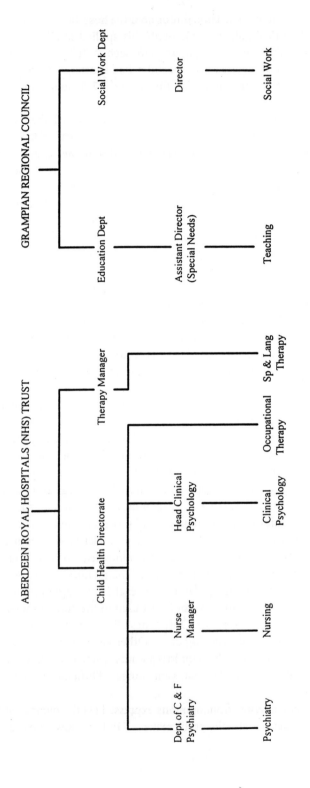

Figure 13.1. Organisational struture and professional input into the Lowit Unit

Table 13.4: Perceptions of Own Role

Profession	Account*	Unique descriptor
Nurses	Caring/Helping child (6); r/ship – with children (2)	[caring/helping child]
Teachers	Teaching (5)	[teaching child]
Doctors	Admin/Mtgs (4); Treatment (3); Teaching staff (3)	[liaison ext. agencies]
Therapists	Assessments (4); Treatment (4)	[advice to staff]
Cl. Psych	Assessment/liaison with staff	[design of behaviour management programmes]
SW	Pre admission and ongoing work with children and families	[pre-admission work]

Numbers providing account given in brackets

was – everyone looked the same, apart from the lady who does the dishes' – as was knowing others' roles and the nature of their input and; (2) the difficulty of knowing procedures – many unwritten and informal. Indeed, it was pointed out that often procedures were unknown to the newcomer and might only be stumbled upon by chance.

Some staff even after a number of years (in particular the social worker and speech and language therapist), still felt they were in the process of clarifying and establishing their role. Moreover, they believed that if they were to move from the unit in all probability the role would be redefined. Worthy of note too is that members of another profession were seen to help an individual in the definition of their own role. A staff nurse said for example '[the social worker] is one of the most outstanding people I know. She probably affected quite a lot initially how I defined my role'.

Underlying staff's remarks regarding their own role was a tacit recognition of overlap with others and yet a need to establish role boundaries:

'Always been a blurring of boundary around psychiatry – can lead to trouble when not clearly defined' (psychiatrist).

'The difference between psychology and psychiatry is regarding approach – it is quite different though we deal with similar cases. We tend to take a problem solving approach, although we are aware of the deeper issues and these are picked up and evolve over time and we may have a reasonable therapeutic outcome. Psychiatry is a very long intervention – need to do proper psychiatric screening, every nuance of family dynamics – do more family work. Some times they take a managerial position and if a lot of input from other agencies manage that case. Would see self in a therapeutic role... therapeutic work with parents or one to one work with children or both... do assessments, observe, collect data and psychometric tests. Psychiatrists gather information by interview... wouldn't do observations but can use drugs' (clinical psychologist).

In addition to a professional role, staff occasionally indicated how this could intersect with other social roles:

'Trying to make friendly relationships – diffuse tension. Teachers as females in particular occupy the peacemaking area. I see my job as getting pupils back to school – helping them to see school in a different light and see teachers as human beings and that there has to be give and take'.

At interview when staff were asked to describe the role of nursing staff many stressed their importance and the demanding nature of the job (for a summary of responses see Table 13.6).

'The work of nurses is running the ward and helping individual child. Working with families and building up family relationships – have the most important role of anyone.'

Yet some staff considered that nursing staff might undervalue it: 'Nurses' role is crucial but I think they undervalue it and wonder if they undervalue it because they see us not valuing it enough' (social worker).

Table 13.5 Main Functions of Nursing Staff*

	N = 29
Care givers	15
Provide structured environment	14
Help child build up relationships	9
Work with families	6
Provide insight/understand feelings	5
Assess/observation	4
Other (role model, liaise, set limits)	13

* more than one function given

Psychiatrists drew attention to the multi-faceted nature of nurses' work and were agreed as to the significance of the role, as can be seen from the following account given by the Medical Director.

> 'Providing for children's physical needs/providing a comfortable physical environment and structures which can be relied on (for example mealtimes). Their role is developing relationships with children. They help modify a child's behaviour by examining with the child what is going on – giving the child choices, alternative modes of responding. They are role models, need to be able to show differences within nursing relationships, respond to difficulties and leave the child feeling safe. They need a good relationship with parents, often difficult, parenting is not always very good... try to understand. They need to know their own authority and use it sensitively, with understanding rather than making the rules.'

Nursing staff duties clearly were regarded as including responsibility for the ward and ward management. Indeed as one teacher stated 'they are the ones who run the unit – think anything else is incidental'. The charge nurse's own description of his role too reflects a significant managerial component: 'co-or-dinator of activities/inter-disciplinary working and staff management. All aspects of clinical work. Promotion of working relationships; development of service; protection of service'. Perhaps the high managerial component of the Charge Nurse's role may account for difficulty some staff experienced in identifying who 'had principal responsibility for the unit'. Five staff, however, identified the charge nurse and a further five the charge nurse *and* one of the consultants. Seven staff replied that they did not know! The comments of a Senior Registrar are indicative of both the issues involved and several staff members' uncertainty in this area. 'It needs a clearly identified leader... needs to be a psychiatrist if it is to function as a medical psychiatric unit... open to debate'.

Multi-disciplinary Teamwork

Throughout the interviews, individuals were asked to comment on a number of aspects of teamwork. In particular discussion focused on: (1) the main factors facilitating and inhibiting relationships between team members; (2) the congruence (or lack of it) regarding standards, methods and practices of members of different disciplines.

Not unexpectedly meetings were identified as the major factors in facilitating relationships – mentioned by approximately half of all staff (although dissatisfaction was often expressed regarding their frequency). It is of interest to note that six staff made specific reference to in-service days as facilitators. By comparison factors inhibiting relationships were more diverse. However, although only eight staff members referred directly to building lay out in response to this specific question the overwhelming majority of staff alluded to it in the course of interviews and discussions. Perceptions of the work of staff was said to be affected by the accommodation provided and the dispersal of team members. Psychiatrists were located 'upstairs' in a different part of the building from the unit, together with the speech and language therapist. Also, clinical psychology and social work were housed in a separate hospital block, necessitating the crossing of two car parks. A staff nurse said 'Feel disadvantaged by the lay out of the building – down here with the children – in a sense feel left with the situation. Psychiatrists value us... not enough recognition of what we all put in' as did a nursing assistant 'Between teaching staff and nurses there is equal respect. Teachers are very dependent on us when they have problems and we back them... other disciplines it's more difficult because of the environment and where we are situated distances us from them. Only been upstairs twice!' Worthy of note is that a therapist remarked 'I feel the unit should function as a unit and not as a unit *people visit*.

In general nurses tended to describe limited contact with doctors and clearly desired to see them having greater interaction with the children and the ward.

Several staff from a number of different disciplines saw the difference in hours worked, 'free time', status and pay as causing resentment among team members: 'Hierarchy interferes with the effectiveness of what we are doing... job status can distance people from being effective... Good now in-service training is mixed – need all in there' (nursing assistant); 'Don't know how much hierarchical set up is a hindrance – nursing staff refer to how much pay doctors get' (registrar).

Teamwork, however, was seen as essential, and fundamental aspects of it were agreed upon, and sometimes vividly visualised 'team effort is all wearing a pair of the same shoes and they fit comfortably. All know what each is doing'.

Differences perceived between professions appeared to relate to the amount of direct contact with children and the nature of input. For example a nurse explained 'Methods (of different professions) are quite entirely different. Psychiatrists and psychologists are more theoretical than nurses – their work is more practical. The relationships are different with children and therefore this leads to a different management of the children. Nurses see kids more as kids – individuals maybe'. Difference with regard to the theoretical 'frameworks' used by staff also emerged as of significance. A psychiatrist who viewed the ward in terms of a biopsychosocial model felt sometimes that social workers and psychologists 'lacked the biopart'. The difficulty of maintaining relationships when situations were challenging or demanding was raised by a number of staff and reflected in the following comment by a teacher 'At times of stress, if a particular child is acting up – everyone starts thinking someone's doing it all wrong. It gets divisive when children are not responding'. Despite differences identified and discussed the majority of staff saw many similarities too: 'I don't see any big difference in opinion. Most people are similar in approach –

Behavioural or family centred – these are the two big strands. There aren't any individuals who stand out who have very different ideas' (psychiatrist).

Several staff cautioned against seeing relationships in terms of professional or discipline grouping: 'Can't even do it by groups; it has to be by individuals' (clinical psychologist); 'Differences in individual approach eg arises out of people's individual experience with children, their personality and previous professional experience – in that order!' (occupational therapist). One teacher in fact advised 'In building relationships it is necessary to get through the stereotype to the personality'. 'The overlying congruent bit is wanting to see good in children and reward the good bit' (clinical psychologist).

The Therapeutic Milieu

Staff's opinions of the key elements constituting a structured environment were sought at interview. The three elements most commonly identified were: (1) daily routine; (2) clear guidelines; and (3) consistency. The latter included consistency between parents and ward staff, as well as consistency between staff members. Staff well appreciated that colleagues had distinctive responses and styles but thought that differences were inevitable: 'you know the way others do it wouldn't work for you' (staff nurse).

> 'Kids suss you out, and know some people are more strict and some more lenient – reasonable so long as you stay the same. There are problems when you are more lenient – you can regret this at the time – things can get out of hand. But also think you can turn people into robots' (staff nurse).

Nevertheless, it was recognised that teamwork imposed constraints.

> 'With teamwork you have to back off a bit because you have a different opinion. At the end of the day the majority rules – you can't steamroll and do your own thing.'

In the course of discussion on consistency often staff's reflections on personal values and style were articulated.

> 'Aware of personal style especially when I came to the unit – see it as run as a middle class value system, but I am not middle class – I don't feel the same values as important as other members of staff' (staff nurse).

Conversely when staff were asked directly about their personal values much material relating to consistency was presented. It was often repeated among nursing staff that as they became more confident so they became less directive, although interestingly teachers tended to feel that with time they had become more directive. Psychiatrists perceived their own directional/non-directional position by reference to their peers:

> 'I tend to be less directive, not very confrontational, reflective. Working with co-therapists it comes to the fore how people handle the situation differently-working with others you see how different your values are.'

> 'I'm more directive than some people. I ask families to do tasks and am more active/interventionist than some... once the task has been achieved I don't carry on in a supportive role, I pull out but am available for consultation.'

Despite staff's ability to discuss the ward environment, several, particularly non-medical staff, found it difficult at interview to examine the unit as a therapeutic milieu, thus helping to explain why there had been such a poor response to a similar question on the questionnaire. It was clear, too, that staff, including psychiatrists, had varying definitions and understanding of a therapeutic milieu. The following comments reflect the discursive, varying and ambivalent nature of responses:

> 'Doesn't operate as a classical therapeutic milieu... Doesn't have regular meetings and a structure associated with a milieu. Although a therapeutic milieu is hard to define it doesn't seem one although I like to think of it as one. Children would be part of a therapeutic milieu having a role in deciding how it should operate. There's no forum for them as a group' (senior registrar).

> 'Children don't take as much responsibility for the running of the unit. Major decision making still retained by staff. The challenging of behaviour is a staff function rather than that of the patient... Could be developed more in the unit' (consultant).

> 'Yes it is. Nursing staff try to build up relationships. There are some systematic behavioural management principles applied which lead to feelings of stability for the child. There is some structure. I see the therapeutic milieu in practical terms rather than as an esoteric ideal... Should be deeper discussion on what we are about' (clinical psychologist).

> 'At times yes and at other times no. There's not a lot of group work or attempts to work with the whole "community" – we should work with them, they would have a say. Say has to be less with children, and issues kept at basic levels but still a lot can be done in giving children responsibility: the little ones under eight years of age in Canada wanted a meeting, It's useful to talk, to get them to look at their behaviour – I don't see that happening here' (associate specialist).

However, when staff at interview were asked about the problems of reconciling individual and group needs much discussion centred on, in fact, the ward milieu. Attention was drawn time and time again to the pressures on admission... 'in reality it's the most pressing case that comes in' and thus as a consequence there 'isn't always the luxury of the best therapeutic group'.

> 'Often there is a risk that children "acting out" can become the dominant culture with some degree of loss or lack of acceptance of authority. Children, who in a different sort of milieu would be OK, can be sucked in... always a balance exists between the pressure to admit and the need to keep the milieu of the ward/culture more constructive.'

Several staff emphasised that the potential always exists that the ward group is unsuitable for a child. Some saw tensions within the group as cyclical 'Sometimes culture counterproductive or productive – often occurs in cycles'. Even where the value of individual work was stressed, the group was seen as being of significance: 'resolution of individual problems may occur within the group' (staff nurse).

Treatment Outcomes

Although some staff voiced doubts regarding pervasiveness of the therapeutic milieu the overwhelming majority of staff were convinced of the effects of admission on the children, as in the words of the staff member 'at the end of the day I feel something is achieved'. Moreover, commonly it was felt that things were capable of change; 'I believe things can always be different. I'm a perpetual optimist – if we look hard enough we can find a way of changing things and see results. Whatever investment we make we may have an effect – even if it's in five years time' (charge nurse).

Where doubts were expressed these was frequently contextualised: 'At times wonder what we are doing but it's part of a normal working day to question effectiveness' (teacher). It was emphasised the effect had to be seen within 'the limits of possible goals' as the Medical Director said

> '[effect] varies from family to family. We work with what is presented and often we are presented with the most disturbed families and we can't make perfect. We can only improve up the ladder one or two rungs – we are not able to change things in a major way.'

Other staff too voiced the view that effects were variable, for instance the social worker who commented

> 'I'm confident enough that for some children in the unit admission is very useful and instructive. It helps families more on to a better way of functioning but I'm not sure it happens enough.'

It was clear from the interviews that staff at all levels and disciplines gave considerable consideration to effects and children's/families' suitability for admission:

'(This is) discussed quite a lot among staff, we're quite good at identifying children who don't have any need of us. We can most readily identify children whose needs are not being met.' (staff nurse)

It was widely recognised, however, that outcomes were not easily quantifiable:

'Forming individual relationships with the children – that is important regardless of outcome. [The Medical Director] says it's important that the children take away a little bit of that relationship forged.' (registrar)

At the conclusion of interviews staff were invited to describe their ideal unit. From the often rapidity and detailed nature of responses it was clear that staff carried with them an image of a unit in which they would like to work and knew the improvements they would like to see. Characteristics of an ideal unit related to three main areas (1) staffing issues; (2) the physical environment: (3) policy and procedures (see Table 13.6). The single aspect mentioned most frequently was that of ward facilities, with 12 staff specifically making reference to sleeping arrangements and desiring to see single rooms or smaller dormitories. In general it was felt that the ward should be 'more cosy'. Few, however, recommended that the unit be situated away from the hospital. Two staff, however, pointed out that in an ideal world such units wouldn't exist!

Table 13.6 Main Characteristics of an Ideal Unit*

	$N = 29$
Physical environment	38
smaller dorms/single rooms	12
better classrooms	5
more rooms	5
more homely/less institutionalised	5
play areas improved	7
other	4
Staffing	25
better trained staff	10
more staff/more settled staff	7
full complement of staff (includ. OT, SALT)	5
other	3
Unit policy and practice	20
clear philosophy	5
more home visits/family work	3
greater participation in community activities	3
no admission over 13 years of age	2
weekend opening	2
other	5

* more than one characteristic provided

Discussion

For nearly half a century, work in psychiatry, in both Britain and the USA, has been based on the assumption that the social environment of in-patient treatment settings could have a substantial impact on the behaviour of psychiatric patients (Price and Moos 1975). Specifically with regard to child residential psychiatric units the whole residential experience has been viewed as its constituting the patient's therapy (Johnson 1982). Yet little detailed knowledge is available on either the organisational features or the day-to-day work of British units which would facilitate identification of the critical dimensions of the ward environment. Those accounts which are available are often dated, impressionistic and written by unit directors. Although it is commonly accepted that in-patients units have tended to develop idiosyncratically, according to local conditions and personalities (Green 1993), there are few, if any, detailed systematic, objective studies which would enable valid comparisons to be drawn and identification of points of convergence and divergence. Indeed, if there is significant diversity, then the potential exists for the exploration of the relationship between type of provision and outcome.

Given that there have been few studies of the dynamics of therapeutic input on a child residential psychiatric ward, appropriate research methods are in their infancy; Wrate et al. (1994) give some indication of both the possibilities and the problems to be overcome. The work reported here indicates one particular approach – a fine-grained and labour intensive method (Pfeiffer and Strzelecki 1990). It well illustrates the time consuming and demanding nature of this manner of investigation and would suggest that such foundation work is necessary before outcome studies can attempt to identify the consequences of particular ward regimes treatments and interactions.

On the basis of the Lowit Unit study, it would appear that the early work dating back to Redl (1959) and Adler (1968) still has much to offer in providing a valuable framework for ward-based studies. For example, the central core common to all residential treatment settings as listed by Adler would in the light of this study still appear valid and reliable:

(1) structured planned living

(2) authority and opportunity for clients to work out feelings

(3) a focus on health rather than pathology of personality

(4) group living

(5) individuality of treatment

(6) identification through the opportunity for forming significant relationships

(7) child–staff interaction

(8) a sense of common purpose

(9) integrating joint planning of treatment programmes by all staff. (Adler
     1968)

There is a need, however, for a greater understanding of processes integral to
elements, for example factors promoting and inhibiting child–staff interaction.
The importance of the relationships between the child and staff is well
recognised: 'The importance of the personal qualities of staff, their interaction
with each other and their ability to form a therapeutic culture is accepted as a
basic building block of residential treatment' (Johnson 1982). Concomitantly
it is acknowledged that issues that diminish the relationship between staff and
patients impede progress to therapeutic goals (Dalton, Muller and Forman
1988). Parry-Jones (1989), in tracing the history of child and family psychiatry,
moreover asserted that much more than in other branches of medicine, the
provision of psychiatric services for children and adolescents is affected by the
character and attitudes of those concerned, at every level, from therapist to
Minister of Health. Yet although Szurek nearly half a century ago in his paper
'Dynamics of staff interaction in hospital psychiatric treatment of children'
(Szurek 1947) highlighted the importance of therapeutic relationships and the
relative infrequency of their study, there have been few empirical attempts over
the years in either Britain or the USA to analyse the characteristic form of such
relationships and their major therapeutic influence.

    To date there has been a paucity of explicit discussion in the ward or
treatment context on *how* education, training attitudes, values and philosophies
affect the therapeutic relationship. Little is known, for example, regarding how
staff's own childhood and their own parenting behaviour or indeed family
status, affects ward environment and patient and parent relationships, even
though potentially these considerations could have a profound influence on the
work of staff. It is of interest to note that in this study that although staff initially
did not identify their own children as having influenced their practice, once
directly asked by the author if this was the case, the majority readily agreed to
the proposition. To date no reference has been found in the literature on child
psychiatric units regarding the effects of staff's attitude to children, their child
rearing practices and beliefs concerning the family, despite the fact that
understanding (and knowledge of) the patient's family is regarded as fundamental to treatment.

    That staff found discussion of the term 'therapeutic milieu' problematic is
perhaps not surprising given the varying definitions of therapeutic milieu which
have evolved over the years and the confusion which has surrounded the use
of such terms as therapeutic milieu, therapeutic community and milieu therapy
(Filstead and Rossi 1973). Among non-medical staff in particular the lack of
clarity regarding such terms is perhaps indicative that in a treatment setting such
terms may become part of staff's vocabulary without a basic questioning of
meaning and applicability or indeed as Johnson (1982) has argued theoretical
orientation tends to lose clarity in the process of implementation. Specific

specialist training for nursing staff in particular, though, may help in providing a stronger theoretical base for working practice. Medical staff's reference to patients' input in the context of discussions on the therapeutic milieu does raise the question whether the Lowit Unit has a lower level of patient participation than other British units or whether British units differ fundamentally in this respect from their counterparts in the USA and Canada. Certainly the overall philosophy of the Lowit Unit, based on an eclectic and problem solving approach appears to fit well with descriptions of other units, by for example Wolkind and Gent (1990).

Staff's on the whole positive perceptions of their colleagues and their practices are of interest in the light of Bettelheim's (1974) comments on social solidarity which he regards as necessary among staff to support them in their relationships with their clients. Furthermore, medical staff's commitment to an eclectic approach, despite differences in therapeutic 'style' is worthy of note in the light of past antagonisms between psychotherapists and behaviour therapists (Graham 1993). Overall, it was evident from interview material that there was recognition of the contribution of other staff members and often this was highly valued.

A major factor inhibiting teamworking was the diverse nature of staff input on the Unit. A crucial factor was whether or not staff had other hospital or community wide commitments. The scattered nature, moreover, of staff accommodation helped produce a situation where some staff were more likely to be seen as 'visitors' to the Unit.

The complexity of line management functions regarding team members, as shown in Figure 13.1, may in the future make work between team members increasingly difficult. The observations of Soni, Steers, Warne and Sang (1989) in the context of adult psychiatry may be equally applicable to child and family psychiatry

> 'Many of the factors that contribute to failure of multi-disciplinary teams in clinical psychiatry relate to the structure, establishment and other factors which are largely intrinsic in the heterogeneous nature of clinical organisation of the delivery of services in psychiatry.' (p.660)

As Soni et al. (1989) have noted, hierarchical structures exist in nursing, social work, occupational therapy and psychological services and multi-disciplinary teams by their nature and composition include members from horizontally as well as vertically organised professions. In a similar vein the authors drew attention to the potentially damaging effects of dual accountability and divided loyalties. Such comments would appear of equal relevance to child and family psychiatry and it may be anticipated that team working may be increasingly difficult to sustain as the non-medical professions become better qualified (two of the ward nurses were graduates) and seek not only parity of esteem but increasing clinical autonomy and a larger part in decision making. In addition, with hospital reorganisation and the creation of clinical directorates, team members may well discover that previous working practices are threatened and new identities and commitments develop. While the Lowit Unit continues to be part of Royal Aberdeen Children's Hospital, the latter is now administered by the Aberdeen Royal Hospitals (NHS) Trust. It seems likely that the full implications of these changes have yet to be known.

As has been noted previously, teams do not have responsibility for the management of resources (Soni *et al.* 1989), and thus are dependent often on managers to release staff and make budgetary commitments. It may be open to question if this arrangement, which perhaps has worked surprisingly well to date, can be maintained in a rapidly changing environment of resource management. A more serious challenge to multi-disciplinary teamwork may thus result from increasing emphasis on business planning and budgeting.

Although it was not foreseen at the beginning of this study, the critical nature of leadership and managerial issues emerged as the work progressed. This may be a reflection of the fact that child residential units are being drawn into tighter managerial structures within hospitals and the residential unit is ceasing 'to be an island within the sea of the greater hospital' (Blotcky *et al.* 1987). Although for many decades unit staff have been working with external agencies in the community, the NHS and Community Care Act (1990), together with new organisational structures (care management) and working practices (assessment of needs), is likely to place different and greater demands on communication and managerial skills. It may well be timely, therefore, to examine the structure and organisation of residential units, their method of resourcing and management training for staff. Clearly the co-ordination of services will continue to be needed but past, and often informal procedures may not be adequate in light of the demands of both health and social care systems.

The high number of staff involved in units, and the variation in the nature and extent of their input, creates considerable difficulties for the evaluation of the work of in-patient residential units. There seems little reason to believe that many of the British audits being carried out will be able to reveal the efficacy of differing therapeutic inputs, particularly since they have highlighted the need for further research. There would appear as much need today as when Pfeiffer and Strelecki (1990) were writing to look closely at 'what factors are required to orchestrate a dynamic, harmonious and penetrating treatment environment' (p.851). If in-patient units are to survive, especially in an increasingly hostile climate, much more needs to be known regarding the manner which hours, days, weeks and months are spent by the patient on the ward. Such research is likely to be slow, and initially unrewarding. It may in the long run provide for a better understanding of the fundamental factors underlying the therapeutic relationship, and lead to improved methods of treatment.

Conclusion

(1) The time consuming and demanding nature of this sort of study was confirmed.

(2) Empirical study of the influence of staff's family experiences on child psychiatric in-patient practice is required.

(3) Confusion about the concept of the therapeutic milieu was found. This has been noted elsewhere (Filstead and Rossi 1973). The value of the classical therapeutic milieu in a modern child psychiatric in-patient setting requires investigation.

(4) A low level of patient participation was found. Comparative studies are required to establish the level and nature of participation that is most beneficial for different age and diagnostic groups. These studies should include assessment of patient satisfaction.

(5) Complexity due to a multiplicity of management pathways and differing patterns of professional organisation was found. These are likely to make adjustment to changes in the NHS and the local authority more difficult.

(6) A degree of confusion over leadership and management issues emerged. It is likely that in the changing climate in the NHS informal arrangements that have worked well in the past now require more formalisation.

Postscript

Units are not static. They can change rapidly with changes in staffing, hospital organisation and administration, and, policy and priorities. Since this study was completed a number of changes have occurred in the Lowit Unit, some indeed possibly as a result of this investigation but others in response to a review by the Trust. In particular, there have been modifications to the fabric of the Unit itself, with the loss of the dormitory and the creation of single and four bedded rooms. The school day has changed and time with nursing staff 'ring fenced'. The number of residential places has been reduced and there will cease to be 'night nurses'; this duty will be taken on by day staff. There has been a change in Medical Director and the new incumbent has moved 'downstairs', sharing an office with the Charge Nurse. Overall practice has become more formalised with the drafting of protocols and a contracting document drawn up with the Trust. There is little, however, to suggest that the children and their problems have changed in any significant respect.

References

Adler, J. (1968) 'General concepts in residential treatment of disturbed children.' *Child Welfare XLVII*, 9, 519–523.

Bettelheim, B. (1974) *A Home for the Heart.* New York: Bantam Books.

Blotcky, M. J., Dimperio, T. L., Blotcky, A. and Looney, J. G. (1987) 'A systems model for residential treatment of children.' *Residential Treatment for Children and Youth 5*, 1, 55–67.

Canfield, M., Muller, J. and Clarkin, J. (1988) 'Issues in research design in psychiatric hospitals.' *Psychiatric Hospital 19*, 11–26.

Dalton, R., Muller, B. and Forman, M.A. (1988) 'The psychiatric hospitalization of children: An overview.' *Child Psychiatry and Human Development 19*, 4, 231–244.

Filstead, W.J. and Rossi, J.J. (1973) 'Therapeutic milieu, Therapeutic Community and Milieu Therapy: Some conceptual and definitional distinctions.' In J.J. Rossi and W.J. Filstead (eds) *The Therapeutic Community.* New York: Behavioural Publications.

Gray, C., Chisholm, D., Smith, P., Brown, M. and McKay, C, (1992) 'The role of the child psychiatrist ward in health care: experiences with different types of admissions over a period of twenty-one years.' *Irish Journal of Psychological Medicine 9*, 17–23.

Green, J.M. (1993) 'Inpatient treatment: personal practice.' In M.E. Garralda (ed) *Managing Children with Psychiatric Problems.* London: BMJ.

Johnson, S. (1982) 'Residential treatment for emotionally disturbed children and adolescents: a review of the literature.' *Canada's Mental Health*, March 1983, 5–8.

Parry-Jones, W.L.I. (1989) 'Annotation: The history of child and adolescent psychiatry: Its present day relevance.' *Journal of Child Psychology and Psychiatry 30*, 1, 3–11.

Pfeiffer, S.I. and Strzelecki, S.C. (1990) 'Inpatient psychiatric treatment of children and adolescents: a review of outcome studies.' *Journal of the American Academy of Child and Adolescent Psychiatry 29*, 6, 847–853.

Price, R.H. and Moos, R.H. (1975) 'Toward a taxonomy of inpatient treatment environments.' *Journal of Abnormal Psychology 84*, 3, 181–188.

Rapoport, R.N. (1960) *Community as Doctor.* London: Tavistock.

Redl, F. (1959) 'The concept of a "Therapeutic Milieu".' *American Journal of Orthopsychiatry 29b*, 721–736.

Research Committee of the Royal College of Psychiatrists (1991) 'Future directions for research in child and adolescent psychiatry.' *Psychiatric Bulletin 15*, 308–310.

Soni, S.D., Steers, L., Warne, T. and Sang, W.H. (1989) 'Multidisciplinary teams and line management.' *Psychiatric Bulletin 13*, 657–661.

Szurek, S.A. (1947) 'Dynamics of staff interaction in hospital psychiatric treatment of children.' *American Journal of Orthopsychiatry 17*, 652–664.

Wolkind, S. and Gent, M. (1990) 'Children's psychiatric in-patient units: present functions and future directions.' *Maladjustment and Therapeutic Education 5*, 2, 54–64.

Wrate, R., Rothery, D., McCabe, R., Aspin, J. and Bryce, G. (1994) 'A prospective multicentre study of admissions to adolescent inpatient units.' *Journal of Adolescence 17*, 221–237.

CHAPTER 14

Contemporary Developments in Child Psychiatric In-Patient Practice

Kasi Brahmanya Gururaj-Prasad

Introduction

In-patient child psychiatric units have recently had to adapt to two major legislative influences: The Children Act 1989, implemented in its entirety from 14th October 1991 in England and Wales; and the National Health Service and Community Care Act 1990 implemented from 1st April 1991. The Children Act 1989, Department of Health (1989a) brought together in one statute hitherto fragmented pieces of legislation concerning children. Further, the Children Act emphasises the paramountcy of the welfare and interests of the child and encourages greater co-operation amongst parents, statutory and voluntary agencies to promote the welfare of the child. The Act incorporates the principle that children are best placed within their natural families, with the parents playing a full part in their upbringing. It uses the phrase 'parental responsibility' in an attempt to clarify the role of the parent, defining the phrase as 'to include all the rights, powers, authority and duties of parents in relation to a child and his property' (Department of Health 1989b). In order to promote co-operation, the Act proposes a 'Non-Interference' principle; that the courts cannot make any order unless it considers to do so would be better than making no order. To assist the courts and implicitly others involved, a welfare checklist (not exhaustive), is provided which includes the following items:

(1) the ascertainable wishes and feelings of the child concerned (considered in the light of his age and understanding)

(2) his physical, emotional and educational needs

(3) the likely effect on him of any change in his circumstances

(4) his age, sex, background, and any characteristics of his which the court considers relevant

(5) any harm which he has suffered or is at risk of suffering

(6) how capable each of his parents, and any other person in relation to whom the court considers the question to be relevant, is of meeting his needs; and

(7) the range of powers available to the court under the Act in the proceedings in question.

The welfare checklist remedies a perception that the courts did not accord due consideration to the ascertainable wishes and feelings of the child. The checklist also requires the court to consider all the options which are available to it (Department of Health 1989b).

The impact of the Children Act 1989 on child psychiatric in-patient units has been more predictable and less unsettling than the National Health Service (NHS) reforms. It is useful to examine the issues within the Act that relate specifically to in-patient units before considering the impact of the NHS reforms:

The Children Act

(1) *Notification of children accommodated* (Sections 85 and 86 of the Children Act) state that health authorities have to notify local authorities when a child is accommodated for a consecutive period of at least three months or if there is the intention that a child should be so accommodated. Hendricks and Williams (1992) state that the intention is to ensure that children do not lose contact with those who hold parental responsibility. However, child psychiatric practice has for long embraced active co-operation with parents and carers so that no major change is required to comply with this guideline, though the practice has now to be formalised.

(2) *Restriction of the liberty of children.* The use of accommodation to physically restrict the liberty of any child is prohibited except when the child is detained under the Mental Health Act 1983 or in secure accommodation which is subject to secure accommodation regulations under Section 25 of the Act. In practice these changes to the secure accommodation regulations mean that a child in an in-patient unit may only be kept in conditions of security, without the authority of a court for up to 72 hours whether consecutively or in aggregate in any period of 28 consecutive days. The court must authorise any placement lasting for longer than 72 hours and the hospital managers will have to apply for the authorisation.

A positive aspect of this legislation has probably been an improvement in recordkeeeping but a worrying implication has been a 'growing paralysis' about the sorts of restraints that can be imposed upon children within in-patient units. Jones (1991) points to a deficiency in the legislation that does not define terms such as 'time-out', 'holding' and 'seclusion', allowing varying interpretations of what is permissible under the Act and what isn't. Wolkind (1993) describes how this resulted in the premature discharge of an aggressive boy whose successful treatment through a time out programme had to be terminated as it was deemed illegal by the local authority. The longest period that the boy who had been sexually abused had spent in the time-out room had been five minutes. However, the local authority suggested that it was appropriate to use physical restraint to counter his violence – a method of restraint that nursing staff thought clearly unsuitable for a boy who had been abused. Staff in residential units face similar difficulties.

(3) *Consent to treatment.* The Children Act specifies that the child must be able to consent to treatment and be able to refuse treatment if he/she is of sufficient understanding to make a decision. The Department of Health places the onus on the doctor by advising that 'this is for the doctor to decide'. Jones (1991) discusses the meaning of consent and states that it is valid if fully informed and freely given by the person concerned. The child must understand why any treatment is proposed, the nature of treatment, its benefits and risks and the consequences of not receiving it. The clinical determination of the capacity to consent is comprised of several elements – age, intelligence, maturity and psychological state – but none of which can be a sole determiner. The age of informed consent remains, however, contentious. The Gillick judgement established that children under 16 years could give legally effective consent to medical treatment, independent of their parents wishes, provided they had sufficient understanding and intelligence.

Shield and Baum (1994) highlight the contradictions of a recent ruling that stated that no one under 18 years has an absolute right to make his or her own decisions on medical treatment, especially when that decision is refusal. The authors state that the ruling has caused disquiet amongst child health professionals. The case in the Court of Appeal in which Lord Donaldson ruled (*Re* W, 1992) deserves close examination by child and adolescent psychiatrists. W, who was born in 1976, was placed in care at an early age and became ill with anorexia nervosa in 1990. Upon attaining the age of 16, she exercised her right to separate representation and challenged the decision to transfer her to an unit specialising in eating disorders. Having lost her case in the High Court, W appealed, stating in one of the grounds that the High Court had no jurisdiction, or alternatively that no jurisdiction should be exercised, to overrule the refusal of a competent minor age 16 to undergo medical treatment. Further W argued that Section 8 of the Family Law Reform Act, 1969, should have been applied in her case. Section 8(1) provides that the consent of a minor who has attained the age of 16 years to any treatment which, in the absence of consent, would constitute a trespass to his person, shall be as effective as if he were of full age. W's condition deteriorated to such a serious extent during the hearing that Lord Donaldson announced that the Court ordered that W be transferred to the specialist unit and receive treatment without her consent for reasons to be given later. Lord Donaldson referring to W's anorexia nervosa stated that although a patient may understand the treatment proposed and the consequences of failure to accept the treatment, certain conditions are capable of destroying the patient's ability to make an informed choice, creating a compulsion to refuse treatment or only to accept treatment which is likely to be ineffective. In his judgement Lord Donaldson stated

> 'There is ample authority for the proposition that the inherent powers of the court under its paren patriae jurisdiction are theoretically limitless and that they certainly extend beyond the powers of a natural parent. There can therefore be no doubt that it has the power to override the refusal of a minor, whether over the age of 16 or under that age but 'Gillick competent'... Prudence does not involve avoiding all risk, but it does involve avoiding taking risks which, if they eventuate, may have irreparable consequences or which are disproportionate to the benefits which could accrue from taking them. I regard this approach as wholly consistent with the philosophy of Section 1 of the Children Act, 1989, and in particular, subsection (3)(a).'

Subsection (3)(a) refers to the first item on the welfare checklist – that is the ascertainable wishes and feelings of the child concerned (considered in the light of his age and understanding). The reasoning of the judgement should allay professional fears and clarify that it was the child's long term welfare being safeguarded. Further, the judgement makes clear the court's authority which extends beyond the powers of a natural parent.

Wolkind (1993) controversially cautions against simply listening to the wishes of the child as it can be detrimental to the welfare of the child. He questions whether the Act is being interpreted to serve narrow professional interests, namely social workers supporting the child's wishes irrespective of long term medical consequences, and some solicitors colluding with social workers. Clark (1994) suggests that child psychiatrists should be familiar with the Mental Health Act 1983, which is more relevant to children and young people suffering from mental disorders. In England and Wales, there is no lower age limit to any of the provisions of the Mental Health Act, 1983 for compulsory hospital treatment. Child psychiatrists in in-patient units may have to use increasingly the Mental Health Act to ensure necessary treatment for children and young people suffering from mental illness. However, Lord Donaldson (Re W, 1992) argues against this approach because of the stigmatising nature of treatment under the Act, viz: 'if the same treatment can be secured upon some other basis, this shall be done'. Clearly there is potential for conflict between the provisions of the Mental Health Act and the Children Act, that only the courts can resolve. Younger children within in-patient units have yet to test provisions of the Children Act, pertaining to consent.

(4) *Legislative Conflicts.* The Act's requirement for co-operation amongst health, education and social services may appear to be in conflict with the marketing concepts and the explicit purchaser/provider split of the NHS Reforms. In-patient units hard pushed to meet contract targets will not be able to respond to the demands of the Children Act, unless service requirements arising from the Act have been negotiated into contracts. There is scant evidence that purchasing commissions have incorporated specific requirements of the Act into contracts. Indeed there is anecdotal evidence of purchasers not funding assessments of children and families requiring in-patient care on the basis that it is too expensive or that it is not part of health care. The Director of Public Health's response to a social worker who had referred a family for residential assessment, following a multi-disciplinary case conference including health professionals, illustrates the difficulties of 'working together'. 'I have recently received an extra contractual referral request for... General Hospital for the residential assessment of the above in the Family Unit under the care of Dr...I am not aware that there has been any involvement in the purchasing authority in the decision to seek this referral and there is no indication of participation of health service staff. I must therefore refuse this referral...'(Personal Communication 1994). The implications of such an approach for in-patient units relying on income from assessment are dire.

The Impact of the NHS and Community Care Act 1990

The internal market reforms passed into law by means of the NHS and Community Care Act 1990 were implemented, by gradualist means, from the

1st of April 1991. Child psychiatric in-patient units have two major challenges with the implementation of the NHS and Community Care Act. (1) The challenge of fragmentation and; (2) the challenge of outcomes. It is useful to consider both these in greater detail.

(1) Challenge of Fragmentation

The key innovation made possible by the NHS and Community Care Act 1990, is the separation of purchasers from providers, creating an internal market (Holliday 1992). General Practitioners through fundholding schemes are now able to purchase certain health services, along with Health Authorities/Boards and private patients from, in theory, any provider of care such as NHS units and /or private sector units, through explicit contracts. NHS provider units, no longer obtain automatic funding for services, unless backed by contracts with purchasers. The contractualism at the heart of the internal market can be a major source of worry for child psychiatric in-patient units, through diversion of scant resources to maintaining contracts rather than to improving service delivery.

Piecemeal creation of 'institutions' such as GP Fundholders means that funding increasingly bypasses the intermediate institutions, such as the District Health Authorities Boards. General Practice Fundholders started with an initial list size of 11,000 which has been gradually reduced to 7000. Once approved, practice budgets are deducted from the allocation of district health authorities and passed directly to the fundholding practice. If fundholders are overfunded, less is available for non-fundholding practices and vice versa. Dixon et al. (1994) have shown that in North West Thames, fundholding practices seem to have been funded more generously than non fundholding practices. There is a £6000 limit on practice liability for any one patient in a financial year so that any expenditure over £6000 is borne directly by the District Health Authority. If a district has a large percentage of fundholders, it can add up to a disproportion-ately adverse impact on the district health authority budget to fund services such as in-patient child psychiatry. Instead of health care provision being decided on a strategic basis by NHS planners, it will increasingly be determined by the purchasing of GP fundholders. GP fundholding may result in a demand-led service, incompatible with the longer term, needs-led strategic thinking that led to the establishment of child psychiatric in-patient units. However, as government policy is to encourage the role of fundholding, child psychiatric in-patient units will have to court this group of purchasers.

As Schorr (1991) points out, the major elements of successful programmes involving children are at odds with the dominant ways that most large systems are funded, and the ways they are expected to assure accountability, quality and equity,

> 'comprehensiveness is at odds, with narrow, categorical funding and multifactored interactions are at odds with our yearnings for one-shot,

quick fixes,... intensiveness and individualisation are at odds with the pressures to assure equity in the face of insufficient funds.' (p 440)

Child psychiatric illness is the product of complex interaction between constitution and the environment and the responses to troubled children and troubled families must be as multifactorial as the troubles themselves.

The extreme fragmentation and thus potentially extreme diversity of provision generated by GP fundholding may drive a wedge between out-patient and in-patient child psychiatric services, reducing the benefits of an integrated child psychiatric service. The probability of competition among providers of routine and inexpensive treatments is high. Therein lies another potential threat to the functioning of child psychiatric in-patient units. While the main purchaser of in-patient services will be the District Health Authority, contracts for out-patient child psychiatric services may well be placed away from in-patient units by GP fundholders. Counsellors, some of whom are directly employed by fundholders, may begin to meet the mental health needs of children in the practice setting, leading to termination of contracts for out-patient child psychiatric services. The delinking of in-patient from out-patient child psychiatric services will threaten the viability of in-patient units. Though fundholders are a genuinely unpredictable element in the new NHS, such a situation probably remains a potential threat, unless the trend to employ unregulated counsellors directly gains momentum. General Practitioners who are fundholders are in a position of conflict – being both purchasers of some services and providers of others. There is no recognition of this conflict by the government and consequently no mechanism to resolve it. Howie, Heaney and Maxwell (1994) studying the effects of fundholding on referral patterns for patients presenting with joint pain found a significant fall in the number of referrals to hospital, following fundholding status. The authors comment that little is known about the effect of fundholding on quality of care and satisfaction of patients.

The fragmentation on the purchasing front has been paralleled by a fragmentation of providers. The emergence of separate acute and community trusts has tested the allegiance of child psychiatric in-patient units to *either* children's services mainly in acute trusts *or* adult mental health services, mainly in community trusts. At a functional level, the establishment of Clinical Directorates has probably led to different members of the multi-disciplinary team belonging to different directorates – child psychiatrists in one directorate, separate from child psychologists, nursing staff, occupational therapists or speech therapists (see Chapter 13). The practice of child psychiatry with its multi-disciplinary and multi-agency ethos is well used to the tensions inherent in multi-disciplinary working. However, the pull of professional allegiances amidst a background of competition and market-forces can only be prevented from impinging on the functioning of the unit by an extremely cohesive staff group.

The fragmentation of purchasers and providers combined with scaling down of purchasing commissions has meant a confusion over who performs certain functions such as needs assessment. General Practitioners are the primary agents in the delivery of health services and, therefore, theoretically in the best position to assess health needs of the local population. However, are General Practitioners assessing needs or demands, and do they have the expertise to assess needs? These are questions that have not been adequately answered to date.

(2) Challenge of Outcomes

Competitive pressures of the internal market are intended to generate a dynamic of increased efficiency and cost-effectiveness. Purchasers are increasingly looking to 'buy right', to compare outcomes and quality, and to incorporate their findings into buying decisions. Parry-Jones (1992) states that therapeutic innovation and service development have been hampered by, amongst many factors, lack of treatment outcome studies and the lack of routine evaluation of intervention programmes. It is recognised that outcomes in relation to contracts are of limited direct value in that most clinical literature examines effectiveness in relation to diagnosing and treating disease, while most contracts are set on a specialty or client group. A further difficulty, as Ward (1994) states, is that the internal market is more suited to services organised in single episodes of in-patient care, such as hip-replacements rather than complex issues of mental health. The contracting process needs greater sophistication to incorporate outcomes, limited as outcomes studies are in Child Psychiatry. However, it is encouraging that the outcomes movement is encompassing broader aspects of health care, thereby increasing its relevance to child psychiatry. For, child psychiatric in-patient units will probably have to rely on outcomes and health gain criteria to justify their usefulness and value. Epstein (1990) points out that the outcomes movement has seen a broadening of focus to include a wider range of outcomes such as functional status, emotional health, social interaction, cognitive function, and degree of disability. Carroll (1993) has produced a list of health gain criteria some of which are relevant to child psychiatric in-patient practice, namely, appropriateness, quantity, quality, effectiveness, acceptability, efficiency and opportunity costs. Orchard (1994), has reaffirmed that medical outcomes are multi-dimensional, most are qualitative and are affected by timing. Orchard further points out that outcomes may not be attributable to specific treatments. Using health gain criteria Light and Bailey (1993) have shown how cost effective Child Mental Health Services are, and argue that it is a prime candidate for joint commissioning between the NHS and local authorities.

In theory, health care should be purchased to maximise health gain, though there are constraints, as Akehurst and Ferguson (1993) point out. The major constraints are the 'initiatives' and 'tasks', such as waiting list initiatives that arise from national policies and emerge from the NHS Management Executive as priorities. These priorities may need to be written into corporate contracts, and Akehurst and Ferguson state that 'concern to meet these constraints could be so overwhelming that no managerial energy may be left to pursue health gain' (p.????). The government can indirectly influence health care in some areas through priorities, while practicing a market philosophy in others. Market forces can be a great leveller. Though there are no centrally collected figures for the number of child and adolescent psychiatry beds, Waite (1994) reports that the number of beds over the last three years has fallen by almost 20 per cent. The Department of Health responded to concerns about the closure of an adolescent unit in Macclesfield by stating 'The scale of residential mental health provision for young people is determined in response to local needs rather than centrally by the department. The number of in-patient places is a matter for individual health authorities to determine and provide appropriate services to meet these needs' (Waite 1994, p.4). It is clear that the lack of a coherent policy on mental health services for young people and the fragmentation of purchasers are partly to blame for the closure of the adolescent unit. Wilson (1994) states that we are living in a state of increasing disconnection, for we are simply not making use of the knowledge we have to coordinate services for children. Wilson argues, too, that the problem of vulnerable children and families must receive government attention, priority and initiative if we are to improve the well-being of our children.

The future for child psychiatric in-patient units appears mixed. Responsive provider in-patient units able to prove positive outcomes and health gain will thrive, especially if purchasing commissions are well developed and able to incorporate outcomes/ health gain criteria into contracts. Where providers are not able to prove cost-effective health outcomes, and the purchasing commissions are poorly developed, the future is gloomy. Much will depend too on which way the political winds blow and how much of a priority the health-policy makers place on child psychiatry.

References

Akehurst, R. and Ferguson, B. (1993) 'The purchasing authority. In M.F. Drummond and A. Maynard (eds) *Purchasing and Providing Cost-Effective Health Care.* Edinburgh: Churchill Livingstone.

Carroll, G. (1993) *Priority Setting in Purchasing Health Care in Rationing in Action.* London: BMJ Publishing Group.

Clark, A. (1994) 'Children's consent to treatment.' *British Medical Journal 308,* 1637.

Department of Health (1983) *The Mental Health Act.* London: HMSO.

Department of Health (1989a) *The Children Act.* London: HMSO.

Department of Health (1989b) *An Introduction to The Children Act 1989.* London: HMSO.

Department of Health (1990) *National Health Service and Community Care Act.* London: HMSO.

Dixon, J., Dinwoodie, M., Hodson, D., Dodd, S., Poltorak, J., Garrett, C., Rice, P., Doncaster, I., Williams, N., (1994) 'Distribution of funds between fundholding and non-fundholding practices.' *British Medical Journal 309,* 30– 34.

Epstein, A.M. (1990) 'The Outcomes Movement – will it get us where we want to go.' *The New England Journal of Medicine 323,* 4, 266–270.

The Family Law Reform Act, 1969 (1970) In D.A. Holden and Butterworths Legal Editorial Staff (eds) *Child Legislation 1969.* London: Butterworths.

Hendriks, J.H. and Williams, R. (1992) 'The Children Act, 1989 – England and Wales: Implications for Healthcare Practice and Schools.' *ACPP Newsletter 14,* 5, 213–220.

Holliday, I. (1992) *The NHS Transformed.* Manchester: Baseline Books.

Howie, J.G.R., Heaney, D.J., Maxwell, M. (1994) 'Evaluating care of patients reporting pain in fundholding practices.' *British Medical Journal 309,* 705–10.

Jones, D.P. (1991) 'Working with the Children Act: Tasks and Responsibilities of the Child and Adolescent Psychiatrist.' In C. Lindsey (ed) *Proceedings of the Children Act Study Day (Occasional Paper 12).* London: Royal College of Psychiatrists.

Light, D. and Bailey, V. (1993) 'Pound foolish.' *Health Services Journal.* February, 16–18.

Orchard, C. (1994) 'Comparing healthcare outcomes.' *British Medical Journal 308,* 1493–1496.

Personal Communication 1994 from Director of Public Health.

Parry-Jones, W.L.L. (1992) 'Management in the National Health Service in Relation to Children and the Provision of Child Psychiatric Services.' *Association of Child Psychology and Psychiatry Newsletter 14,* 1, 3–10.

Re W, 1992 3 WLR 758.

Schorr, L.B. (1991) 'Children, families and the cycle of disadvantage.' *Canadian Journal of Psychiatry 36,* 6, 437–441.

Shield, J.P.H. and Baum, J.D. (1994) 'Children's consent to treatment.' *British Medical Journal 308,* 1182–83.

Waite, J. (1994) Radio 4's 'Face the Facts' reported in *Young Minds Newsletter 18,* 2–4.

Ward, P. (1994) 'The mental health market.' *Psychiatric Bulletin 18,* 538–540.

Wilson, P. (1994) 'Out of touch.' *Young Minds Newsletter 18,* 1.

Wolkind, S.N. (1993) 'The 1989 Children Act: A cynical view from an Ivory Tower.' *ACPP Newsletter 15,* 1, 40–41.

CHAPTER 15

Issues Relating to Child Residential Psychiatric Units

Rosemary Chesson and Douglas Chisholm

Low Visibility

Although units have been in existence in Britain for over 40 years, as outlined in Chapters 1 and 3, it would appear that there is a lack of public awareness of them. Even health care professionals, social workers and teachers, may not know of such provision or be unclear as to methods of referral. Certainly, there has been very little public debate concerning the need for in-patient units and while 'solutions' continue to be sought for 'anti-social' children exhibiting extreme forms of behaviour, there has been little specific reference to psychiatric treatment. Interestingly, much of the discussion which occurred regarding adult psychiatry in the 1960s and 1970s has never emerged within the context of child psychiatry. In particular, there is little evidence of the mad/bad debate (Turner 1987), which may be particularly relevant to children admitted to residential units. There is a dearth of material in non-psychiatric publications questioning the ability to diagnose children as mentally ill given: (1) the very young age of many of the children seen, and concomitantly, their incomplete emotional and behavioural development; (2) the prevalence of physical illness among those admitted (Gray *et al.* 1992); (3) the severe social deprivation of some of the children referred; and (4) the multi-faceted nature of the children's problems, as indicated for example in Chapters 3 and 9. In the light of responsibility by adult members of society for the young and the news worthiness of child-related stories, especially those of a medical or criminal nature, the lack of discussion, both within and outwith specialist publications, seems all the more surprising.

Regarding the murder of James Bulger by two 10-year-old boys in 1993, debate focused on the punitive aspects of the case and issues relating to the need for protection of the public. Very few indeed of the medical and health journals gave serious consideration to the case, especially in the context of psychiatric in-patient treatment, although an exception was the *British Journal of Nursing.* An editorial in the latter highlighted that there had been little mention of other important considerations. However, emphasis was placed on responding to the needs of surviving siblings and the 'long-term darker side of grieving' (Notter 1993). Interesting to note, nevertheless, was the attention paid by the media, especially the 'quality' newspapers to the views of child psychiatrists. Their reported comments were in stark contrast to the general reporting of events, as Black said 'the terms "evil" and "monster"' are not psychiatric diagnoses. I think children vary in the way they have been socialised; how well they have been taught to behave, curb their impulses and how to empathise and feel for others' (Waterhouse 1993, p.6). Similarly, Dr Sheldrick, consultant in child and adolescent forensic psychiatry at the Maudsley Hospital suggested that 'children who committed horrendous crimes were "sad rather than bad"' (Neuslatter and Hunt 1993).

In the same year, but independently, journalists were describing a sharp rise in the number of children admitted to psychiatric hospitals. Once again psychiatrists were interviewed and reported as 'blaming' the figures on increasing psychological pressure on children as well as drawing attention to the fact that children's homes had been closed together with special schools, and that child guidance clinics were being run down (Rickford 1993). More recently, increases in the numbers of children with mental illness have been headlined (Cohen 1995) together with reports regarding 'children as young as five being expelled from school' (MacLeod 1995, p.4). Little systematic review of existing facilities and approaches has occurred concurrently.

It might be expected that the relatively long term hospitalisation which so frequently accompanies admission to a child psychiatric unit would, in itself, prompt comment. In the treatment of physical illness, for example, length of stay has been reduced, *inter alia*, in response to the perceived undesirability of separating children from their parents and other family members (Zetterstroem 1984). In-patient psychiatric treatment in addition creates the risk of negative labelling and, indeed, stigmatisation. It is, perhaps, worthy of note, too, that there have been few attempts to analyse the effects of stigma in childhood by either sociologists, psychologists or psychiatrists. Indeed, is it, in fact, the case that attendance at a residential unit is stigmatising for the child and his or her family and if so, can this be shown to have long term implications? It could well be the case, however, that where psychiatric units are located within a children's hospital stigmatisation is reduced.

In a recent study of parents' and children's perceptions of psychiatric hospitalisation, however, it was found that both were unclear regarding the main reasons for admission to a child psychiatric unit (Chesson, Harding, Hart and O'Loughlin 1995). Of particular significance was that the children tended to see the unit as a school, rather than as a medical, or particularly psychiatric, facility (Chesson *et al.* 1995). The value of seeking consumers' views also was well demonstrated by the latter investigation.

It is only too apparent from the literature that there has been little attempt to date to determine children's views of psychiatric units. This is despite an increasing emphasis on consumerism (Subotsky 1992) and children's rights. For example Article 12 of the UN Convention of Rights of the Child encapsulates the 'child's right to express an opinion and to have that opinion taken into account, in any matter or procedure affecting the child' (cited by Blair and Billingham 1993). While eliciting children's opinions may be fraught with difficulties, the experience of one of the authors (RC) would suggest that these are not insurmountable. (Chesson *et al.* 1995).

Why then has so little attention been focused on such units? Currently, any general discussion on visibility can but be speculative, given the lack of empirical enquiry. It seems likely, nevertheless, that any one explanation will be inadequate. Possible explanations will need to take into account social attitudes towards mental illness in children. Is there an underlying discomfort among the adult population with the very notion that children – some as young as five years of age – should experience emotional and behavioural problems. The Grampian school survey, described in in Chapter 7, indicated that teachers tended to report children's difficulties in social/motivational terms rather than in medical/illness terminology. As public awareness of the interaction between psycho-social and physiological factors in producing mental illness increases, so does, in fact, public disquiet increase proportionally; some responsibility for problems may need to be accepted by society.

It is noteworthy that there have been few reports of patient abuse in child psychiatric units, in contrast, for example, to the situation regarding child residential homes.

Comparison of In-Patient Units and Children's Homes

Arguably, some of the children referred to psychiatric units could have been admitted to child residential homes as indeed some in-patients are, following discharge. Conversely, in some cases, referral to a psychiatric unit might be regarded as more appropriate than home placement. In order to explore this issue it may be helpful, therefore, to compare and contrast in-patient units and children's homes.

In-patient Units and Children's Homes

To date, there has been little systematic investigation of the role of units *vis à vis* children's homes. This is despite a common belief among practitioners that there is a 'random' element in allocation see, for example, Chapter 11. In particular, there have been few attempts to examine placement and referral in the context of all available alternatives for children for whom removal from the family home becomes necessary. To the best of the authors' knowledge, there has been no previous detailed documentation of the characterisation of in-patient units and British children's homes.

Population Characteristics

(1) The residents in most children's homes are predominantly adolescents, while child psychiatric in-patient units cater for children, mainly of primary school age. However, some children are admitted to homes and some younger adolescents to child psychiatric in-patient units.

   Adolescent psychiatric in-patient units are the relevant NHS provision for older youngsters and many of the points that follow apply equally well to them.

(2) Although residents in children's homes are known to have a raised incidence of psychiatric disorders, all children in child psychiatric in-patient units are perceived to have a psychiatric disorder (or did at time of admission or were suspected of having one). While in both, children with conduct disorders will be found, it is to the psychiatric units that children with severe psychiatric disorders with acute symptoms are likely to be admitted.

(3) Many of the children in both will come from families with psychosocial problems. However, evidence would suggest that there is more deprivation among the families of children admitted to homes.

(4) The children in an in-patient child psychiatric unit have a home base outwith the unit. Although this is frequently the case for children in a children's home, it is not necessarily so.

Functions and Staffing

(1) Although both children's homes and child psychiatric in-patient units provide care, assessment and treatment, in child psychiatric units, the primary tasks are assessment and treatment, while this is true only of some of the more specialised children's homes.

(2) Qualified staff of children's homes are mainly trained in social work, whereas qualified staff in child psychiatric in-patient units undertaking the day-to-day care of the children are mainly trained in nursing, usually in the specialities of paediatric or mental illness nursing or less commonly in child psychiatric nursing. There are important overlaps in the education and training of staff working in both sectors, however. It is still the case that many staff in both will be unqualified and will have received inadequate training.

Many similar skills and insights are required in both to enable workers to meet the needs of children with emotional and behavioural difficulties and of their parents and families and to work with the other professionals involved. Nonetheless, some skills are specific to the different settings, for example, for nurses administration of medication in child psychiatric units.

Both sets of workers will be exposed to stress from having to relate closely to disturbed and demanding children who may raise problems of control including showing aggressive behaviour to staff or others. The nature of the work in both setting is such that staff tensions readily arise.

Organisation and Administration

Children's homes are either administered by local authorities through their social services departments, or social work departments in Scotland, or are run by voluntary agencies. By contrast, all child psychiatric in-patient units are NHS provisions. These differences in administration have a significant effect on resource management and the day-to day running of the homes and units. Although the residents in children's homes may receive psychiatric treatment, their care in the home does not become the clinical responsibility of a child and adolescent psychiatrist, as it is in an in-patient unit. The extent of his/her involvement is not likely to be as great. In an in-patient unit treatment too from other specialities is often more readily available and more easily co-ordinated. Multi-disciplinary teamwork is more common in a unit rather than a home and usually includes a wider range of professionals who work closely together.

Commonalities

Despite the differences between children's homes and units, given their common ground, it is likely that much could be gained through increased contact and communication. There are many issues that are equally relevant for both, and knowledge and experience as to what constitutes good practice in one setting is likely to be largely applicable in the other. The relevance of knowledge of good practices in residential care to child psychiatric in-patient units is highlighted by the requirement in the Children Act of health authorities that they notify local authorities of children accommodated for more than three months (see Chapter 14). Issues of importance in both settings include:

- the need for improved planning for the individual child
- developing approaches with parents and measures to promote partnership
- the need to be aware of the risk of abuse by staff or other children and to have measures to prevent it

- the gap between children's concerns and staff's perceptions of these
- the importance of objective evidence being gathered for decision-making
- the need for the integration of units with the wider community.

Studies such as those of Colton (1988) demonstrating the greater child-centredness of foster homes as compared with residential homes and the work of King, Raynes and Tizard (1982) on patterns of child management in hostels, homes and hospitals for handicapped children, raise the question of the extent of child-oriented practice in child psychiatric in-patient units, an issue Barker (1974) had already identified as meriting investigation. It is a cause for regret that, to date, there has been little cross fertilisation of ideas in child care and that child residential and psychiatric services have had a tradition of separate development.

Indications for In-patient Admission

It has been pointed out that child psychiatric in-patient units might have disappeared once they were no longer needed for the post-encephalitic behaviour disorders that prompted their introduction (Perry 1989). Instead, at this relatively early stage in their history they changed their role and began to cater for a wide range of emotional and behavioural disorders that could not be catered for in the community. Since then, as described in Chapter 3, units have had to make further changes in the children admitted so that in the USA a much larger proportion of the children are suffering from severe conduct disorders (Jemerin and Phillips 1988, Hendren and Berlin 1991). There is less information available about the children treated in in-patient units in the UK.

Wolkind and Gent (1987) discussed changes that have occurred in the cases admitted to the unit at the Maudsley Hospital. They point out that their unit is part of a supraregional hospital run by a Special Health Authority and not necessarily typical of other child psychiatric in-patient units. They state that with refinement and greater availability of family therapy and behaviour therapy, school phobia, habit disorders and pre-pubertal anorexia nervosa are usually treated successfully as out-patients, whereas in-patient treatment might well have been considered to be required in the past. They categorise the children admitted into psychoses, neuropsychiatric disorders, severe emotional disorders, 'psychosomatic' disorders (broadly defined) and conduct disorders. The latter is the largest group, which frequently occurs against a background of physical, emotional or sexual abuse. However, they make it clear that it is considerations of the severity, complexity, and unusual nature of the disorders, and of the multi-modal nature of treatment needs that lead to admission.

Gray et al. (1992) also categorised the children into diagnostic groups which were broadly similar to those of Wolkind and Gent (1987), but highlighted the finding that almost 20 per cent of the admissions suffered from a physical disorder. Unlike Wolkind and Gent, they did not identify any trend for admissions of children with encopresis to become less frequent. This difference may well reflect the supraregional role of the Maudsley Unit.

Green (1992) categorised children not by diagnostic groups but into those for whom out-patient treatment is insufficient including those where the child is at risk; those needing residential assessment to clarify their problems; children in crisis situations; and those requiring controlled trials of medication. As regards the crisis admissions he made the important distinction between family breakdown in the context of psychiatric treatment, and care and control issues where reception into social services care would be more likely to be indicated. Both he and Wolkind and Gent pointed to a role for child psychiatric in-patient units in the assessment of parenting with Green mentioning specifically the possibility of Munchausen's Syndrome by Proxy.

Hersov (1994) in his description of children for whom in-patient admission is the treatment of choice grouped the children somewhat differently to Green (1992) but appears to be covering a similar population. He does not mention specifically, however, those in crisis situations and those who required drug trials. He refers specifically to the need to establish whether cognitive impairment is due to neglect. He also makes the comment that there must be a realistic likelihood that in-patient treatment can help.

In Scotland, an National Audit primarily of out-patient services is underway (Hoare 1994). The first year of this identified a group of children who met the criteria for inclusion in the Audit and who received in-patient treatment. The preliminary findings seemed generally to support the information from the papers previously mentioned.

Although Wrate and Wolkind (1991) have said that there would not be agreement about which children should be admitted to child psychiatric in-patient units and Green (1992) comments on differences between units in children admitted the papers quoted above appear to indicate a good deal of common ground as regards the children for whom in-patient admission is the treatment of choice, at least at the level of detail that is available. However, the scene is a changing one, partly for financial reasons but also determined by other factors such as

(1) Advances in assessment and treatment removing some cases from the group who require in-patient provision but perhaps introducing approaches that require an in-patient stay for their implementation.

(2) New groups of patients who would respond well to in-patient treatment being identified. Children with HIV infection, with AIDS or coming from families where another family member has AIDS are likely to form one such group.

Gray et al. (1992), too, raised the question of whether children with mild mental handicap should be treated in child psychiatric units to a greater extent than they are at present. Currently with research into mental handicap moving ahead rapidly in response to advances in molecular genetics and the neuro-sciences, and with it being known that genetic disorders can lead to mild mental handicap (Rutter 1995) this question requires active consideration. The increasing knowledge about behavioural phenotypes – the behavioural, cognitive, linguistic, social or psychiatric features associated with a genetic or chromosomal disorder (Flint and Yule 1994) – underlines this as does psychiatric disorder being three times more common among children with mild mental handicap than with children in general. There is evidence from Wrate *et al.* (1985), too, that some of these children benefit particularly from hospital-based services. The proposition that some mildly mentally handicapped children might be appropriately treated in child psychiatric in-patient units may appear to clash with the move to accommodate even the more severely handicapped outwith the hospital, but this is a superficial impression only as the aim of admission would be to re-establish the child living as full a life as possible in the community.

As Mant and Bucher (1994) point out there remains a need for well designed trials to establish the effectiveness or otherwise of in-patient treatment for specific conditions. One would expect the results of such trials to affect the type of children admitted to in-patient units although it is well known that research is not always implemented (Davidoff, Haynes, Sackett and Smith 1995). To a small extent this process may well have happened already: for example, it has been demonstrated that behaviour change achieved in autistic children through operant conditioning in child psychiatric in-patient units does not generalise to home (Rutter 1985) so that such children would not be admitted for that reason. Certainly, it would seem desirable that children receive in-patient treatment on the basis of such evidence, and on the basis of well informed assessments of need which have been identified as a major role for purchaser health authorities (Mant and Bucher 1994), rather than in a piecemeal and unco-ordinated way in response to pressures purchaser feel under, possibly because of gaps in other provisions or fears of adverse publicity.

Care in the Community

Care in the community for children may well be seen as the preferred option, in the light of government commitment to family values and a prevailing anti-institutional ideology. As Wells (1995) has suggested regarding adolescent units 'community good, hospital bad' propaganda has led to a reduced emphasis on investment in residential units. However, fundamentally underpinning the concept of community care is family care. Yet for many of the children referred to units, family care had proved insufficient even with domiciliary support and out-patient treatment. Indeed, the child's problems with the associated difficulties in the parent child relationship often are crucial factors in bringing about admission. Whatever the extent of the other difficulties, the child has family problems, and the inability of a family to resolve them may lead them to seek help or lead to intervention by statutory bodies.

In addition the need of the child for educational psychology may be making explicit that children's problems can no longer be dealt with in the classroom. Specialist help is viewed as appropriate given the nature and extent of the children's difficulties. Exclusion from school, furthermore, precludes support from the educational mainstream community. Such children, who may subsequently be referred to a child psychiatric unit, may well be ones whom not only parents, but also schools cannot support. Clearly, in such circumstances as described above, community care simply is not feasible. Indeed, it has been asserted in the context of adolescent psychiatry that a substantial percentage of referrals only can be 'effectively, safely and economically' treated on a residential unit (Wells 1995).

It is indisputable, however, that in-patient treatment is expensive as the estimated costs of mental health packages calculated by Light and Bailey (1993) demonstrate. Yet, as the latter point out, the Home Office and Social Services, together with the education departments of local authorities, spend substantial sums in relation to disturbed children, often to no apparent effect. Light and Bailey (1993) thus propose, given the purchasing milieu, that contracts are drawn up, between child mental health services and those social institutions that might benefit from appropriate provision. In particular, they conclude that 'it is (child mental health) a prime candidate for joint commissioning between the NHS and local authorities' (Light and Bailey 1993, p.17). Further support for this approach is to be found in Mant and Bucher's report of market research to establish the market for a sub-regional child and adolescent psychiatric unit (Mant and Bucher 1994). They discovered a demand, albeit limited, for in-patient services in some districts, although the result demonstrated a rather more widespread demand for out-patient services. Considerable interest was shown by educational authorities regarding developing links with a sub-regional child and adolescent psychiatric unit which was seen by Special Education senior staff and local child guidance personnel as being able to provide more detailed assessment than could be achieved in child guidance clinics. Worthy of note is that this ability was seen as enhanced by the presence of an in-patient unit. Mant and Bucher (1994) speculate that in the future, potential purchasers might include Social Services departments, schools and GP fund-holders. Finally, Mant and Bucher (1994) forewarn that if regional in-patient facilities are significantly reduced, perhaps as a consequence of market trends, then children are likely to be admitted to adult mental hospitals. Thus a case may be made for a continuing role for in-patient units. The major shifts to community and purchasing may, given a supportive environment and an imaginative approach by the units, create a pivotal role for in-patient facilities as they establish themselves as community resources and centres of expertise, working closely with the educational and social sectors.

At the Crossroads

Much of the ground covered in this book centres on the extent to which child psychiatric in-patient units, and the children treated in them can be considered to be 'at the crossroads'. Child psychiatric units may be seen to be 'at the crossroads' in a number of respects:

- in their relationships to other medical specialties, especially paediatrics and adult psychiatry
- in their relationship to the wider community and the different agencies operating in it
- and as regards their own future.

It is clear that child psychiatric in-patient units have important relationships with both paediatrics and adult psychiatry. The relationship with paediatrics is important in child psychiatric practice in general since it is always important to attend to both the physical and mental health of the child. However, this is particularly the case in relation to in-patient practice, in view of the relatively high incidence of concurrent, and sometimes inter-related, physical disorders among in-patients, and the need for shared care for certain children, for example in many cases of anorexia nervosa or of psychiatric disorder in association with epilepsy. The importance of adequate physical assessment of the children with their often severe and complex disorders has also been discussed in Chapter 12. In that chapter, too, the need for links with adult psychiatry when a family member is suffering from severe psychiatric disorder is examined. This happens much less frequently, however, than does the occurrence of significant physical disorder among the children, but when it does happen it underlines the importance of maintaining these links. The relevance of training in adult psychiatry and paediatrics for child psychiatrists was also considered in Chapter 12.

The close relationship of child psychiatry with both paediatrics and adult psychiatry may raise particular problems as to which of the two represents the most appropriate management structure for child psychiatric services. Clearly, this has implications for units. Harrison (1994) has discussed with regard to mental health services in general their distribution among acute, community, mixed or specialist mental health Trusts. For child psychiatry, unless mental health services and child health services are part of the same Trust, a painful choice may have to be made. If the decision is reached to be within the same Trust as child health services, particular efforts will have to be made to maintain links with adult psychiatry. It also raises a significant issue regarding adolescent psychiatry. Either the child psychiatric and the adolescent psychiatric services have to follow separate paths or adolescent psychiatry must be separated from adult psychiatry. With the close links that are required clinically, especially at the upper end of the age range, this may well be unacceptable. On the other hand, if child psychiatry and adolescent psychiatry services become parts of different Trusts, particular efforts will be required to allow as seamless psychiatric care as possible to take place as the transition occurs for patients from childhood to adolescence. Close attention will need to be paid to the joint planning of services and service development. The fact that child psychiatric and adolescent psychiatric services may well be on a small scale in many areas may facilitate these efforts and make for success.

A closely related question is that regarding the appropriate trust setting for child psychiatric in-patient units. Although there may be arguments that a community base would allow child psychiatric in-patient units to be more accepted by and integrated within the community, the authors would argue that the advantages of close links with child health services, and of ready access to hospital facilities, together with the greater acceptability to parents of a hospital base, outweigh these. Clearly which road is the choice as regards this has profound implications for the nature of the child psychiatric in-patient services provided. Close links with paediatrics and a paediatric hospital tend to strengthen the medical base of the unit and that can preserve its capacity to assess and treat the children with severe psychiatric disorders, often with an important physical/medical component, who cannot easily be managed elsewhere.

As has been mentioned on a number of occasions previously, child psychiatric in-patient units have a long tradition of maintaining flexible boundaries which allow close community links to occur. These links are essential since child psychiatric in-patient treatment is only one phase in the management of the children admitted, and the responsibility for the children and for their care and treatment is likely to lie with parents and agencies in the community after discharge. The complexity and intractable nature of the problems of many of the children admitted often mean that there are several different professionals from different agencies (local authority, voluntary and other parts of the NHS) involved when a child is admitted and when he or she is discharged. The extent of this involvement is reflected in the size of case conferences, which are an important part of the management of many in-patients.

As regards their own future, child psychiatric in-patient units are very much standing at a crossroads. There is clearly a great deal of uncertainty about their future. Although there is almost a 50 per cent increase in psychiatric admissions of 10–14 year olds recorded by the Department of Health (Wells 1995) and the recognition of the need for child psychiatric in-patient units (Kurtz 1992), child psychiatric in-patient units are closing. In addition, others are being directed into the path of converting to day units or to five-day assessment units although it is believed that the picture is patchy and that some services are considering expanding. Nonetheless, the overall effect is likely to be one of continuing contraction in the numbers of child and adolescent psychiatric in-patient units available, unless the process can be reversed by effective partnerships being forged between purchasers and providers, as described by Williams and Farrer (1994), and purchasers can be convinced of the value of psychiatric in-patient units. If this does not happen when children with psychiatric disorders reach a critical juncture in their lives the help they require may simply not be available.

References

Barker, P. (ed) (1974) *The Residential Psychiatric Treatment of Children*. London: Crosby, Lockwood and Staples.

Blair, M. and Billingham, K. (1993) 'Information, children and power.' *Primary Health Care 3*, 10, 14/15.

Chesson, R., Hart, C., Harding, L. and O'Loughlin, V. (1995) *Parents' and Children's Perceptions of Psychiatric Hospitalisation*. Report to the Home and Health Department, The Scottish Office.

Cohen, J. (1995) 'Mental illness among children jumps 50%.' *The Sunday Times*, 19 March, 7.

Colton, M. (1988) 'Dimensions of foster and residential care practice.' *Journal of Child Psychology and Psychiatry 29*, 5, 589–600.

Davidoff, F., Haynes, B., Sackett, D. and Smith, R. (1995) 'A new journal to help doctors identify the information they need'. *British Medical Journal 310*, 1085–1086.

Flint, J. And Yule, W. (1994) 'Behavioural phenotypes.' In M. Rutter, E. Taylor And L. Hersov (eds) *Child and Adolescent Psychiatry: Modern Approaches*. Oxford: Blackwell.

Green, J. (1992) 'In-patient psychiatry units.' *Archives of Disease in Childhood 67*, 1120–1123.

Gray, C., Chisholm, D., Smith, P., Brown, M. and McKay, C. (1992) 'The role of the child psychiatric ward in health care: experiences with different types of admission over a period of 21 years.' *Irish Journal of Psychological Medicine 9*, 17–23.

Harrison, J. (1994) *Psychiatric Bulletin 18*, 8, 469–471.

Harrison, R.L. and Berlin, I.N. (1991) (Eds) *Psychiatric In-patient Care of Children and Adolescents: A Multicultural Approach*. New York: Wiley.

Hersov, L. (1994) 'Inpatient and day hospital units.' In M Rutter, E. Taylor and L. Hersov. *Child and Adolescent Psychiatry: Modern Approaches*. Oxford: Blackwell.

Hoare, P. (1994) 'Child and adolescent services – child and adolescent psychiatric services in Scotland.' In C.A. Dean. *Slow Train Coming: Bringing its Mental Health*

Revolution to Scotland. Glasgow: Greater Glasgow Community and Mental Health Services NHS Trust.

Jemerin, J.M. and Philips, I. (1988) 'Changes in in-patient child psychiatry: consequences and recommendations.' *Journal of the American Academy of Child and Adolescent Psychiatry 27,* 397–403.

King, R., Raynes, N.V. and Tizard, J. (1982) *Patterns of Residential Care.* London: Routledge and Kegan Paul Ltd.

Kurtz, Z. (1992) *With Health in Mind: Mental Health Cure for Children and Young People.* London: Action for Sick Children.

Light, D. and Bailey, V. (1993) 'Pound foolish.' *Health Service Journal,* 11 February, 16–18.

Mant, J. and Bucher, J. (1994) 'Is there a market for regional units in child and adolescent psychiatry?' *Journal of Public Health Medicine 16,* 3, 305–309.

MacLeod, D. (1995) '5 year-olds expelled as classes grow.' *The Guardian,* 31 January, 4.

Neuslatter, A and Hunt, L. (1993) 'The Bulger murder: young criminals are "sad rather than bad".' *Independent,* 25 November, 3.

Notter, J. (1993) 'Implications of the James Bulger case for community nurses.' *British Journal of Nursing 2,* 5, 255.

Perry, R. (1989) 'The medical in-patient model.' In R.D. Lyman, S. Prentice-Dunn and S. Gabel (eds) *Residential and In-patient Treatment of Children and Adolescents.* New York: Plenum Press.

Rickford, F. (1993) 'Big rise in children "dumped" in mental hospitals.' *The Independent on Sunday,* April, 1.

Subotsky, F. (1992) 'Psychiatric treatment for children – the organisation of services.' *Archives of Diseases in Childhood 67,* 971–975.

Turner, B.S. (1987) *Medical Power and Social Knowledge.* London: Sage.

Waterhouse, R. (1993) 'Children who kill are not evil say doctors.' *The Independent,* 15 December, 6.

Wells, P. (1995) 'Adolescent units – wither on the vine? A meeting with the under-secretary for State.' *Psychiatric Bulletin 19,* 248–249.

Williams, R. and Farrar, M. (1994) 'Child and adolescent services – commissioning child and adolescent mental health services.' In C. Dean. *A Slow Train Coming: Bringing its Mental Health Revolution to Scotland.* Glasgow: Greater Glasgow Community and Mental Health Services NHS Trust.

Wolkind, S. and Gent, M. (1987) 'Children's psychiatric in-patient units: Present functions and future directions.' *Maladjustment and Therapeutic Education 5,* 2, 54–64.

Wrate, R.M., Kolvin, I., Garside, R.F., Wolstenholme, F., Hulbert, C.M. and Leitch, I.M. (1985) 'Helping seriously disturbed children.' In A.R. Nicol' (ed)

Longitudinal Studies on Child Psychology and Psychiatry: Practical Lessons from Research Experience. Chichester: John Wiley and Sons.

Wrate, R., Rothery, D., McCabe, R., Aspin, J. and Bryce, G. (1994) 'A prospective multicentre study of admissions to adolescent inpatient units.' *Journal of Adolescence 17*, 221–237.

Zetterstroem, R. (1984) 'Responses of children to hospitalisation.' *Acta Paediatrica Scandinavia 73*, 289–295.

Appendix

In-patient and Day-patient Units in the United Kingdom

Area	Unit	Age	Type of Unit	No. of Beds	Comments
Avon	Department of Child and Family Psychiatry Lumsden Walker House Bristol Children's Hospital Bristol B52 8BJ	0–14	IP & DP	4 IP 6 DP 10 total	
Berkshire	Paxton Family and Young Person's Unit 57 Bath Road Reading, Berkshire RG32 BAH	0–18	IP & DP	8 IP 8–11 DP	Extensive group programme
Buckinghamshire	Child and Family Guidance Clinic Amersham Health Centre Amersham, Buckinghamshire HP6 5AH	0–18	IP & DP	2 IP	Combined inpatient and daypatient between 2 units. Two IP beds plus day placement as needed.
Buckinghamshire	Department of Child Mental Health Wycombe Clinic, High Wycombe, Buckinghamshire HP13 6PQ	0–18	IP & DP		See above
Cambridgeshire	Brookside Family Consultation Clinic Adolescent Unit, Douglas House Trumpington Road, Cambridge	11–17	IP & DP	9–10	8–10 IP beds 6 DP beds
Cambridgeshire	The Croft Children's Unit 28/30 Long Road Cambridge, Cambridgeshire	0–12	IP & DP	8	6–8 IP beds 6–8 DP places

In-patient and Day-patient Units in the United Kingdom

Area	Unit	Age	Type of Unit	No of Beds	Comments
Cambridgeshire	Department of Child and Family Psychiatry Peterborough District Hospital Edward Jenner Unit Peterborough	5–11	DP		
Cheshire	Regional Young People's Centre Pine Lodge 77 Liverpool Road, Chester CH12 1AW	13–19	IP	10	
Cleveland	Young People's Centre, St Luke's Hospital Martin Road, Middlesborough	12–19	IP & DP	10	also 2 ECR and 5 day paients
Cumbria	Ashfield Child Guidance Centre High Street Workington, Cumbria CA14 4ES	n/k	IP	n/k*	
Cumbria	Department of Child Psychiatry Cumberland Infirmary, Carlisle	0–18	DP		
Derbyshire	Child Psychiatry Department Oaklands 103 Duffield Road, Derby	0–16	DP		
Devon	Young People's Centre Mount Gould Hospital Mount Gould Road Plymouth, PL4 7QD	14–20	IP & DP	6	Also 10 day patients Will soon be family day service for children up to 14
Devon	Child Adolescent and Family Service Matford Lodge Exeter, Devon EX2 4UD	2.5–12	IP DP	IP OP 10 DP	IP will be phased out this year. Outpatient group and programmes.

* not known

In-patient and Day-patient Units in the United Kingdom (continued)

Area	Unit	Age	Type of Unit	No. of Beds	Comments
Devon	Larkby Adolescent Unit Victoria Park Road Exeter, Devon EX2 4NU	13–18	IP DP	12 IP 6 DP	Primarily inpatient/day patient service
Durham	Aycliffe Centre for Children Newton Aycliffe Co. Durham, DL5 6JB	11–18	DP & IP	114	National Centre for Disordered Adolescents (46 secure beds and 68 open facilities beds)
Durham	Department of Child and Family Psychiatry Dryburn Hospital Durham City, Co. Durham	0–18	DP		
Durham, South	Marian Centre Darlington Memorial Hospital Darlington, Durham DL3 6HX	0–16	OP		Now combined with Deparment of Child and Family Psychiatry, Westfield Bishop Auckland Inpatient Services, St Lukes, Middlesbourgh
Essex	District Psychology Service c/o Mental Health Unit Basildon Hospital, Nethermayne Basildon SS16 5NL	0–18	IP & DP	n/k	
Essex	Longview Unit 216 Turner Road Colchester, Essex CO4 5JR	13–16	DP & IP	10	
Essex	Child Development Centre Galen House Clinic Fourth Avenue Harlow, CM20 1DT	0–18	IP	n/k	

	In-patient and Day-patient Units in the United Kingdom (continued)				
Area	Unit	Age	Type of Unit	No of Beds	Comments
Essex	London Borough of Havering Raphael House 64 Western Road Romford, RM1 3LR	0–18	DP OP	n/k	
Gloucestershire	Clinical Psychology Department 10 West Lodge Drive Coney Hill Gloucester GL4 7QJ	0–18	DP & IP OP	n/k	
Hampshire	Leigh House Hospital Regional Unit Chandlers Ford Eastleigh SO5 1JP	Adoles cent	IP & DP	12–15	
Hampshire	Merlin Centre 19 Villiers Road Southsea, Portsmouth	0–12	DP & IP	15	Admis of families – index child 0–12 Admis mother with pst-natal depress Admis children 7–12 (in own right)
Hampshire	Brookvale Adolescent Service 30 Brookvale Road Portswood Southampton SO2 1QR	16–19	DP	n/k	
Hampshire	Bursledon House Department of Paediatrics Southampton General Hospital Southampton SO9 4XY	0–16	DP & IP	12 IP 6 DP 18 Total	

	In-patient and Day-patient Units in the United Kingdom (continued)				
Area	Unit	Age	Type of Unit	No of Beds	Comments
Hertfordshire	Hill End Adolescent Unit Hill End Hospital St Albans Hertfordshire AL4 0RB	12–16	IP	n/k	
Humberside North	West End Community Adolescent & Family Service 2062–2068 Hessle Road Hull, HU13 9NW	12–18	IP & DP	6 IP 6 DP 12 Total	
Humberside North	Child and Family Unit Main Street Willersby Hull, HU10	0–14	DP & IP	12	
Humberside South	Child and Family Unit Grimsby District General Hospital Scarths Road, Grimsby DN33 2BA	0–16	DP		IP beds available in North Humberside Services when necessary (2–3 yr)
Humberside South	Clinical Psychology Department Scunthorpe General Hospital Cliff Gardens, Scunthorpe DN15 7BH	0–18	DP		
Isle of Wight	Department of Child and Family Psychiatry 7 Pyle Street, Newport Isle of Wight, PO30 1JW	0–18	DP		
Kent	Beech House St Augustine's Hospital Chartham Down Canterbury, CT4 7LL	11–18	IP & DP	6	6 IP and 10 DP

Area	Unit	Age	Type of Unit	No of Beds	Comments
	In-patient and Day-patient Units in the United Kingdom (continued)				
Kent	Ellington Children's Hospital 1 Grove Road Ramsgate, Kent, CT11 9SH	0–18	DP		
Kent	Department of Child and Family Therapy 51 London Road Canterbury, CT2 8LF	0–12	DP	1	
Lancashire	Department of Child & Family Psychiatry Queen's Park Hospital Blackburn, Lancashire, BB2 3HH	0–18	DP		
Lancashire	Red Oak House Piccadily, Scotforth Lancaster LA1 4PW	0–12	IP & DP	12	4 DP and 12 IP
Lancashire	Bickerstaffe House 53 Garstang Road Preston PR1 1LB	0–16	IP & DP	4 IP 4 DP 8 Total	
Lancashire	Department of Clinical Psychology Royal Preston Hospital PO Box 66 Preston PR2 4HT	0–18	IP	n/k	
Lancashire	Child and Adolescent Unit (Psychiatry) Birch Hill Hospital Rochdale, Lancashire, OL12 6BA	0–18	DP		
Lancashire	Child and Adolescent Psychiatry Sandy Lane Skelmersdale, Lancashire, WN8 6BA	0–16	DP		

In-patient and Day-patient Units in the United Kingdom (continued)

Area	Unit	Age	Type of Unit	No of Beds	Comments
Lancashire	Department of Child Psychiatry Queen's Park Hospital Blackburn, BB2 3HH	n/k	DP		
Lancashire	Child and Family Services Bolton General Hospital Farnworth, Bolton, BL4 0JR	n/k	DP		probably become 10 DP's
Lancashire	Department of Child & Family Psychiatry Burnley General Hospital Casterton Avenue, Burnley, BB10 2PG	n/k	IP	n/k	
Leicestershire	Tanglewood Children's Resource Centre Westcotes Drive Leicester, LE3 0QU	0–11	DP		
Leicestershire	Oakham House Adolescent Unit Towers Hospital, Leicester	12–16 (18)	IP & DP	13	
Lincolnshire	The Health Centre Lincoln Lane Boston, Lincolnshire, PE21 8RU	8–16	DP	6	
Lincolnshire	Ash Villa Adolescent Unit Rauceby Hospital Sleaford, Lincolnshire, NG34 8PP	8–16	IP & DP	16	
London – East Postal District	Department of Child & Family Psychiatry The London Hospital Whitechapel, E1 1BB	0–18	IP	up to 4 as needed	

In-patient and Day-patient Units in the United Kingdom (continued)					
Area	Unit	Age	Type of Unit	No of Beds	Comments
London – North Postal District	Simmons House Adolescent Unit St Luke's Woodside Hospital Woodside Avenue, London, N10 3HU	13–18	IP & DP	10 IP) 12 2 DP)	
London – North West Postal District	Department of Child & Family Psychiatry Day Unit of the Tavistock Clinic 33 Daleham Gardens London, NW 5BU	0–10	DP		18 DP
London – North West Postal District	Department of Child & Family Psychiatry Royal Free Hospital Hampstead, London, NW3 2QS	0–18	IP	n/k	Access to paediatric beds
London – North West Postal District	Regional Adolescent Unit Northgae Clinic Goldsmith Avenue, London, NW9 7HR	16–21	IP	20	10 male and 10 female
London – North West Postal District	Mildred Creak Unit Great Ormond Street Hospital London, WC1N 3JH	8–15	IP	8	
London – South East Postal District	Department of Child & Family Psychiatry St Thomas' Hospital London, SE1	0–18	IP& DP	n/k	
London – South East Postal District	Department of Child & Family Psychiatry Bloomfield Clinic, Guy's Hospital St Thomas Street, London SE1 9RT	7–14	IP & DP	8	
London – South West Postal District	Department of Clinical Psychology Queen Mary's University Hospital Roehampton Lane, London SW15 5PN	0–18	IP	n/k	

In-patient and Day-patient Units in the United Kingdom (continued)

Area	Unit	Age	Type of Unit	No of Beds	Comments
London – South West Postal District	Child and Adolescent Service and Emanuel Miller Unit Lanesborough Wing St George's Hospital Tooting, London SW17 0QT	0–18	DP		
London – South East Postal District	Collingham Gardens Child and Family Psychiatric Unit 5 Collingham Gardens London SW5 0HR	0–13	Ip & DP	12	Catchment area – all North West Thames
Liverpool	Child Psychological Services 6 Rainhill Road, St Helen's Merseyside, WA9 5DB	n/k	IP	n/k	
Liverpool	Dewi Jones Unit Department of Psychological Medicine Royal Liverpool Children's Hospital Liverpool, L12 2AP	5–14	IP & DP	3 DP 10 IP 13 Total	Regional IP Service for 5–14 year olds
Liverpool	Family Support Service Adcote House Oxton Village, Wirral	0–17	DP	n/k	OP also
Liverpool	Child and Family Unit Cherry Tree Hospital Cherry Tree Lane Stockport SK2 7PZ	5–17	IP & DP	n/k	5 day unit 5–11 day places 11–17 6 day/IP places

In-patient and Day-patient Units in the United Kingdom (continued)					
Area	Unit	Age	Type of Unit	No of Beds	Comments
Manchester	Department of Child & Family Psychiatry Booth Hall Children's Hospital Charleston Road, Blackley, M9 2AA	0–18	IP & DP	10 IP 8 DP 18 Total	
Manchester	Forensic/Adolescent Unit Gardner Unit/McGuiness Unit Prestwich Hospital Prestwich, Manchester, M25 7BL	n/k	IP	16	Forensic adolescent Unit
Manchester	Department of Child Psychiatry Royal Manchester Children's Hospital Pendlebury, Manchester, M27 1HA	n/k	DP		8 places
Norfolk	Department of Child & Family Psychiatry Thurlow House, Kings' Lynn Norfolk, PE30 5PD	0–18	DP		
Norfolk	'Hightrees' Foxhall Road, Ipswich	n/k	IP	10	No DP places at present
Northamptonshire	Springfield Cliftonville, Northampton, NN1 5BE	0–18	DP		
Northamptonshire	Ken Stewart Family Centre Northampton	n/k	DP		Child and Adolescent DP
Northumberland	Residential Unit	8–16	n/k	10	Jointly funded by SW and NHS – function will be reviewed 1994
Nottinghamshire	Thorneywood Unit St Ann's Hospital Nottingham, N53 6LF	0–16	IP & DP	n/k	

	In-patient and Day-patient Units in the United Kingdom (continued)				
Area	Unit	Age	Type of Unit	No of Beds	Comments
Oxfordshire	Highfield Family & Adolescent Unit Warneford Hospital Warneford Lane Oxford, OX3 7JX	13–18	IP & DP	18	
Oxfordshire	Park Hospital for Children Oxford	0–13	IP & DP	25	
Somerset	Regional Unit Merrifield Family Adolescent Unit Tonevale Hospital Norton Fitxwarren Taunton, TA4 1DB	11–18	IP & DP	28	soon to be 24 and may become 12
Staffordshire	Wall Lane House Young People's Centre St Edward's Hospital Cheddleton, Leek, ST13 7EB	11–18	IP & DP	12	
Surrey	Stepping Stones – Child & Adolescent IP Psychiatry Unit Queen Mary's Hospital for Children Carshalton, SM5 4NR	0–18	IP	10	
Surrey	Regional Adolescent Unit Long Grove Hospital Horton Lane, Epsom, KT19 8PU	11–18	IP & DP	n/k	
Surrey	Child & Adolescent Clinical Psychology Department of Health (Paediatric Dept) Kingston Hospital, Kingston-upon-Thames Surrey, KT2 7QB	0–19	DP		

In-patient and Day-patient Units in the United Kingdom (continued)					
Area	Unit	Age	Type of Unit	No of Beds	Comments
Sussex, West	Adolescent Unit Colwood Hospital Haywards Heath West Sussex, RH17 7SH	11–18	IP & DP	18	
Tees, North	Woodlands Unit Child, Adolescent and Family Psychiatry North Tees General Hospital Hardwick, Stockton-on-Tees	0–18 (5–16 for DP)	DP	15	No inpatient service. CPN carers all of age range. Also run peripheral clinics
Tyne and Wear	Young People's Unit Newcastle General Hospital Westgate Road Newcastle-upon-Tyne, NE4 6BE	13–19	IP & DP	n/k	
Tyne and Wear	Department of Child, Adolescent and Family Psychology Sunderland District General Hospital Kayll Road, Sunderland, SR4 7TP	0–16	DP		
Tyne and Wear	Fleming Nuffield Unit Burdon Terrace Jesmond, Newcastle	n/k	IP & FP	20	2 IP and 13 DP
Tyne and Wear	Department of Child & Family Psychiatry Queen Elizabeth Hospital Sheriff Hill, Gateshead, NT9 6SX	n/k	DP		
Tyneside, South	Department of Child and Family Psychiatry South Tyneside District Hospital South Shields, Tyne and Wear NE34 0PL	0–16	DP		

In-patient and Day-patient Units in the United Kingdom (continued)

Area	Unit	Age	Type of Unit	No of Beds	Comments
West Midlands	Irwin Unit for Young People Hollymoor Hospital Northfield, Birmingam, B31 5EX	12–17	IP & DP	5 DP 20 IP 25 Total	May merge soon with Charles Burne Clinic
West Midlands	Charles Burns Clinic Paediatric Department Moseley, Birmingham, B13 8QD	0–15	DP	19 DP 12 IP	
West Midlands	Child Clinical Psychology Services Paediatric Department Dudley Road Hospital Birmingham, B18 3QL	0–16	IP & DP	n/k	
West Midlands	District Clinical Psychology Service 208 Monyhull Hall Road Kings Norton Birmingham, B30 3QL	0–20	IP & DP	n/k	
West Midlands	Child Psychiatry Department The Children's Hospital Ladywood Middleway Ladywood, B16 8ET	0–16	IP & DP	10 IP} 15 5 DP}	
West Midlands	Clinical Psychology Department Cross Street Health Centre Dudley, West Midlands, DY1 1RN	0–18	IP	n/k	
West Midlands	Child Psychiatry Department Birmingham Children's Hospital Birmingham	0–16	IP & DP	5 DP 10 IP 15 Total	

In-patient and Day-patient Units in the United Kingdom (continued)					
Area	Unit	Age	Type of Unit	No of Beds	Comments
Wiltshire	Swindon and Marlborough Child and Adolescent Mental Health Service Marlborough Children's Hospital Hyde Road, Marlborough, SN8 1JT	3–16	DP	6 in Adolescent Unit	
Wiltshire	Child and Family Guidance Centre Wyvern House Theatre Square (Off Regent Circus) Swindon, AN1 6RE	3–7	DP		
Yorkshire, North	Lime Trees Child, Adolescent and Family Unit 31 Shipton Road, York, YO3 6RE	0–18	IP & DP	16	
Yorkshire, South	Department of Child & Family Psyciatry Chatham House, Doncaster Gate Rotherham, S65 1DJ	0–16	IP & DP	n/k	
Yorkshire, South	Maple House Day Hospital for Adolescents	11–16	DP	12	
Yorkshire, South	Shirle Hill Children's Unit 6A Cherry Tree Road Sheffield, South Yorkshire, S11 9AA	5–11	IP & DP	6	IP (6–11 emergency bed) DP 12
Yorkshire, South	Adolescent Unit Northern General Hospital Sheffield, South Yorkshire, S5 7AU	11–18	IP & DP	13	13 IP and 12 DP
Yorkshire, West	Department of Child Psychiatry Halifax General Hospital Salter Hebble, Halifax, HX3 0PW	0–18	IP	n/k	

In-patient and Day-patient Units in the United Kingdom (continued)

Area	Unit	Age	Type of Unit	No. of Beds	Comments
Yorkshire, West	Department of Child and Adolescent Psychiatry St Luke's Hospital, Crosland Moor Huddersfield, HD4 5RQ	0–19	IP & DP	n/k	
Yorkshire, West	Kanner Unit High Royds Hospital Menston, Ilkley, LS29 6AQ	0–12	IP & DP	12	
Yorkshire, West	Linton House Menston, Ilkley, West Yorkshire, LS29 6AQ	12–16	IP	12	
Yorkshire, West	Airedale Child and Family Service Hillbrook, Mayfield Road Keighley, BD20 6LD	0–18	DP		
Yorkshire, West	Department of Child and Family Psychiatry St James' University Hospital Leeds, LS9 7TF	0–16	DP	12	
Wales					
Glamorgan, South	Harvey Jones Adolescent Unit Velindre Road, Whitchurch, Cardiff South Glamorgan, CF4 7JG	10–18	IP & DP	14	number of beds under review
Glamorgan South	Child and Family Clinic Trehafod, Waunarlwydd Road Cockett, Swansea, SA2 0UZ	0–16	DP	20	6 nursery and 14 child and adolescent
Gwent	Child and Adolescent Psychiatry Services Nevill Hall Hospital, Abergavenny, Gwent	0–18	IP & DP	n/k	

In-patient and Day-patient Units in the United Kingdom (continued)					
Area	Unit	Age	Type of Unit	No of Beds	Comments
Wales, South	Gwynfa Residential Unit Pen-y-Bryn Road Upper Colwyn Bay, Clwyd, LL99 6AL	11–18	IP	18	
Wales, South	Paediatric Clinical Psychological Service Paediatric Dept: Wrexham Wrexham, Clwyd, LL13 7TD	0–18	IP	n/k	
Northern Ireland					
Northern Ireland	Forster Green Hospital Sainfield Road, Belfast, BT8 4HD	0–13	IP & DP	20 IP 5 DP	IP 20 and DP 5
Northern Ireland	Young People's Centre 10 College Gardens, Belfast, BT9 6BQ	14–18	IP & DP	6	6 IP 4 DP
Northern Ireland	Paediatric Department, Waveney Hospital Antrim, Co Antrim	n/k	IP	25	
Scotland					
Dumfries and Galloway	Ladyfield House Glencaple Road Dumfries DG1 4TE	4–18	IP, DP	12 IP, 2 DP child [12 IP, 2 DP adolescent]	
Fife	Playfield House Stratheden Hospital, Cupar, Fife	12–18	IP, DP	16 IP	Plans to increase DP numbers to that of IP
Fife	Forteviot House Royal Hospital for Sick Children Edinburgh	up to 12	IP, DP		5 Day short stay assessment Unit (under review)

In-patient and Day-patient Units in the United Kingdom (continued)

Area	Unit	Age	Type of Unit	No of Beds	Comments
Fife	YPU Royal Edinburgh Hospital	13–22	DP	20 DP 20 DP	Day programme for 13–19 years and separate unit for psychotics 13–22 years
Fife	Willowgrove Craigshill Livingstone E654 5LL	12–18	IP	12	Adolescent Unit
Grampian	Lowit Unit Royal Aberdeen Children's Hospital Cornhill Road, Aberdeen, AB9 2ZG	up to 14	IP, DP	6 IP, 10 DP	
Strathclyde	Hospital for Sick Children, Yorkhill Royal Glasgow, G3 8SJ	5–12	IP, DP	8 IP 6 DP	Open 5 days a week
Strathclyde	Adolescent Unit Gartnavel Royal Hospital 1055 Great Western Road, Glasgow, G12 0XH	12–16/17	IP	10	
Strathclyde	Glasgow Communication Disorders Unit Dept of Child and Family Psychiatry Royal Hospital for Sick Children Yorkhill, Glasgow	0–16	DP	6–8	specialist day unit
Strathclyde	Larkfield Child and Family Centre Larkfield Road Greenock PA16 0XN	0–16	DP	10	2 day per week
Strathclyde	Child and Family Centre Hawkhead Hospital, Hawkhead Road Paisley	0–18	DP		21 day places per week
Tayside	Dudhope House 15 Dudhope Terrace Dundee	3–12	IP, DP	CW 8 IP YPU 7 IP, 1 DP	Children's Ward and Young People's Unit. 5 Day Ward for pre-school to 12 years (with provision to open 4 days if necessary)

Notes on Contributors

Madeline Brown: Formerly had medical responsibility for the Lowit Unit. Is a graduate of Aberdeen University and has spent most of her working life in Aberdeen, although spent some time early in her career at Edinburgh City Hospital.

Rosemary Chesson: Currently Reader in Health Services Research, School of Health Sciences, The Robert Gordon University and formerly Senior Research Fellow, Department of Child and Family Psychiatry, Royal Aberdeen Children's Hospital. Is a sociology graduate from London University, with a higher degree from Bath University. Has lectured in sociology at Massey University, New Zealand and prior to moving to Aberdeen worked as a Research Officer for the National Foundation for Educational Research. While in Aberdeen has had an input into a number of health related research projects. Has recently completed a Scottish Office funded project on parents' and children's perceptions of psychiatric hospitalisation. Is currently convener for Clinicians and Educators Research Forum and acts as an adviser/consultant on research to Aberdeen General Hospitals, Grampian Healthcare.

Douglas Chisholm: Currently Consultant Child and Adolescent Psychiatrist, Department of Child and Family Psychiatry, Royal Aberdeen Children's Hospital (RACH) and Clinical Senior Lecturer, Department of Mental Health, University of Aberdeen. Is a graduate of Aberdeen University and trained at the Royal Cornhill Hospital and RACH. Has had previous appointment at the Clarke Institute of Psychiatry, Toronto. Previously Chairman Grampian Family Conciliation Service and for Grampian branch of the Association for Family Therapy. Presently is a member of the co-ordinating committee for the Scottish National Audit Project: The provision and effectiveness of child psychiatric services in Scotland.

Jackie Flewker-Barker: Is a Senior Occupational Therapist at the Royal Aberdeen Children's Hospital. She worked as a nursery nurse for five years prior to training as a therapist.

Leonora Harding: Is a psychology graduate (University of Durham) who initially qualified as a teacher working for ILEA prior to obtaining an MSc in Clinical Psychology from the University of Newcastle upon Tyne. She worked as clinical psychologist prior to becoming a lecturer in Special Education at the University of Ulster (1973–85). Currently is a clinical psychologist employed by the Royal Aberdeen Children's Hospital. Is a committee member of the UK

Special Interest Group working with children (DCP). At present is editing a series on psychological assessment.

Jane Jones: Is a specialist clinical adviser in child psychiatry for Scottish Region (College of Speech and Language Therapists) having recently joined the Royal Aberdeen Children's Hospital (RACH). She qualified from the Birmingham Polytechnic School of Speech Therapy (University Central England) and spent her post qualification years largely providing general speech and language therapy for children in hospital and school settings. This was followed by two years specialised work in special schools for children with moderate to severe learning difficulties and in a school with behavioural and emotional problems. Prior to joining RACH worked in Camphill/Rudolf Steiner Schools. Has a special interest in speech and language in-put into child psychiatry.

Lindsey Mackie: Is Head Teacher at the Royal Aberdeen Children's Hospital (including Head Teacher and full-time teacher in the Lowit Unit). Initially qualified MA (Hons) Psychology and Political Economy, St Andrew's University, and qualified as a teacher at Moray House College Of Education. In 1979 obtained an M.Litt. in Educational Psychology from the University of Aberdeen and in 1983 a Diploma in Special Education.

David McLeod: Is currently a staff nurse on the Lowit Unit where he has worked for the past three years. In 1982 he graduated with a BSc (Social Sciences) from the University of Edinburgh and was awarded recently a Diploma in Nursing. He acted as co-worker at Newton Dee Village (Campbell Village Trust), Aberdeen, prior to entering nursing, training as a Registered Mental Nurse, and working in a Day hospital before joining the unit.

Victor O'Loughlin: At present is Consultant Child Psychiatrist, South Eastern Health Board, Waterford, Eire and formerly was Senior Registrar, Child and Family Psychiatry, Royal Aberdeen Children's Hospital. Was educated and trained in Dublin and worked at the Royal City of Dublin Hospital, Baggot, prior to moving to Aberdeen. Worked as a research assistant at the Clinical Research Centre, Royal Cornhill Hospital, Aberdeen, prior to his appointment at the RACH.

Royston Paice: Is Charge Nurse on the Lowit Unit. Is a Registered Mental Nurse, qualifying in 1974. Worked in adult psychiatry in Aberdeen prior to joining the unit.

Kasi Brahmanya Gururaj-Prasad: Since 1991 Consultant Child and Adolescent Psychiatrist, and since 1993, Clinical Director (Child Health Services) Community Health Care, North Durham National Health Service Trust and member of Directors' Group of Trust. Has an active interest in the management of children's services. Trained in child and adolescent psychiatry in Aberdeen from 1987 to 1991. He has publications on autism and is currently involved in examining the areas of deliberate self-harm and auditing the role of the child psychiatrist.

Nan Riddell: At present social worker, Social Work Department, Royal Aberdeen Children's Hospital, and has had input into the Lowit Unit for 10 years. Prior to graduating from Aberdeen University (M.A. Social Sciences) and qualifying as a social worker she was a youth worker in Glasgow.

Elizabeth Stephenson: Worked in acute psychiatry in Aberdeen after obtaining her Diploma in occupational therapy from the Astley Ainslie Hospital. Subsequently was a paediatric occupational therapist at Corseford School run by the Scottish Council for Spastics. Has a particular interest in children with motor learning difficulties and has initiated research in this area. Is a past chairman of a UK (occupational therapy) study group on perception and is a group member of the National Association of Paediatric occupational therapists.

Ronnie Wilson: Ronnie qualified as a Home Teacher for the Blind in 1964. He worked with the local Society for the Blind in Aberdeenshire until 1972. After qualifying as a social worker he worked in a city centre team from 1974 – 1978. At that time he took up his present post as Senior Social Worker in the Royal Aberdeen Children's Hospital. In 1989 he obtained the Diploma in Advanced Social Work (Child Protection) at Dundee University.

Subject Index

Author Index